DISTANT ALLIANCES

DISTANT ALLIANCES

PROMOTING EDUCATION FOR GIRLS AND WOMEN IN LATIN AMERICA

EDITED BY
REGINA CORTINA AND
NELLY P. STROMQUIST

ROUTLEDGEFALMER
NEW YORK & LONDON

Published in 2000 by
RoutledgeFalmer
29 West 35th Street
New York, NY 10001

Pubished in Great Britain by
RoutledgeFalmer
11 New Fetter Lane
London EC4P 4EE

10   9   8   7   6   5   4   3   2   1

Library of Congress Cataloging-in-Publication Data

Distant alliances : promoting education for girls and women in Latin America /
edited by Regina Cortina and Nelly P. Stromquist.
   p. cm. — (Garland reference library of social science ; v. 1415.
Reference books in international education ; (v. 51)
   "The essays in this book were initially presented and discussed at the Pre-
LASA conference on Gender and Education in Latin America, September
22–23, 1998, at the John Nuveen Center for International Affairs, University of
Chicago . . . The Pre-LASA98 conference preceded the International Congress
of the Latin American Studies Association"—Acknowledgments.
   Includes bibliographical references and index.
   ISBN 0-8153-3375-7 (alk. paper)
   1. Women—Education—Latin America—Congresses.   2. Sex differences
in education—Latin America—Congresses.   3. Educational equalization—
Latin America—Congresses.   4. Feminism and education—Latin America—
Congresses.   5. Sex discrimination in education—Latin America—
Congresses.   6. Education and state—Latin America—Congresses.
I. Cortina, Regina.   II. Stromquist, Nelly P.   III. Garland reference library of
social science ; v. 1415.   IV. Garland reference library of social science.
Reference books in international education ; vol. 51.

LC1912 .D57 2000
371.822'098—dc21   00-057279

Printed on acid-free, 250-year-life paper.
Manufactured in the United States of America

Contents

Series Editor's Foreword

This series of scholarly works in comparative and international education has grown well beyond the initial conception of a collection of reference books. Although retaining its original purpose of providing a resource to scholars, students, and a variety of other professionals who need to understand the role played by education in various societies or world regions, it also strives to provide accurate, relevant, and up-to-date information on a wide variety of selected educational issues, problems, and experiments within an international context.

Contributors to this series are well-known scholars who have devoted their professional lives to the study of their specializations. Without exception these men and women possess an intimate understanding of the subject of their research and writing. Without exception they have not only studied their subject in dusty archives but have lived and traveled widely in their quest for knowledge. In short, they are "experts" in the best sense of that often overused word.

In our increasingly interdependent world, it is now widely understood that it is a matter of military, economic, and environmental survival that we understand better not only what makes other societies tick, but also how others, be they Japanese, Hungarian, South African, or Chilean, attempt to solve the same kinds of educational problems that we face in North America. As the late George Z. F. Bereday wrote more than three decades ago in *Comparative Methods in Education*: "[E]ducation is a mirror held against the face of a people. Nations may put on blustering shows of strength to conceal public weakness, erect grand façades to conceal shabby backyards, and profess peace while secretly arming for conquest, but how they take care of their children tells unerringly who they are" (New York: Holt, Rinehart and Winston, 1964, p. 5).

Perhaps equally important, however, is the valuable perspective that studying another education system (or its problems) provides us in understanding our own system (or its problems). When we step beyond our own limited experience and our commonly held assumptions about schools and learning in order to look back at our system in contrast to another, we see it in a very different light. To learn, for example, how China or Belgium handles the education of a multilingual society; how the French provide for the funding of public education; or how the Japanese control access to their universities enables us to better understand that there are reasonable alternatives to our own familiar way of doing things. Not that we can borrow directly from other societies. Indeed, educational arrangements are inevitably a reflection of deeply embedded political, economic, and cultural factors that are unique to a particular society. But a conscious recognition that there are other ways of doing things can serve to open our minds and provoke our imaginations in ways that can result in new experiments or approaches that we may not have otherwise considered.

Since this series is intended to be a useful research tool, the editor and contributors welcome suggestions for future volumes, as well as ways in which this series can be improved.

Edward R. Beauchamp
University of Hawaii

Acknowledgments

The essays in this book were initially presented and discussed at the Pre-LASA98 conference on Gender and Education in Latin America, September 22–23, 1998, at the John Nuveen Center for International Affairs, University of Illinois, Chicago. We would like to thank the Spencer Foundation for its generous support of the conference. Mary K. Vaughan, professor of history and Latin American studies, and Ariani Friedl, director of the John Nuveen Center, who graciously agreed to host the conference, and Mary Niemiec, her successor who oversaw the conference, provided additional funding and local arrangements. Nora Bonnin coordinated multiple conference activities and last-minute details at the Chicago campus. The Pre-LASA98 conference preceded the International Congress of the Latin American Studies Association.

We also want to acknowledge the timely support from the Ford Foundation to translate, revise, and edit the original conference papers and to prepare the corresponding Spanish-language edition of this book. We are grateful for the support in the preparation of this book that Regina Cortina received from the School of Education and the Center for Latin American and Caribbean Studies at New York University. The director and staff as well as the students in the center provided logistical support during the project. In the editing and revision of the manuscript, we owe special debt of thanks to Patricio Navia. The assistance provided by the Rossier School of Education at the University of Southern California is also acknowledged with thanks. Caroline E. Parker, a graduate student in the Graduate School of Education at Harvard University, translated most of the chapters from Spanish to English, capturing with accuracy and style the original ideas. We also want to acknowledge the contribution of Gloria Bonder (Universidad de Buenos Aires, Argentina) in the initial phase of the project.

As this book finds readers concerned about the topic, we would like to salute the women who have done pioneering work in the field of women's education and who have shown unfailing commitment to bettering the lives of all women. Those leaders—in communities, academic institutions, government, and nongovernmental organizations—are further distinguished by their ability to reflect upon relevant issues and to articulate them in written form. We hope that this publication will advance the debate on education policy in relation to gender equity.

DISTANT ALLIANCES

Introduction

The education of women and girls emerged in the 1990s as a top priority in three arenas of international dialogue. The World Conference on Education for All, convened in Thailand in 1990, demonstrated a clear consensus across national and cultural boundaries on the importance of education for eliminating poverty. Parallel to that consensus, a series of international meetings addressing the rights and opportunities of women around the world, convening first in Mexico City in 1975 and culminating in Beijing in 1995, created a platform for action that included the education of women and girls as one of its central planks. While those strong commitments were taking shape in the world of education and the women's movement, a similar consensus appeared among donor countries in 1996. The world's major industrial powers in the Organization for Economic Cooperation and Development (OECD) agreed to include basic education and gender equity as a high priority in bilateral and multilateral cooperation. The confluence of these three lines of consensus in education, the women's movement, and economic assistance to the third world was followed by numerous international forums addressing the transformation of schooling and education more generally in developing countries, with the aim of dramatically improving the education of women and girls as part of the larger goal of reducing poverty and creating sustainable development.[1]

The essays in this book explore the reality of education in Latin America in the aftermath of these international initiatives. The priorities identified through such initiatives are broader than the changes that have taken place in the region since the beginning of the decade. This book

1

explores tensions and achievements in the region following widespread recognition that more should be done to address the educational needs of women and girls in developing countries. A central goal of this volume is to learn from different experiences with the rhetoric of reform and the realities of change in Latin American countries. We also hope to identify probable areas of education reform and policy activity in the future for both the formal and nonformal systems of education. When referring to the education of girls, we mean public and private systems of schooling where girls go for their years of formal instruction. When discussing the education of adult women, we mean nonformal education or the many forms of organized learning that are taking place in civil society. Civil society can be understood as "organized in various ways and sectors, including individuals, the private sector, labor, political parties, academic, and other non-governmental actors and organizations." Invigorating civil society through community participation to give "depth and durability" to democracy is one of the commitments to the Plan of Action— signed by all the nations in the Americas.[2]

Latin America is recognized for virtually universal access to basic education. The United Nations' education statistics for the region suggest that there is parity between girls and boys in access to primary schooling.[3] However, educational conditions are far from ideal. When detailed analysis of education at the community level is taken into account, Guatemala and Bolivia are the countries in the region with the most significant gender gap in education.[4] Primary school completion is a severe problem for both boys and girls. Overall in Latin America, only half of the girls and boys who start primary school complete their basic education. Among the large majority of boys and girls participating in public schools, grade repetition and high dropout rates are common in all countries across Latin America. In addition to the issues of access and retention, a seemingly intractable problem is the education of all those adults who were not able to finish primary school and for whom the nonformal system is necessary but not adequate. Latin America has the lowest adult illiteracy rate in the third world, but substantial pockets of illiterates exist among the indigenous population and groups of African descent.[5]

This book aims to go beyond the description of educational indicators to probe measures and initiatives to correct undesirable situations affecting the education of girls and women. In an ideal scenario, economic policies would facilitate the well-being of all citizens and thus compensatory and equity measures for certain groups would not be necessary. In the absence of such policies, it becomes indispensable to rely on social policies, particularly education, to ensure equity for all groups in society. In this collection, we examine public policies to advance the condition of women and thus minimize gender asymmetries. Important initiatives are occurring outside the government; hence, we must be attentive to the work of nongovernmental organizations (NGOs) and, particularly, women-led NGOs. Since social international agreements have been signed in the last twenty-five years on fundamental aspects of education and gender, we are concerned throughout this book with knowing how such agreements are influencing public policy in Latin American countries.

The structure of this book reflects three strategically important actors in the quest to improve education for women and girls in Latin America: national ministries of education and their plans for education reform; organizations in civil society that provide nonformal education for adult women; and international cooperation agencies that channel financial and technical assistance to national governments and to the organizations in civil society that are providing education to adult women.

National ministries of education are key actors because they have the power to shape policies and provide funding. All over Latin America, education systems are undergoing transformation as they adjust to new global economic realities and respond to demands from increasingly vocal constituencies. Education is showing signs of considerable change as new curricula are implemented, new textbooks are used, and new teachers are hired. One might assume that it is always possible to make room for change. This book examines the degree to which gender can and should be taken into account when new policies and initiatives are framed. In most cases, national efforts are seldom evaluated, which explains the need to study each country's experience in detail to understand the possibilities for improvement. Because the policy changes taking place across different countries in Latin America are influenced by international organizations, to some extent causing different countries in the region to move in the same direction when implementing new programs, the similarities among their policy initiatives make it possible to generate interesting patterns among country-specific case studies.

The organizations in civil society that are often referred to collectively as NGOs have multiple functions. Serving a clientele with limited income, they are rarely economic self-sufficient institutions since they provide services free of charge or at extremely low cost for poor and marginalized groups. These NGOs are usually funded by external sources, in some cases directly by donor countries and international organizations chartered under the United Nations or representing coalitions of wealthy countries, including development agencies of the Western industrialized countries representing their own interests.

NGOs operating at the local level in Latin America often receive a substantial amount of funding from foreign organizations and agencies. They focus intensively on local issues since they are operating within small communities. Local NGOs also receive money from the international NGOs. With such mixed support financially, they are relatively independent of the government of the donor country as well as from the government of those countries in which they function. For that reason, they are flexible and frequently provide assistance in innovative ways, focusing on needs that might not be sanctioned under local legislation, such as HIV-AIDS education, preventing violence against women, sex education, or reproductive health. NGOs devoted to women have had the freedom to commit themselves to various gender issues, in countries where gender equity is not a priority in public policy. Yet, despite the accomplishment of NGOs in the field of education and gender equity, there are few written descriptions and even fewer probing interpretations beyond what is offered in this book.

NGOs have been quite active in Latin America, perhaps more than any other region of the world. They played an important role during the period of authoritarian regimes in the Southern Cone, helping to hold together and provide vitally needed forms of education, social networks, and human services in civil society during times of severe repression by the military and the government. There is also a thirty-year history of NGOs working in the region on sustainable development. NGOs tend to focus on specific fields of action, such as human rights, environmental conservation, and democratization. NGOs that focus on women's education and gender awareness have been able to provide leadership training and empowerment consistent with the vision of the international women's movement. Efforts of this nature are being conducted by relatively small staffs with limited resources, devoted to program development and fund raising with much less time available to reflect upon or systematize their experience. Women operating in such networks do not often intersect with the academic world. Another central goal of this book, therefore, is to bring to light the learning that has taken place within those NGOs.

The funding that international development agencies provide for education in Latin America is dwarfed by the much larger total expenditure for education by national and state governments in the region. Nevertheless, international funding is of great importance for the poor, the indigenous groups, and the adult population that has limited access to the formal systems of education. Since the 1980s, Latin America has been confronted by a prolonged economic crisis, which has been devastating to social expenditure, especially to education. As countries have been struggling to maintain their education funding, assistance provided by international organizations has been crucial in strategic areas of educational need in the region.

In the case of women and girls, the progressive positions taken by development agencies such as UNESCO and two major NGOs funded by the Dutch Ministry of Foreign Affairs have been instrumental in generating a public discussion of gender disparities within society, politics, and education. The ways in which these agencies frame an understanding of gender and the types of projects they are willing to fund exercise a visible influence on the work done in Latin American countries. Within the world of international assistance agencies there are salient differences in philosophy, which in turn are reflected in the aims and structures of the programs they sponsor. During 1996, in a meeting sponsored by OECD, donor countries pledged to increase funding to their bilateral agencies to ensure universal basic education in the third world, thus reiterating a commitment made in Jomtien, Thailand, in 1990.[6] This commitment increased the number of donor countries participating in Latin America, and it provided an opportunity not only for new approaches but also for a broader vision of how to support education. The stimulus provided by the OECD-sponsored meeting furnishes us an excellent opportunity now to take stock of what has been done. Accordingly, the goal of the last section of this book is to examine the contributions of bilateral and multilateral aid in the region.

Reflecting on the importance of the three actors identified in the foregoing paragraphs, this book is organized in three sections. The first examines gender equity policies and programs in several countries. The chapter on Paraguay by Carmen Colazo traces the trajectory of PRIOME (Programa Nacional de Promoción de la Igualdad de Oportunidades para la Mujer en el Area Educativa) and highlights its protagonists, opponents, and accomplishments. Colazo describes how a model previously conceived in Argentina influenced public policies on gender equity. She describes and interprets the education reform that has taken place in the 1990s and describes the financial assistance and technical support from the Netherlands at the launching stage, along with continuous support from the *Agencia Española de Cooperación Internacional* (AECI).

The chapter by Cecilia Lazarte and Martha Lanza describes efforts in Bolivia to improve gender equity since 1994, when that country's comprehensive education reform defined national identity as multilingual, multicultural, and rooted in popular participation. The legislation described includes not only young girls in school but indigenous and rural women, focusing on both formal and nonformal education, and calling for implementation of complementary programs in both systems. As in the case of Paraguay, the financial assistance and technical support from the Netherlands had been crucial in the development of this project.

The chapter by María Clara di Pierro offers a detailed historical review of public policies on adult education in Brazil. She finds that nationwide policy on literacy has traditionally been weakly implemented. She also finds that such policies fail to address the specificity of women's conditions and end up serving younger women and older men, denying the future benefits of literacy for women aged thirty and above, who not only comprise a large category of adult illiterates but who are also most likely to be heads of households and raising children. Thus, those with the largest potential to break the effects of intergenerational illiteracy are underserved by government literacy programs.

The second section of the book examines the direct engagement of NGOs in providing education for adult women. Nelly P. Stromquist looks at women-led NGOs as expressions of a social movement, in this case the feminist movement. Her chapter reviews the activities of women-led NGOs in formal, nonformal, and informal education. She finds that these groups are making a rich contribution to gender awareness, organization, and mobilization of women particularly through nonformal and informal education. The latter, although not usually the subject of investigation, offers many possibilities for individual and collective agency. Her chapter closes with a typology of NGO-sponsored educational activities.

Describing an initiative in Mexico, Malú Valenzuela y Gómez Gallardo presents an account of how a feminist NGO has been able to develop a project to understand gender relations in preschools and how mothers, fathers, and teachers influence the learning of gender roles by girls and boys. A notable feature of this model is the inclusion of both teachers and parents in gender training. The project has been extended to other preschools funded by the local government.

As international agencies have increasingly required that recipients of their funds pay special attention to gender, a market has been created for courses of gender training. The chapter by Jeanine Anderson and Rosa Mendoza focuses on new linkages between academics and activists/practitioners to provide mutual support in the creation and provision of courses on gender and development. They compare programs in two different institutions in Peru, assessing constraints as well as accomplishments. The linkage between theory and practice is difficult to establish given the myriad forms that problems at the community level tend to have. The chapter confirms that evaluations have not been done on the gender training packages supplied by international agencies, and strongly recommends revision of these packages because they are outdated both in the images they present on gender relations and the theory of gender that supports them.

Alejandra Valdés focuses on the emergence of women's leadership as a central component in the political culture of our times. Valdés describes a leadership training program in Chile for women who have already played leadership roles in their organizations. The training program considered the importance of "individuation" skills as opposed to "identicity" traits and promoted in its trainees the capability to face conflict, to accept visibility as leaders, and to develop trust in and respect for other women leaders. Since under conventional frames of mind, neither men nor women believe it is proper for women to engage in forms of assertive and much less confrontational behavior, efforts to train women for formal leadership meet considerable resistance.

The chapter by María Bonino and Celia Eccher focuses on the contribution of the largest network of NGOs led by women working on education in Latin America, known as REPEM (*Red de Educación Popular Entre Mujeres de América Latina y el Caribe*). This chapter presents an account of what has been learned through network collaboration about working with national governments, international agencies, and local communities. These authors emphasize that the greatest challenge today is to bring implementation of international agreements to the local level.

The third section inquires into the role of international agencies in promoting education and gender awareness for women and girls in Latin America. The chapter by Regina Cortina analyzes global imperatives for education reform in light of local predicaments faced by people struggling to maintain families and community institutions. The chapter argues that short-term investment by international agencies for project-level support is not furnishing sustained capacity building. The predicament at the local level is that without serious investment by the state in teacher training, the learning that has been achieved through such projects will not ensure lasting influence in the educational systems of the region. Moreover, the projects being funded could succeed in improving the completion rate in primary schools without promoting the expansion and completion of middle school opportunities.

María Luisa Jáuregui describes several shifts in UNESCO programs that have moved from more universalistic to more specific problem-focused approaches. This chapter also considers the new practice of interorganizational cooperation, designed to better address the educational problems in the region. The chapter offers a useful picture of the dauntingly wide range of problems that UNESCO is trying to address in Latin America.

Regina Cortina with Helen Porter look at new developments in bilateral aid resulting from agreements in the 1990s by donor countries. New players such as Spain are present in Latin America today. Other countries such as Canada, the Netherlands, and the United States are revising their bilateral goals. The chapter draws comparisons among the different ways these countries implement their bilateral cooperation. European countries tend to rely on their NGOs, whereas USAID does direct implementation with U.S. subcontractors who work in partnerships with the government and private sector of the recipient country. The chapter presents an interpretation of the policies and types of projects present in Latin America today.

The chapter by Nelly P. Stromquist and colleagues assesses a major project of USAID in Guatemala to increase the retention of rural girls in primary schools. The chapter reviews project goals and assumptions regarding the engagement of civil society, the role of the private sector in resource generation, and the provision of scholarships to encourage the attendance and retention of girls who would otherwise remain unschooled. The project succeeded in increasing the retention of girls in primary schools, but the community and government dynamics needed to provide lasting support for the projects did not materialize.

The contribution by Fúlvia Rosemberg offers a rare probing of the unintended effects of a low-cost policy aimed at providing preschool education for children of poor families. With the assistance of statistical data broken down by ethnicity, age, school grade, and geographical location, she finds that, although more Afro-Brazilian children are entering preschool, they also represent a disproportionate share of those being retained in preschool for several years. Moreover, the teachers of these children tend to lack teaching credentials and usually have low levels of education. The intersection of poor children and poor teachers creates cause for alarm and illuminates yet another manner by which social class, gender, and ethnicity compound the difficulties of forming an educated citizenry.

In this book, we are presenting country-specific case studies, and project evaluations and policy analysis, as a synthesis of what we have learned during the 1990s about how to address the educational needs of women and girls in Latin America. We hope this book will be helpful in clarifying the complementary roles of women-led NGOs and international cooperation in bringing about policy change in support of gender equity in education at the national level. We also hope that studies in this volume will help to illuminate the kinds of programs and projects most likely to produce urgently needed change so that it will be possible to secure greater educational opportunity for women and girls in Latin America.

Regina Cortina   Nelly P. Stromquist
New York University   *University of Southern California*
June 1999   *at Los Angeles*

NOTES

[1]OECD, *Shaping the 21st Century: The Contribution of Development Cooperation,* 1996.

[2]One of the points of the Plan of Action promulgated by the Summit of the Americas, signed by all the presidents of nations in the hemisphere, in Miami in 1994. The definition of civil society is the one adopted in this document.

[3]For the most recent statistics, see *The Equity Gap: Latin America, The Caribbean and the Social Summit* (Santiago de Chile: United Nations, 1997); and UNICEF, *The State of the World's Children 1999, Education* (New York: UNICEF, 1999).

[4]For gender gap in education, see Population Action International, *Educating Girls: Gender Gaps and Gains,* 1998 Report. For Bolivia, see Lazarte and Lanza in this volume, and for Guatemala, see Stromquist ct al. also in this volume.

[5]For issues of educational quality and repetition, see The *Equity Gap.*

[6]See OECD, *Shaping the 21st Century.* The Netherlands has had a co-financing arrangement with four major NGOs since 1980. The two most important in terms of gender and education are NOVIB (Netherlands Organization for International Development Cooperation—Non-Denominational) and HIVOS (Humanist Institute for Cooperation with Developing Countries). Together the four NGOs receive 10 percent of the Dutch budget for foreign assistance.

REFERENCES

OECD. *Shaping the 21st Century: The Contribution of Development Co-operation,* 1996.

Population Action International. *Educating Girls: Gender Gaps and Gains,* 1998 Report.

United Nations. *The Equity Gap: Latin America, The Caribbean and the Social Summit.* Santiago de Chile: United Nations, 1997.

UNICEF. *The State of the World's Children 1999, Education.* New York: UNICEF, 1999.

PART I

Gender Equity in Education Policy

Accomplishments, Obstacles, and
Future Directions in Latin America

Public Policies on Gender and Education in Paraguay
The Project for Equal Opportunities

CARMEN COLAZO

INTRODUCTION: THE HISTORY OF GENDER EQUITY IN PUBLIC POLICY IN PARAGUAY*

Paraguay is a small country sandwiched between Argentina and Brazil in the center of South America. It has experienced long periods of isolation, which have favored a nationalist culture with prolonged stages of authoritarian centralization. Historically, it has suffered under severe dictatorships, which have left rigid patriarchal patterns that are difficult to modify in the medium term.

Despite the rigid patriarchy, women reconstructed the country after the two great wars, which decimated the masculine population. First, after the War of the Triple Alliance (1870) with Argentina, Brazil, and Uruguay, where boys as young as twelve years old were killed. Later, in the war against Bolivia, or the Chaco War (1935), that leaves a recent memory of a country populated by women. But women never took advantage of these situations to take more power or protagonistic positions. They continued with their daily work, promoting men in public and visible leadership positions.

The periods of greater freedom for Paraguayan women coincided with historical stages of the advance of feminism internationally. There was a large public campaign to win women's vote at the beginning of the

*In the text, various articles from the National Constitution of the Republic of Paraguay have been cited. Official Edition, Spanish and Guaraní, June 1992.

century, and the campaign was finally won in the 1960s, under the dictatorship of General Alfredo Stroessner Matiauda. Finally, since 1987, women's organizations, as social movements, have been consolidating around working for legislative change, for quotas in decision-making positions, and for a Women's Secretariat at the ministerial level.[1]

For the first time since the coup on February 3, 1989, that overthrew the Stroessner dictatorship that lasted for more than thirty-five years, the country finds itself in a transition toward democracy that is not without difficulties. After General Andrés Rodríguez (1989–1993), Stroessner's son-in-law, was removed by force, the first free elections in years were planned and an electoral agenda was organized that included constitutional reform.

The country's first democratic constitution was passed in June 1992, and it included as many of the demands as the organized women could get included. Later, the country was run for the first time in decades by a civilian leader, Juan Carlos Wasmosy (1993–1998). Important gender issues were addressed within this emerging democratic framework. For the first time, during the government of General Rodríguez, a woman headed up a ministry when Cintya Prieto was the Minister of Health and Social Welfare from November 17, 1989, until 1993.

That government administration addressed women's issues within the National Development Plan, and women's organizations played an active role in the development of laws and the promotion of specific public policies. The First Civil Code developed by a feminist organization, the Women's Coordination of Paraguay, was passed in 1992, with minor modifications by the legislature. The women fought for a participation quota of no more than 60 percent for either sex in decision-making posts, but won only a 20 percent women's quota in the 1995 Electoral Code reform, by pressure from another organization: the Network of Political Women. This group also proposed the law to create the Women's Secretariat at the ministerial level, which was instituted under Law 34 of 1992.

The Wasmosy government formed the Women's Secretariat in 1993. The first minister was Cristina Muñoz, who, despite competing against the daughter of President Rodríguez, obtained the post because of her ability, her political involvement, her commitment to gender issues, and the support of an important sector of Paraguayan women. The Women's Secretariat has now been functioning for more than six years.

Through its Education Office, the Secretariat began to organize, coordinate, and monitor the country's gender equity policies.

It was difficult, however, to get the Ministry of Education and Cul-

ture (MEC) to support the dissemination of these new contents and practices. Initially, it was practically impossible to work intersectorally in
this area. The Women's Secretariat designed a project of equality of
opportunities and results for women in education, emulating the Argentine Program of Equal Opportunities for Women (PRIOM). The idea was
that MEC would implement the project and be one of its beneficiaries.
The project was designed and structured with the advice and support of
the former head of the Argentine PRIOM, Gloria Bonder, working with
Carmen Colazo, the head of the Paraguayan Education Office of the
Women's Secretariat.

This was the beginning of PRIOME, the Project for Equal Opportunities and Results for Women in Education, which embodied the primary
political and strategic objective of the Secretariat, to work for interinsti-
tutional gender equity policies in education. The Secretariat was aware
that the educational reform, which had been in process since 1990, could
not continue moving forward without broad, clear, and concrete support
for gender, and the only institution that could do this efficiently was
the Women's Secretariat, as the coordinator of the state's gender equity
policies.

The educational reform was initiated by presidential decree 7.815
on November 26, 1990, with the formation of an Advisory Council. Of
the twelve founding members of the Council, only two were women, and
currently there is only one woman member. None of the women have had
experience in gender issues.[2]

The national educational reform incorporates equality of opportunity between men and women in its educational goals. But it does not
speak of coeducation, nor does it mention gender as a broad-reaching
component, but instead speaks of "family education." It has been conceived of and implemented from the Ministry of Education and Culture
with criteria of complementarity between the sexes for marriage, the
affirmation of the traditional role assigned to women, and other concepts
and practices considered discriminatory from the feminist position.

This demonstrates that at the level of public policy, there is still a
lack of understanding or acceptance of the significance of gender in education and its consequences for individual and social development. There
is not an understanding of its true human and political dimension, or its
support for the analysis of social inequalities and the value of its integration in the solution of social inequalities. The existence of this gender
component in Paraguayan public policy is more linked to the people who
are committed to gender and who find themselves in certain positions

where they can push it. There is not a global concept at the state level or strategic criteria about gender.

It is common to find within national public policies that certain ministries, institutes, or state offices are given to certain party sectors, power factions, or pressure groups. This makes national policy a difficult puzzle to put together, with compartmentalized and sometimes even contradictory characteristics, which can be understood only by taking into account the complexity of the distribution and exercise of power.

The Catholic Church has had, and continues to have, significant influence in Paraguayan educational policies. The 1992 constitution, which for the first time separates church and state, and leaves behind the confessional church and official religion, also recognizes and expressly thanks the Catholic Church for its support of national culture. This institution has demonstrated its power both by holding posts in the Ministry of Education and Culture, by proposing people linked to the church for positions of minister and vice minister, as well as by participating in the formulation of educational policies. The Educational Reform Council, an autonomous consulting body, which is responsible for the reform's "philosophy," has a majority of members who are recognized in Paraguay for their contribution to education and close links to the Catholic Church. Several of them are, or have been, priests. The educational reform reflects the religious position of the Council and the Ministry, and reinforces the population's cultural traditions, which have visible feudal and patriarchal characteristics. These coexist with the modernizing tendencies of globalization and its demands. The reform has also had critical support from the World Bank and Harvard University, which have also influenced its tendencies to promote educational criteria emphasizing labor needs, in accordance with current neoliberal and globalization demands.

THE PRIOME PROJECT AND THE PRIOME PROGRAM

The PRIOME Project was designed within the Women's Secretariat, thanks to initial Swedish Cooperation and later support from the Spanish International Cooperation Agency (AECI), which helped to implement the project. An accord between the Paraguayan and Spanish governments established shared tasks to put into practice article 48 of the constitution, which addresses equality between men and women.

A Tripartite Commission was organized between the Women's Secretariat, the Spanish International Cooperation Agency, and the Technical Planning Secretary in order to decide on activities and budget. The

PRIOME Project was the cornerstone from which the Women's Secretariat could initiate direct conversations with the Ministry of Education and Culture to initiate an Equal Opportunity Program for Women in Education, to develop four priority areas: (a) curricular reform with a gender component; (b) review and analysis of texts and materials from a gender perspective; (c) teacher training in gender; and (d) raising the awareness of public opinion around the importance of the inclusion of gender in education.

Thus began in the country an institutional process to slowly introduce a gender focus in education. It also introduced a different experience of working together through the gender specialist team within the country linked to the feminist movement and to nongovernment organizations, working together with state technicians and teachers.

The PRIOME Project initiated an Inter-ministerial Accord between the Women's Secretariat and the Ministry of Education and Culture, which initiated the program of the same name. The program became part of the Curriculum Department of the MEC, which designs the Ministry's basic educational policies, through an office that includes a technical operating unit with a director and two consultants, one a gender specialist and one an education specialist. The PRIOME Program has the specific function of fulfilling the cross-curricular component of gender in Paraguayan education, as expressed in the accord signed by the Minister of Women and the Minister of Education and Culture.

PRIOME PROJECT ACHIEVEMENTS
IN SHARED WORK WITH THE PROGRAM

The project teams organized working plans around the educational reform implementation, to work with it and enrich it with gender support. The project's members worked with the Ministry of Education and Culture to build contacts with those responsible for the respective areas and to try to introduce suggestions for the curriculum, for teacher training with directors, teachers, and trainers, as well as for texts and materials. They developed analysis matrices in each of the project areas and theoretical documents addressing the areas, taking into account gender considerations and indicators. Listed below are the most important achievements of this part of the project:

1. Began to work interinstitutionally in order to establish gender across the curriculum in the educational system, within an

education that is accustomed to speak in masculine terms to identify all people, and which has not taken into account dignity and equality of rights between men and women as a priority—and even less has considered respect for differences—in the context of a pluriethnic and multicultural country that has only just begun to weakly leave behind excluding nationalism.

2. Initiated a change in curricular images and content, giving suggestions to modify the absence of women from history and science, and in general, highlighting women's diverse contributions to culture, in contrast to the traditional and stereotyped image of woman as mother, daughter, symbol of the homeland, teacher, partner in procreation and patroneis supporting great achievements of men.

3. Analyzed the transmission through educational practices of hatred, love, care, generosity, evil, activity, and inactivity. Identify who was assigned which roles and why, and what have been the cultural consequences; and develop analysis matrices so that teachers and others who work in nonformal or informal education can identify them and work to change them.

4. Collaborated in buying books and materials, reviewing them from a gender perspective, and making clear and concrete suggestions for change.

5. Structured and developed a gender module, together with another on sexuality, within the teaching training of more than fifteen hundred directors, teachers, workers in the educational system, and trainers from teacher training centers. During these modules, issues were addressed that were almost considered taboo within the traditionalist, stereotyped, and rigid cultural structure as manifested in curriculum, texts, and so on.

6. Initiated a debate about sexuality—a taboo issue within Paraguayan culture, resisted in the education sphere—beginning with dialogue about gender and heterosexuality, and eventually talking openly and respectfully about different sexual identities. This motivated, on the teachers' part, the sharing of experiences within their educational practices, in terms of issues brought up by girls and boys about their homosexuality and with respect to other sexual identities, not in terms of the abnormal, the prohibited, the dirty, the ugly, but from the powerlessness of ignorance, perceived rejection, or the shame of teaching what they do not

know enough about or about which they have their own preconceptions. There was a positive dialogue with teachers of both
sexes around the reasons that there are statistically high levels of
sexual confusion among young people and adults in a society
that hides and prohibits free speech about these experiences.
Participants also looked at why there is a problem with teenage
pregnancy, as early as twelve years old in rural areas, as well as
other problems in a world bombarded by media images of sex,
without the possibility for children to dialogue with adults who
can listen, understand, and help them.[3]

7. Wore down existing resistance to coeducation within the teaching force and to see how, little by little, interest was piqued in
knowing more about it and putting it into practice.

8. Noted how the Guaraní have a hard time translating certain Spanish words that describe the reproductive apparatus, which leads to
jokes in class, and how teachers would rather tear pages out of
books than pronounce certain words to their students, and how
understanding the language issues can help in understanding the
problem and finding possible solutions.[4]

9. Debated why girls are not encouraged to study math and science, but are pushed to play with dolls, to practice domestic
tasks and the roles of wife and mother. Why boys are at the top
of the list and girls appear at the end, without using an alphabet-
ical ordering that would be nondiscriminatory, but where all,
both boys and girls, equally suffer the violence of a hierarchical
and authoritarian system that in many schools is translated into
physical blows against students "so that they will learn."

10. The project was able to plan the incorporation of gender in education for a five-year period and to organize instruments for monitoring and evaluation. At the same time, the project has also
developed materials and texts to incorporate gender into education.

In sum, it was an achievement to have been able to address these
issues with people from different social strata in the country, and to see
how all of them participated in placing the intimate and daily into the
public sphere. Throughout this process, international cooperation that is
committed to incorporating gender into education has been critical, gam-
bling on change and a future in democracy, providing experts and finance
for the process.

OBSTACLES TO THE PRIOME PROJECT

One of the major obstacles that the project faced was the difficulty of changing ingrained bureaucratic MEC structures. This made it difficult for people from nongovernment sectors to understand certain indispensable hierarchical codes, like who writes a note and who signs it, and the power that these actions imply, which is often expressed in the outlook that expresses: What can they teach those of us who already know? All of this requires negotiations.

Another obstacle was the difficulty, for people from the private sector with their particular concept of work, of adjusting to the single preset schedule of officials who work in the public sector, as well as adjusting to their patterns and rhythms. For instance, the MEC did not have an annual plan, but organized activities throughout the year, which presented a major obstacle for the gender project work. Even the dress code seems to divide the two almost irreconcilable worlds: that of the formal world and that of the informal world.

It was also difficult for people to recognize the gender component as a questioner of women's traditional roles, within a socializing structure that considers mothers and teachers (second mothers) as almost sacred archetypes, and that understands women's classic role to be the best way to socialize boys and girls and to prepare them for future families. This attitude persists despite the articles in the constitution that speak of equality, no discrimination in education, and respect for different kinds of families (Article 46 on equality, Article 73 on education and culture, and Article 49 on the rights of the family).

At various times, the PRIOME team members faced a problem with dogmatic religious beliefs, whose proponents resisted the incorporation of the gender component. The team members even found that people within Family Education—the term used in the education reform—presented ideas of the complementarity of the sexes and antifeminism. They found these attitudes among authorities, teachers, and other people involved in the process. The most extreme example of these positions was found in the courses, where there were different opinions expressed that opposed the incorporation of a gender perspective in education, which are worth sharing.

Participants of both sexes offered reasons for not including the gender component in education. They said that the gender perspective goes against the Catholic religion and other religions for the following reasons: (a) it speaks of equal opportunities between men and women when men and women are not and should not be equal; (b) there cannot be equality because it goes against cultural norms established by religion; (c) the Bible expressly states that God the Father is male and that He created us, that Christ was also a man, and that Maria, his mother, had a specific role as woman-mother; (d) the Bible states that woman was made from the rib of man and thus is complementary to man, not superior to him; (e) women should remain in their places as wives and mothers and should not want to have other roles that would destroy the family through their own fault, as is currently happening when mothers work outside of the home; (f) feminists are seeking women's superiority over men and they are foreigners and extremists who do not understand the country's culture; and (g) if girls and boys are educated with a gender focus, boys will become homosexuals when they do girls' activities, and girls will become tomboys when they do boys' activities. There was extreme fear that boys and girls would "become homosexuals" if nonsexist education was instituted.

Another interesting aspect for analysis was the teachers' difficulty in talking about sexual pleasure. It was noted that in almost all the images and concepts that are communicated in materials, texts, and classes about the genital organs, the feminine reproductive organs were not explained in detail because it was difficult to explain the functioning of some of the organs. There was fear that if teachers explained that the clitoris was an organ expressly for pleasure, this could imply that sex is pleasurable, which might provoke young people to engage in sexual relations and face serious problems of early pregnancy, "promiscuity," "immorality," and so on.

With respect to the debate that emerged around other sexual identities, there was also significant fear expressed by both men and women participants. They feared that they might influence the socialization process or push girls and boys into "premature" sexuality, or sexuality that is considered "abnormal" if they give them the opportunity to explore their sexuality with specific materials and texts.

The team also faced some resistance to the idea of interculturality. Participants questioned the fact that some consultants were of other nationalities. This occurred even though at the beginning of the course it was explained that international cooperation supported the project economically and it was also supported by the work of some experts at the Spanish Women's Institute and some young Spanish collaborators. At various times the participants insinuated that the gender issue was for other countries, not for Paraguay, and that is why foreigners had to come in to inculcate them. However, not all people spoke this way, though a considerable number of teachers did.

We share these positions because they are the clearest expression of the reality that we confront when we introduce the gender component in Paraguayan education, and because they must be considered when analyzing the achievements and obstacles to incorporating into education feminism's beliefs in equal opportunity between men and women, respect for differences, and support of equitable human development.

LESSONS LEARNED AND FINAL CONCLUSIONS

The work carried out by me as the Women's Secretariat's leader, first as director of education, and later as a promoter for the PRIOME Program and designer of the PRIOME Project, offers some lessons that are worth sharing.

As we know, the incorporation of gender in education is an arduous task that will take many years. The educational system, as an agent of the socialization process, is generally structured to reinforce patriarchal and sexist cultural practices, not to change values, attitudes, and behaviors, and this is especially true in Latin America.

Public policies that seek to modify such entrenched cultural patterns are both necessary and revolutionary, but are strongly resisted by the dominant culture. The obstacles are powerful, and are expressed by the institutions or sectors with the greatest interest in preventing change, that is, by the most conservative elements of society.

The degree to which gender policies can be implemented, weakened, or disappear depends on the political-ideological sector holding state power at any one time. In Paraguay, this is fundamentally related to the state's religious or dictatorial commitment. The more the state tends toward religion or dictatorship, the more difficult it will be to implement gender policies, because: (a) the Church generally does not conceive of women as people with the same opportunities and rights as men, and they see in women's individual and social freedom the seeds of the destruction of the family because of the abandonment of traditional roles; and (b) Paraguayan populist dictators favor the preeminence of the military *caudillo* figure and strengthen classic feminine stereotypes that complement that image.

In addition, the degree to which schools are linked to religious or dictatorial criteria has a direct relation to their resistance to accepting gender concepts, even more so if we consider the possibility of inserting content that expresses people's right to have other sexual identities. Boys and girls who can feel, manifest, and/or define in themselves a different sexual identity will continue to be painfully discriminated against in this educational system, as are all those people who do not adjust to the norm.[5]

Another aspect to be pointed out is that international cooperation has generally favored the inclusion of the gender component and has almost obligated that it be included in order to get funding. However, when cooperation ends—since the funding is supposed to promote plans, programs, projects, but not to sustain them for many years—many of the programs will end. Efforts vanish and the people who implemented them get burned out.

That is why the PRIOME Project runs the risk of not having continuity if international cooperation ceases. The state does not appear to have emphasized its necessity and has not assigned the necessary budget to the program. But the strategy of organizing the national program and legitimizing it by an accord between ministries offers hope that not everything will be paralyzed and that work will continue.

Despite the insistence on and the training about the importance of incorporating a gender component in education to authorities and other involved sectors, the individuals and institutions involved did not internalize the idea that is part and parcel of the gender perspective, the sense of equity and social justice implied by gender. What it means, exactly, is that girls should have the same opportunities in the future as boys in Paraguay. We say that gender discrimination is cultural, and this ends up being an empty sentence.

Many strategies have yet to be considered, and much patience is needed to continue fighting against the trends: from avoiding conflict and seeking negotiation in order to avoid greater tensions, to standing firm behind certain ideas. It is important to continue the discourses, investigation, and compiling of statistics. It is important to plan, knowing that sometimes large steps are less effective than small steps that might go unnoticed in certain situations.

It is important to note the interest of many male and female teachers in gender once they begin to understand its transforming magnitude, and even their manifested desire to continue to receive training from this perspective. We could see interest in organizing gender projects in the different areas they were working in and how, little by little, they left behind prejudices and preconceptions to support this component and use its multiplier effect within the educational process, which requires the deconstruction of earlier patterns, to find a more human and democratic synthesis within the school, society, and the state.

I have also come to the conclusion that despite the fact that we are accustomed to saying that no one is irreplaceable, this is not always true. There are irreplaceable people in the gender issue, because when someone really committed to gender leaves a certain post, years of work can be lost in just a short time. The commitment of feminist women is invaluable, because they are committed to and skilled in a transforming ideology. It is always important to support women's organizations, and individual women, who share and support our work.

Gender equity in public policy in Paraguay has begun to be institutionalized, especially because of the existence of a permanent program, which now has clear priorities, and thanks to a pioneering project that is currently making plans for four more years of work. However, it must be recognized that, given the rapidly changing situations in our Latin American realities, that is no guarantee for the future.

Thus, now is the time to continue the project in its impact study phase, and to solidify new and better products, and it is also the time to design and implement new projects within the PRIOME Program. It is also the time to connect them to the National Plan for Equal Opportunities already designed by the Women's Secretariat and to its operating plan, based on the Platform for Action endorsed in the Fourth International Women's Conference in Beijing, China, in 1995.

The PRIOME Program has great possibilities for future development, but it needs greater autonomy and a larger budget. It should focus on the modification of the "family education" component to incorporate gender criteria. It should work toward coeducation, and should be capable of arguing and defending itself to authorities, teachers, and society. It also needs a support team to implement training projects, which should be solidified in an accord with the NGOs that have the human resources and experience in this area.[6]

The PRIOME Program has the future challenge of designing ministerial norms in gender and education, designing the research that is required, working with all levels of formal education and projecting toward nonformal education, in coordination with interested organizations.

PRIOME can become a space where people can denounce incidents of sexual harassment, rape, and any other type of violence in the educational sphere, as long as there is no other specific body for that task. It can also connect to other organizations that work on that issue. PRIOME should establish agreements to fulfill and implement its Action Plan.

This program was supported by cooperation from AECI, which gambled on a pioneering project that will only see fruits in the long term. But it is also clear that the responsibility for its continuation in the national and international sphere must be supported by the political will of governments that are initiating cultural change toward a sustainable development with social justice. It is the people who have the national political decision-making power who should be valuing these tools and who should give them the budget support they need to achieve the required modifications.

It remains clear, finally, that only gender solidarity—such as the support for this work from the Women's Institute and from Argentine PRIOM, and support from individual women like Gloria Bonder, Pilar Gonzalez, Ana Manero, Concepción Jaramillo, Francisco Venegas, on the international level, and Cristina Muñoz, Esther Prieto, Graziella Corvalán, Line Bareiro, and Marta Melgarejo, on the national level, and so many others—will make possible the construction of different societies, if we remain committed to our work for a better world that is more just, more equitable, and more united.

NOTES

[1]See: Line Bareiro, Clyde Soto, and others, *Alquimistas* (Asunción: Centro de Documentación y Estudios, 1996); Cecilia Silvera Alvarez, *Telémaco Silvera, Un demócrata Republicano (Vida y escritos)* (Asunción: Editorial Saleciana, 1992); Esther Prieto (ed.), *"Igualdad ante la Ley," New Legislation in Paraguay* (Asunción: Presidencia de la República, Secretaría de la Mujer, Ediciones La Rural, 1996).

[2]Fundación En Alianza, *Reforma Educativa. Compromiso de Todos, Informe de Avance del Consejo Asesor de la Reforma Educativa* (Asunción: Ediciones Koé-Yú, 1992).

[3]See: María Victoria Heikel, *Ser Mujer en Paraguay. Situación sociodemográfica y cambios registrados en el período intercensal. 1982–1992* (Asunción: Presidencia de la República, Secretaría Técnica de Planificación, Dirección General de Estadísticas, Encuestas y Censos, Fondo de Población de las Naciones Unidas [FNUAP], 1996); Cándida Mereles and Angélica Roa de Beca, *Ahora ya saben todo. Vivencia de la sexualidad de las adolescentes. Factores socioculturales y expresiones de una conducta sexual de riesgo en adolescentes de zonas urbano marginales del Paraguay* (Asunción: Fondo de Población de las Naciones Unidas [FNUAP]), QR Producciones Gráficas, 1996).

[4]Throughout the project many teachers talked about tearing out page N52 from the third-grade book distributed by the Ministry of Education and Culture as part of the free materials from the educational reform. This book had been

solicited, analyzed, and approved by the Ministry. The page spoke about the sexual act in technically simple terms, but it said that it was an act that gives pleasure to those who engage in it. There was dialogue in the courses about this issue. Women and men teachers shared their difficulties with expressing that sexuality is pleasurable because of the fear of promoting "unleashed" sexuality, and they also talked about the difficulty of translating the terms used in the page into Guaraní, because in that language they are very "strong" and cause laughter.

[5]Bejamín Arditti, *Circuito Norma-Diferencia* (Asunción: Centro de Documentación y Estudio, 1989). We clarify that when we speak of boys and girls we are referring to the age contemplated in the International Convention on the Rights of the Child, which identifies people as children until eighteen years of age.

[6]Paraguay has been going through a difficult stage in its process of transition to democracy. In 1998, during the presentation before Parliament of a law dealing with violence against women by the Coordination of Women of Paraguay, a demonstration by military *caudillo* Lino Oviedo, supporter of the country's real power during the government of Cubas Grau—who just resigned after a period of impeachment proceedings by the Parliament supported in great measure by the population, and which cost the lives of six young demonstrators—called the women who accompanied the presentation "crazy feminists" and other offensive terms. Today, after a period of great national agitation, the country finds itself with a new government that is talking of returning to more respectful forms of interaction and that favors the continuation of programs and projects like PRIOME.

REFERENCES

Arditti, Bejamín. *Circuito Norma-Diferencia.* Asunción: Centro de Documentación y Estudio, 1989.
Bareiro, Line, Clyde Soto, et al. *Alquimistas.* Asunción: Centro de Documentación y Estudios, 1996.
Fundación En Alianza. *Reforma Educativa. Compromiso de Todos, Informe de Avance del Consejo Asesor de la Reforma Educativa.* Asunción: Ediciones Koé-Yú, 1992.
Heikel, María Victoria Heikel. *Ser Mujer en Paraguay. Situación socio-demográfica y cambios registrados en el período intercensal. 1982–1992.* Asunción: Presidencia de la República, Secretaría Técnica de Planificación, Dirección General de Estadísticas, Encuestas y Censos, Fondo de Población de las Naciones Unidas (FNUAP), 1996.
Mereles, Cándida and Angélica Roa de Beca. *Ahora ya saben todo. Vivencia de la sexualidad de las adolescentes. Factores socioculturales y expresiones de una conducta sexual de riesgo en adolescentes de zonas urbano marginales del Paraguay.* Asunción: Fondo de Población de las Naciones Unidas (FNUAP), QR Producciones Gráficas, 1996.

Prieto, Esther (ed). *"Igualdad ante la Ley,"* *New Legislation in Paraguay*. Asunción: Presidencia de la República, Secretaría de la Mujer, Ediciones La Rural, 1996.

Silvera Alvarez, Cecilia. *Telémaco Silvera, un demócrata republicano (Vida y escritos)*. Asunción: Editorial Saleciana, 1992.

Gender Equity in Bolivian Educational Policies
Experiences and Challenges

CECILIA LAZARTE AND MARTHA LANZA

INTRODUCTION

In 1996, the Bolivian government issued a legal document declaring that all schools segregated by sex should become coeducational. This action provoked irate protests from both students and teachers who defended the "tradition" of boys' schools, while directors argued that they did not have any girls' bathrooms. The girls who took on the challenge of registering at these schools in the face of such prejudice stated:

> We women have a right to come here. We are equal to them. Saying that the discipline will be too strict and that we won't be able to bear it is only an excuse. Let them realize we are ready for it![1]

This dramatic episode in the history of Bolivian education and in the search for equality of opportunities makes clear once again that there is still a long road to travel, the opportunity cost is still very high for women, and coeducation is still a goal that must be reached. There have been important steps, however. The Undersecretary of Gender Affairs was formed in 1994 (*Subsecretaría de Asuntos de Género,* SAG) within the *Ministerio de Desarrollo Humano* (Ministry of Human Development),[2] and that same year the Educational Reform Law was approved. Both actions, happening at the same time, have allowed important advances and at the same time have offered challenges for the future.

In this context, it is important to note that Swedish and Dutch cooperation finance both the state gender institute (SAG) and the educational reform, which has been an advantage when promoting gender equity policies, because the breadth and flexibility of the objectives and orientations of this cooperation have led to a broad margin of autonomy in the design and implementation of policies during the period that we analyze.

These elements make up the framework through which we will attempt to look at the education and gender field. We will review women's educational situation in Bolivia, the educational policies promoted by the state in the 1994–1997 period, and the experience of mainstreaming the gender focus in educational reform during that period. Finally, we will point out some of the lessons we have learned and the challenges the study has highlighted.

EDUCATIONAL SITUATION OF WOMEN IN BOLIVIA

Bolivia is a country with marked geographic, ecological, and cultural variety, and therefore has great social inequities. One of the unique characteristics of the country's educational issues is the linguistic and cultural diversity as expressed in spoken languages: 30 percent speak only Spanish; 14 percent speak a native tongue which could be Quechua, Aymara, or Guaraní, and 60 percent of the population is bilingual. Sixty percent of the population is indigenous, which complicates the situation of Bolivian women even more because gender inequities are mixed with ethnic, cultural, and social inequities. According to Silvia Rivera, "to be woman, indigenous (*chola* or *birlocha*), as well as poor, is a triple stigma which keeps a growing number of people from accessing a status dignified of human beings."[3]

In that framework, a woman's educational situation in recent decades has undergone important advances that have been expressed in the significant reduction of the illiteracy rate and an increase in school attendance. However, it is also evident that important gaps in linguistic terms continue, as well as gaps based on geography, rural or urban location, gender, and age.

Rural illiteracy rates are higher than urban illiteracy rates, and illiteracy among women is higher in both rural and urban areas, mostly affecting women over 44 years old. Other significant data indicates that 27 percent of the economically active feminine population from 15 to 64 years old is illiterate, a problem that affects the women themselves, their homes, and the country in general.[4] The persistence of illiteracy among women has to do with a diversity of associated factors. Among these we note the marginalization these women experienced when they were girls in school, and the high levels of female dropouts from primary school.

Both of these contribute to the high levels of illiteracy due to lack of practice. This phenomenon, at the same time, is the result of various cultural and economic practices that affect women in the majority—practices that are closely linked to the issue of access and retention of women in the educational system. In effect, diverse studies carried out in this area demonstrate that the greatest obstacles are sociocultural; the perception is that a girl's education is not important because there is no return for the girl or for her family. Sociocultural issues include the domestic tasks assigned to oldest daughters in a family, such as caring for younger siblings and animals, and other tasks. These responsibilities increase with the extreme poverty that characterizes rural indigenous families, the impact of which can be observed in Table 1.

In terms of school attendance rates, the Bolivian educational panorama has been transformed, improving educational conditions for the population in general, but with persistent and significant gaps between the urban and rural sectors. In both cases, however, the female population still finds itself marginalized and excluded, especially at the secondary, technical, and higher education levels.

As demonstrated in Table 2, school attendance levels have increased above all in the 6 to 14 year old population;[5] however, once again rural women are those with the lowest attendance rates. In general terms, girls between 16 and 19 years old in rural areas appear to suffer the most. At the national level, we see schooling rates of 84 percent; 86 percent for males and 82 percent for women. While these differences are not very high, at the

Table 1. Illiteracy Rates among the Population over 15 years, by Sex and Urban and Rural Residence, 1976 and 1992

Area	1976			1992		
	Total %	Men %	Women %	Total %	Men %	Women %
Nation	36	15	53	20	9	36
Urban	24	6	37	11	4	23
Rural	48	23	68	27	15	50

Source: Undersecretary of Gender Affairs, Report on Women's Advances in Bolivia, 1994. Population and Housing Census of 1976 and 1992.

local level the differences are accentuated. Of the 311 Bolivian municipalities, 75 percent experience inequity for women, 5 percent experience gender equity, and close to 20 percent experience inequity for men.[6]

It has been calculated that almost 60 percent of boys and girls who
enter school do not speak Spanish or a popular Spanish (that is, a Spanish
adapted to the structural logic of their mother tongue), which places
them at a serious disadvantage in the learning process based on formal
Spanish.[7] Other critical factors have to do with the lack of security and
the irrelevance of what is learned. The ways of transmitting knowledge
and the social relations established in the educational process also have
an influence, as do self-esteem and attitudes toward life. All of this joins
with the quality of the educational process and the lack of equal opportunities for women.

CONSTRUCTING GENDER EQUITY IN EDUCATION

The gender gaps described here demonstrate the need to develop policies
and strategies oriented toward broadening women's education, especially
for indigenous girls, and eliminating gender discrimination in terms of
access and retention, fundamentally affecting the quality of education. In
that framework, we cite some antecedents to contextualize the scene, looking at actions and strategies that worked to incorporate a gender perspective in the Bolivian educational policies in the period we analyze.

The process of making women's marginality visible and transforming it in public policies has been in gestation since the beginning of the

**Table 2. School Attendance Rate among the School-Age Population
from 6 to 19 Years, by Sex and Urban and Rural Residence, Bolivia,
1992**

Age Groups	Urban Total %	Urban Women %	Urban Men %	Rural Total %	Rural Women %	Rural Men %
6 to 19 years	82	81	84	63	59	66
6 to 14 years	91	90	92	75	72	78
15 to 19 years	66	63	69	29	24	34

Source: Population and Housing Census 1992.

women's movement, whose most immediate reference point has been the fight for democracy at the end of the 1970s, where the participation of women miners and housewives was fundamental, although they lacked a significant role in the decision-making process and the implementation of public policies. In the 1980s, nongovernmental organizations emerged with the perspective of affecting women's situation, generating what Sonia Montaño[8] calls a "social convergence between women and the state, promoting models, projects and criticisms against the state and against discrimination."[9]

The National Plan for Women was designed in 1993[10] as part of the policies of the National Organization of Women and the Family (*Organismo Nacional de la Mujer y la Familia,* ONAMFA).[11] This initiated a new period in policy analysis aimed at improving women's condition and situation. In 1994, a new process of social and economic reforms was launched. It included the reform of the executive power. These changes responded to a new focus on sustainable human development based on the decentralization process and the strengthening of local democracy. Undoubtedly, this new environment was conducive to the design, management, institutionalization, and legitimization of policies aimed at promoting diversity, equal opportunities, and equity.

In this framework of the state reforms, the Undersecretary for Gender Affairs (SAG) was founded. It was responsible for policies directed at women in the Bolivian state, with the mission of "creating the conditions and strengthening the institutional bases for the design and implementation of national public policies, oriented to the achievement of equal opportunity for women."[12] It is important to mention that this principle was considered to be a pillar of sustainable human development and of the strengthening of political, social, economic, and family democracy. The SAG strategies were based on the trilogy of investment, equity, and autonomy: *Investment,* to overcome the old notion of social spending and to use the high returns to invest in women; *equity,* to achieve not only a redistribution of income but more fundamentally the redistribution of power; *autonomy,* to transcend the focus on *woman = family unity* and to advance toward a recognition of a woman's ability to decide individually about forms of organization, political participation, reproductive roles, and economic participation. The creation and institutionalization of SAG was a fundamental achievement of the women's movement; a product, according to Sonia Montaño, of "the existence of a reformist political agenda that facilitated the coming together of state willingness and women's social determination."[13]

Parallel to the creation of the SAG, the Educational Reform Law was approved in July 1994, which introduced an innovative pedagogical concept, implying a recognition of the country's ethnic and cultural diversity and establishing as fundamental pillars interculturality, popular participation, and situated and active learning. In addition, the principle of equality of opportunities permeated the beginning and end of education. In effect, the law notes that education "is intercultural and bilingual, because it assumes the country's sociocultural heterogeneity in an atmosphere of respect between Bolivian men and women."[14] In terms of the goals of education, the law stipulates: "generating gender equity in the educational atmosphere, stimulating women's greater active participation in society."[15]

With regard to the curriculum and pedagogical approach, the new law "incorporates the concept of gender equity throughout the curricular design process."[16] This aspect is articulated by taking into account *transversal competencies,* incorporating social issues in the development of educational content, thus notably enriching educational quality. The *transversal competencies* considered were education for gender equity, democracy, sustainable development, health, and sexuality.

Without a doubt, the inclusion of these elements in the legislation represents a significant step toward a more pluralistic, gender-respecting, and integrating education for girls and boys. According to Elizabeth Salinas,

> the Educational Reform Law aimed at developing a more democratic and pluralistic society, receptive to our community's development needs, conscious of its responsibility to form new generations to be a part of an ever changing and growingly complex world, and capable of offering women and men from all walks of life the same opportunities and possibilities to fully develop their interests and capacities. The Law would take an active role in generating equal opportunities in different areas of the community.[17]

POLICY ORIENTATIONS

The incorporation and treatment of the gender perspective in Bolivian educational policies was developed based on two basic considerations: in the first place, the need to understand mainstreaming as a determining factor in the construction of educational quality, and as a result, the need to mainstream this approach throughout educational policies in a permanent and integral way. From this perspective, mainstreaming the gender approach was suggested in the following areas:

- By identifying basic learning needs in a program called NEBAS (Spanish acronym).
- Through its relationship with the intercultural approach from a critical vision of cultural values and practices in a context of equity.
- Through equity in male and female participation in management and control of the educational process.
- In the entire process of educational planning, including the diagnosis, planning, implementation, monitoring, and evaluation phases.
- In the process of curricular innovation, specifically in the contents and activities, and the criteria to redesign the classroom space and learning spaces.
- In teacher's training and professional development.

The intention was to assume gender equity as a focus directly related to the criteria of innovation of pedagogical practice. This innovative focus assumes that one sees, thinks, and does things differently based on new conceptions that help to interpret, question, and modify daily practices. In this framework, however, educational quality acquires a social sense that should be complemented by an individual sense of recognition and valuing, and responses to personal needs for full development without any kind of bias.

The second consideration was the recognition that gender discrimination is part of a series of discriminations (based on ethnic, cultural, social differences, etc.) equally harmful for social and individual development, and all of which call for the generation of a collective individual conscience. Added to this is the notion of the other and positive acceptance of difference in relation to interculturality and gender, within the elemental respect afforded by human rights.

This idea coincides with the intercultural education focus promoted by the Educational Reform Program, which proposes a perspective to place the subject in his or her own culture and to prepare him or her for a process of critical and selective appropriation of the elements of other cultures. It was an attempt to promote a pedagogy of difference and respect for all people, to view reality based on universal values related to human rights.

A VIEW OF THE PROCESS

The mission of the Undersecretary of Gender Affairs refers to developing norms for gender policies within public policies. In reality, the real process has gone beyond the normative sphere. There is gradual movement toward the formulation of a five-year strategy that, according to Ivonne Farah, contemplates four fundamental areas of public policies: "policy design, implementation, legitimization and institutionalization."[18]

In the educational field, this is expressed in a series of proposed measures to incorporate a gender focus in educational reform. In the first stage of the process, the central objective of the policies is to incorporate a gender focus in the curricular and pedagogical proposals, fundamental spheres for educational reform, in the degree to which these define the how and what of educational processes. The efforts centered on the design of general orientations and curricular content for the first three years of schooling, above all for the area of social sciences and natural sciences ("life sciences" in the new curriculum) based on some general criteria that informed the process: (a) including materials that emphasized contributions, experiences, and needs of girls and boys; (b) including images that portrayed girls and boys doing different things; (c) promoting the participation of girls and boys in all kinds of activities; (d) preventing sexism in the language used.

The training of pedagogic consultants (teachers whose new function, after a training process, is to implement the new educational reforms in the classroom and to advise classroom teachers) was another fundamental issue in this process. There were workshops and materials about gender equity. However, despite having conducted programs with more than 500 pedagogical aides (almost 100% of the entire group), the time allocated for the activity was insufficient (3 hours in many instances and a one-day program in a few cases). Gender equity was not made a part of the training curriculum. In this sense, it is evident that without systematic training processes, simply building awareness is totally insufficient to achieve the proposed equity goals, because despite the efforts made, training of teachers and pedagogical consultants continues to be an urgent task that must happen continually. The awareness-promoting activities were accompanied by the development of specific materials for the teachers and pedagogical consultants.

In this first moment, the SAG education team faced various dilemmas. Is there enough technical capacity to face such a complex and conservative sector like the education sector (even though it is in the middle of an education reform)? Does SAG's organizational structure permit opening lobbying spaces within the sector in equal conditions? Are there enough inputs to sustain and legitimize the proposals elaborated by the SAG?

These questions grow out of a permanent conflict of interests between the policies designed by the SAG and the policies designed in the educational reform framework. In effect, when considering gender equity in the framework of sector policies, there is an emergence of prejudices, values, ideologies, points of view, that is, all the elements that filter problems, evaluate them or reject them and define their consideration in the sector agenda (education). This leads to the complexity of the process of incorporating gender equity.[19] Beginning with these reflections and as a product of this experience, specific strategies have been designed for the sector with relation to the political atmosphere mentioned above.

Policy Design

For policy design, and given the lack of information about women's situation in education, there has been a generation of inputs through research that addresses issues like the structure of teaching and the teachers' role, violence and discrimination in school, and others. This information has allowed the design of proposals and strategies for policies related both to access and to quality of the educational processes and their incidence in gender equity.

Another important and successful strategy has been the implementation of pilot projects, like the Program for the Prevention of Violence in Schools (PPVE). This pilot experience had financial support from UNICEF, was developed in schools linked to the Catholic Church, and allowed the SAG to have a proposal for how to address the gender focus in the classroom, based on permanent teacher training. The concept that guided the design and implementation of this pilot project were based on the recognition of the difference that is established by sex, and the assignment of a series of stereotyped and/or exclusive responsibilities, rights, and roles according to sex, which convert difference into inequality, discrimination, and violence. The programs concentrated on training for teachers, directors, and parents, on the organization of various activities, on the development of specific materials, on participatory action research, and finally, on follow-up, evaluation, and permanent adjustments.

At the same time, the methodology used verification, experimentation, and confrontation through observation as a permanent resource in the teacher training process. This brought it closer to real life experiences, deepening the analysis of the practice of discrimination and fostering a conscious decision to promote change. When discrimination was identified in the participating schools, we used it to address the problem

and to make sure we all understood that it concerned everyone. One of
the first changes we aimed at was precisely to affect how the particular
case of discrimination was perceived to help transform the private and
public behavior that led to it. Otherwise, the intervention would not
make sense. We influence a certain behavior because we realize that it
can change. Based on our experience, the PPVE developed into a program aimed at:

- establishing a knowledge base of the practices of violence and
  gender discrimination, analyzing their causes and designing
  strategies to confront them;
- generating the conditions whereby, through training, there can be
  a diagnosis made and action taken directed toward teachers, students, and parents;
- promoting the appropriation of issues as a resource to motivate
  and develop mutual commitment between the participants in the
  process;
- developing facilitating teams as a link between the school and
  external agents, to receive demands, to resolve conflicts, and to
  evaluate achievements;
- validating the strategy of training and intervention in the framework of addressing the gender focus in education; and
- identifying policies to be transferred to the sector.

In almost 24 months of implementation, the PPVE has managed to
broaden its coverage to the main nine cities in Bolivia and has developed
more than 40 teams through the participation of 200 facilitators, who
have developed activities with 1,253 teachers and 23,348 students at the
primary and secondary levels.

The implementation process faced diverse obstacles, some related to
obtaining immediate changes, as demonstrated by some comments from
the facilitating teams: "even though the actions were completed, the
changes have still not taken place as we had hoped," or, "there is a resistance to change, because the results would produce new concerns and
initiatives for which we are still not prepared."[20] In that sense, it is evident that the recognition of the problems of violence and gender discrimination, within and outside of the school, are still far from resulting in a
change of attitudes or of ways of confronting that reality. In this sense, it
is evident that acknowledging the problems of violence and gender-
based discrimination within and outside the school will not automati-

cally bring about a change in attitude that will face and change that reality. The process of change is not simple. It does not stop at questioning a common behavior; it also implies the belief that such behavior can be changed.

Perhaps one of the greatest institutional obstacles has been the influence of the political context. The change of government in 1997 brought with it changes in personnel in the departments of education, which meant that once again new personnel had to be trained. This situation has weakened program implementation because these processes require systematic follow-up and, above all, continuity.

The achievements were significant. School directors incorporated PPVE activities in their school programs. Teachers and facilitators undertook a series of activities that varied from campaigns to installing complaint boxes for students, and they themselves educated parents. Moreover, it was possible to transform the issue of violence into a theme for discussion and debate. This led to a generalized practice of calling into question violence and seeking ways to prevent and combat violence in schools.

On the other hand, this experience has led to reflections on the true limitations of schools, because while the issue must be addressed in school, it is also necessary to develop systematic actions in other spheres: the family, the state, and civil society.

One of the biggest achievements has been the signing of an agreement to implement the PPVE as part of the educational reform, which is an important reference point around how to mainstream public policies. The experience also offered inputs to the curriculum and teacher training proposals for the educational reform. Finally, the PPVE has highlighted the issue of gender discrimination as a serious problem that affects educational quality.

Legitimacy

Reflecting on some key concepts related to institutional changes, we consider that keeping the issue of gender equity in education on the public agenda and legitimizing the proposals and advances thus far are fundamental to institutionalizing both policies and their effects at the social and cultural level. Diverse activities are carried out with this goal: articles are periodically written and published, the media is permanently involved, there are publicity campaigns, and so forth. All of this helps to generate greater opening of the sector and to plan, inter-sectorally, a program of positive action to confront the issue of girls' access to and retention to schools in rural areas, which contemplates a series of measures aimed at addressing this in the areas with the highest dropout rates for girls. This action program is currently a component of the Educational Reform II and is in its first phase of implementation.

Institutionalization

The institutionalization of gender policies is a long and complex process. The instruments and mechanisms used have demonstrated their fragility in the degree to which the agreements that have been signed and the organizations that have been created for follow-up have been the result of decided processes that have been agreed to and that have not been reflected in legal documents. Despite this, they are totally valid instruments to advance in the processes of integration, because they are important political commitments despite their temporal character. In this framework, agreements have been signed between the SAG authorities and the Ministry of Education to implement joint activities (like the implementation of the International Gender and Education Seminar and the implementation of research on specific issues) or activities that the SAG implemented in the framework of sector actions, like the training of pedagogic consultants, the training of educational reform technicians, the incorporation of the gender focus in the curriculum, among others. Finally, an agreement has been signed through which the Program for the Prevention of Violence in Schools was transferred from the gender office (SAG) to the education sector. For the completion and follow-up of these agreements, Gender and Education Committees were formed at the central, departmental, and municipal level with the participation of authorities and technicians from both areas. The Five- and Ten-Year Plans for Women were designed (elevated to the level of resolution by the current government), all of them as mechanisms and instruments destined to institutionalize gender equity as a public policy, but also to give continuity to the processes already begun.

It is important to emphasize the role of foreign cooperation both for institutionalization and for legitimization of gender policies in the sector. Foreign cooperation has contributed to having the authorities of the education sector be willing to consider the issue in their agenda, to open spaces for dialogue and working together. Perhaps one of the most effective forms has been the incorporation of specific recommendations in the reports of annual reviews of the educational reform process made by the

World Bank, which was achieved through an intense lobbying process between the SAG gender institute and Swedish and Dutch cooperation to detect the problematic points and to design strategies that collaborate with the efforts carried out by the SAG to integrate the gender focus in educational policies, with which negotiation conditions are improved.

Implementation

The implementation of public policies is an issue of crucial importance. In effect, the organizational structure, the hierarchies, the functions, the style of work, and the forms of internal relationships are all fundamental factors to the degree that they can be problems or obstacles at the moment of negotiating, establishing alliances, seeking consensus with the sector with which one wants to work together, in this case the education sector. In the SAG's experience, the development of a work team and its placement in the SAG organizational structure has been fundamental, because it allowed them to negotiate the proposed measures in better conditions with the sector. Evidently, the political importance of the educational reform for the government always gives the gender issue a second level priority, by which, despite the existence of equal hierarchies, the negotiation conditions can only end up being equally beneficial with great difficulty.

We are in fact talking about the construction of an integrated strategy that assumes advances in policy formulation, its legitimation and a determined implementation and institutionalization strategy of the same within the education sector and within the gender institution.

MOVING THE PROCESS FORWARD: LESSONS AND CHALLENGES

The experiences described here have been a source of important learning, on the one hand, from the perspective of integration of the gender focus in education, and on the other hand, from the perspective of the role of cooperation in these processes. We continue now by looking at five issues that allow the visualization of some lessons learned but that at the same time are challenges that merit a broader and deeper reflection to continue advancing. These issues have to do with dilemmas like the following: Is it enough to incorporate a gender focus in laws and norms? When specific projects are implemented by the gender institute, does the institute's role as norm-setter disqualify them? How can those processes that have begun have guaranteed economic and social sustainability? Finally, what are the limits, time frames, and intensities of the integration processes of the gender focus in educational policies?

Political Will and Management Ability

Political agreements do not guarantee the implementation in practice of the normative and operational proposals. Political support of the issue is fundamental to generate agreements among the hierarchical levels; however, the what, the how, and the when of incorporating the gender perspective in education also depends on the technical proposals, on human resources, and fundamentally on the management ability and the mechanisms of institutionalization that are adopted.

The Normative and the Operational

The consideration in the Educational Reform Law of aspects that refer to gender equity is an important advance in and of itself. However, this reference has not been sufficient to incorporate and operationalize these objectives and concepts in practice. From there emerges the discussion about the character and attributes of the gender institutes in the state. In the Bolivian case, the SAG mission is eminently normative of the gender policies and defines as a fundamental strategy the mainstreaming of a gender focus in sector policies.

From this perspective, the fundamental challenge is to guarantee that the education sector accepts the responsibility to offer quality education to boys and girls, equality of opportunities and equal benefits to all, as noted in the law. But this has required, and continues to require, the implementation of specific actions in coordination with the sector, from the sector or toward the sector. That is, to guarantee that the norms are fulfilled requires a level of operational ability, which in the Bolivian case can translate into pilot projects with a limited character in time but with a clear intentionality of becoming part of sector policy.

The Continuity of Gender Policies

The Bolivian reality still demonstrates signs of institutional weakness, expressed in the fact that inevitably all changes in government (in this case the 1997 presidential elections) include personnel changes and many times changes in policy orientations. This fact generates a series of difficulties and/or opportunities. This is a crucial issue not only with regards to financial support offered by foreign cooperation, but also with regards to the women's movement, because it has to do with the legitimacy of gender policies. In the Bolivian experience the politization of the gender space (today the Vice Ministry of Gender, Generations and Family) has weakened its position, and it is in the midst of a process of re-engineering itself in search of its inner strength and its role in civil society.

INSTITUTIONALIZATION AND SUSTAINABILITY OF THE PROCESSES

The processes of institutionalization depend on a diversity of aspects—it is evident that one of the most important factors refers to financial resources. In effect, a key indicator is when and in what the government is willing to invest for gender equity. To date, the greatest support continues to come from international cooperation, while contributions from the national treasury barely cover 10% of the SAG budget.

This fact presents an important challenge to foreign cooperation, because among their objectives they include the establishment of financial sustainability for the programs. This also presents a challenge to the state gender institutes because the possibility of implementing policies is closely linked to the conditions of sustainability. In this sense, the key questions are: Until when and in what quantity will outside financing be necessary? What strategies should be implemented to achieve levels of sustainability? Are gender policies possible in the current conditions of development? This issue about sustainability of public gender policies is an unresolved issue and merits attention in the near future, since it is critical to overcome current levels of dependence and move toward designing sustainable strategies that demonstrate our countries' real abilities.

Finally, it is necessary to remember that the process has only been recently begun and there is still much to do. Given the advances, teachings, and challenges, it is pertinent to think about and assume that the solidifying of some and the resolving of others will depend in great measure on the type of relations that are established between the women's movement, the state gender institute, and foreign cooperation, among whom new spaces of dialogue and working together should be generated that permit the advancement and deepening of this process.

NOTES

[1]Testimony of an adolescent girl written at a boys' school in La Paz, in *Boletín Sendas,* no. 38, 1997.

[2]In 1997, the Under Secretariat of Gender Issues became the General Directorate of Gender Issues, which diminished the hierarchy of the institute.

[3]Silvia Rivera Cusicanqui et al., "Being an Indigenous, *Chola* or *Birlocha* Woman in Post-Colonial Bolivia in the 90s" (La Paz: Ministry of Human Development, Undersecretary of Gender Affairs, 1996).

[4]Instituto Nacional de Estadistica (INE), *Grupos Vulnerables Niños, Jóvenes y Mujeres en Bolivia* (La Paz: Fondo de Población de las Naciones Unidas e INE, 1997).

[5]Sonia Montaño, "Invertir en la equidad. Políticas Sociales para la mujer en Bolivia" (La Paz: Unidad de Análisis de Políticas Sociales y Organismo Nacional de la Mujer y la Familia, 1992).

[6]Secretaría Nacional de Educación, "Información Estadísticas de Indicadores Educativos en el Componente Acceso y Permanencia de la Niñas Rurales en la Escuela" (La Paz: Secretaría Nacional de Educación, 1997).

[7]The Index of Educational Inequity is calculated based on the difference between feminine and masculine school attendance and its relationship to the school-age population.

[8]Sonia Montaño is a sociologist by profession, and a participant in the women's movement. She was the first Undersecretary of Gender Affairs, and her participation was transcendental for the institutional process of the state space.

[9]Sonia Montaño, "Bolivia. Crónica de una agitada vida," *Cuarto Propio Revista Especial Fempress* V, 1998.

[10]The National Plan for Women was designed in the framework of a long process of meetings, alliance building, and consensus-seeking between different women's NGOs, base organizations, and the financial support of international cooperation, from which somehow the women's agenda was developed.

[11]The Women's Social Action Team was formed in the 1970s, and was an autonomous organization led since then by wives of presidents, whose supportive actions were directed fundamentally to women and children. In 1990, it was transformed into the National Organization of Assistance to Children and Families, without rejecting its central characteristics. However, because of political circumstances, there was a possibility of designing strategies for women from a gender perspective, and the national Women's Program was begun at that time.

[12]Undersecretary of Gender Affairs, "Report on Implementation, Constructing Equity" (La Paz: SAG, 1997).

[13]Montaño, *op. cit.*

[14]Law number 1565, Educational Reform Law, approved July 7, 1994. Article 2, page 8.

[15]Educational Reform Law, 1994.

[16]Law number 1565.

[17]Elizabeth Salinas et al.,"Guía Jurídica de la Mujer y Familia" (La Paz: SAG, 1997.)

[18]Ivonne Farah was the second Undersecretary of Gender Issues between 1995 and 1997. She contributed to the institutionalization of gender policies in the nation via the design of the aforementioned areas affected by those policies. See *Plan Quinquenal para la Equidad de Género 1997–2001.* SAG, La Paz, 1997–2001.

[19]Martha Lanza, "Gender Equity as a Public Policy," *Revista CIDES* No. 4, La Paz, 1998.

[20]Undersecretary of Gender Affairs, "Report on Implementation, Constructing Equity" (La Paz: SAG, 1997).

REFERENCES

Bonder, Gloria. "Equidad de Género en la Educación." La Paz: Ministerio de Desarrollo Humano, Subsecretaría de Asuntos de Género (SAG), 1997.

Bonder, Gloria. *Mujer y Educación en América Latina: Hacia la igualdad de oportunidades.* Madrid: Fero, 1994.

Departamento de Evaluación de Políticas y Operaciones. *Evaluación del Programa de Desarrollo de los Países Bajos en Bolivia.* IOV La Haya: Ministerio de Asuntos Exteriores de los Países Bajos, 1998.

Instituto Nacional de Estadística (INE). *Censo de Población y Vivienda.* La Paz, 1992.

Instituto Nacional de Estadística. *Grupos Vulnerables Niños, Jóvenes y Mujeres en Bolivia.* La Paz: Fondo de Población de las Naciones Unidas (FNUAP) e INE, 1997.

Instituto Nacional de Estadística (INE). *Grupos vulnerables niños, jóvenes y mujeres en Bolivia, INE, FNUAP.* La Paz, 1997.

Lanza, Martha. "La Equidad de Género como Política Pública: Reflexiones desde la Practica." La Paz: CIDES, Muela del Diablo, 1998.

Lanza, Martha. La equidad de género como política pública. *Revista CIDES* no. 4 (1998).

Lanza, Martha and Nora Mengoa. "Memoria Seminario Internacional de género y educación." La Paz: Subsecretaria de Asuntos de Género (SAG/Grupo Design), 1997.

Lazarte, Cecilia, et al. "Guía de Orientación del Programa de Prevención de la Violencia en la Escuela (PPVE)." La Paz: Subsecretaría de Asuntos de Género (SAG), 1997.

Ministerio de Desarrollo Humano. *Ley de Reforma Educativa.* La Paz, 1994.

Ministry of Foreign Affairs. Women and Development Division. *Girls and Primary Education.* The Hague: Ministry of Foreign Affairs, 1997.

Montaño, Sonia. "Bolivia. Crónica de una agitada vida." *Cuarto Propio Revista Especial Fempress* V (1998).

Montaño, Sonia. "Invertir en la Equidad Políticas Sociales para la Mujer en Bolivia." Unidad de Análisis de Políticas Sociales (UDAPSO) y Organismo Nacional de la Niñez y la Familia (ONANFA), 1992.

Pimentel, Juan Carlos, et al. "Memoria Seminario Reforma Educativa y Género." La Paz: Huellas, 1994.

Rivera, Silvia, et al. "Ser Mujer Indígena, chola o birlocha en Bolivia Postcolonial de los años 90." La Paz: Ministerio de Desarrollo Humano Subsecretaria de Asuntos de Género, 1996.

Salinas, Elizabeth, et al. "Guía Jurídica de la Mujer y Familia." La Paz: Subsecretaría de Asuntos de Género (SAG), 1997.

Secretaría Nacional de Educación. "Información Estadísticas de Indicadores Educativos en el Componente Acceso y Permanencia de la Niñas Rurales en la Escuela." La Paz, 1997.

Subsecretaría de Asuntos de Género (SAG). "Plan de Igualdad de Oportunidades para las mujeres." La Paz: Ministerio de Desarrollo Humano, 1997.

Subsecretaría de Asuntos de Género. *Plan quinquenal 1997–2001.* La Paz: Subsecretaría de Asuntos de Género, 1997.

Subsecretaría de Asuntos de Género et al. "Informe sobre el Avance de la Mujeres en Bolivia." La Paz: Ministerio de Desarrollo Humano, 1994.

Public Policy and Adult Education for Women in Brazil

MARÍA CLARA DI PIERRO

INTRODUCTION

In addition to having one of the most inequitable income distribution systems in the world, Brazil also has a highly inequitable education system. An analysis of public policies and proposals for alternative policies to promote educational equity must take both phenomena into account, because focusing exclusively on improving the education system will not solve the system's problems. Educational policies must encompass the socioeconomic and cultural conditions that limit groups or individuals from having access to or benefiting from educational opportunities.

In the complex matrix of selection, discrimination, and exclusion factors that make up Brazilian education, gender structures barely emerge. This invisibility results in part from the relative equality of educational opportunities for men and women observed in the last four decades and the subsequent assumptions that the "gender problem" has been resolved (Table 1) and in part from the fact that the field of gender studies is still relatively new in Brazilian educational research.

Thinking about gender emerged in the field of social science and was recently incorporated in Brazilian educational research. Gender issues appeared at the end of the 1970s, when new social actors—urban social movements of women and feminists among them—simultaneously awoke academic interest among sociologists, political scientists, and teachers with the introduction in the country of literature that was called feminist studies. From then on, a small portion of Brazilian educational research incorporated gender in its analysis, focusing on teaching

Table 1. Brazil: Average Years of Study by Sex, 1960–1996

Sex	1960	1970	1980	1991	1996
Men	2.4	2.6	3.9	5.1	5.7
Women	1.9	2.2	3.5	4.9	6.0

Source: IPEA, 1998.

as a women's profession, women as the actors in education-focused social movements, sexist stereotypes in textbooks and in children's and young adults' literature, and the reproduction of gender hierarchies and sexual roles in the school socialization of children. In the 1990s, international organizations introduced the economic perspective, using cost-benefit analysis to establish that girls' and women's education has positive impacts on the reduction of fertility levels and infant mortality rates and favorably affects other poverty indicators.

Several authors have noted that gender no longer explains existing educational inequalities in many Latin American countries (Brazil among them), but rather combines with other variables such as social class and economic status, geographic region, urban or rural location, race, age, and occupational status.[1] On the other hand, demographic studies reveal three clear shifts in Brazilian women's social position in past decades: Women not only reached educational levels equal to men but have even slightly surpassed men in terms of access to and achievement at all educational levels. The increase in educational levels has favored the rapid incorporation of women in the labor market, although they still receive substantially lower remuneration than men and occupy those spaces culturally typified as feminine. Fecundity rates have been decreasing rapidly (from 4.4 percent in 1985 to 2.5 percent in 1995) in close negative correlation with women's educational level. This relative success obtained by women as a whole in their recent insertion in the Brazilian school system has, however, allowed other dimensions of gender relations and education to remain hidden. In particular, certain variables of discrimination such as race and age in relation to gender deserve more careful study.

This chapter analyzes recently developed public policies on basic education for young people and adults, highlighting age as an important factor of discrimination in women's struggle for educational rights.

PUBLIC POLICIES ADDRESSING ADULT EDUCATION IN BRAZIL

Brazilian legislative documents and educational policies have referred to basic education for adults since the end of the nineteenth century. Public action organized around adult education grew in importance after 1945, when 25 percent of the National Fund for Primary Education resources were directed to literacy programs and campaigns. These federally coordinated programs and campaigns expanded in the following ten years, as did the formal school system. The expansion, together with urbanization and industrialization, contributed to a decrease in adult illiteracy rates from 65 percent in 1920 to 40 percent in 1960.

Brazil underwent intense political and social turmoil at the beginning of the 1960s. Unions, student organizations, peasant leagues, religious groups, and political groups, often supported by the government, implemented adult literacy programs influenced by Paulo Freire's pedagogical approach, which encompassed a broad popular education and culture movement. These initiatives culminated in a national literacy campaign sponsored by the federal government, but they were suspended by the military coup in March 1964.

The military government's adult education policies did not take shape until 1971 with the Brazilian Literacy Movement, *MOBRAL* (*Movimiento Brasileiro de Alfabetização*), and with the passage of Law No. 5692, the National Education Law, which included an entire chapter on Supplementary Education.[2] MOBRAL worked throughout Brazil until 1985. It remained linked in the nation's memory to the authoritarian government's ideological propaganda, to poor educational outcomes, pedagogical authoritarianism, waste of resources, and inefficient and poor teacher training. Supplementary Education also tried to respond to demands to train the labor force for the exclusionary economic development model introduced by the military regime and ended up creating compensatory education models for youth and adults that continue to be operative today.

Throughout the two decades of the military regime, popular education and culture movements were reborn in scattered and small-scale literacy programs for youth and adults. Volunteers from Catholic ecclesiastical communities linked to liberation theology promoted literacy programs, as did urban and rural unions, community associations, and nongovernmental organizations (NGOs) devoted to education. The NGOs contributed to grassroots organization and mobilized resistance to the military dictatorship through education, culture, and the defense of human rights.

In the last half of the 1980s, during the period of political transition toward democracy, MOBRAL was eliminated and replaced by the *Educar* Foundation, which abandoned direct provision of literacy and post-literacy services, instead working out agreements with local municipalities or civil society organizations. This administrative shift allowed youth and adults to have different basic education experiences, informed by the popular education paradigm, and supported by public resources or incorporated in municipal education systems governed by directly elected progressive parties.

One of the achievements of the democratic transition period was the legal recognition of youth and adult education rights within the 1988 Constitution. The new constitution guaranteed access to public and free basic education for all. Previously, education had been guaranteed only to children and adolescents between seven and fourteen years.[3] The new constitutional text led to expectations of a substantial expansion of the youth and adult education programs. Hopes for this expansion were nourished by the United Nations, which declared 1990 the International Year of Literacy during the World Conference on Education for All held in Thailand, of which Brazil is a signatory. As one of the world's nine most populated countries with high illiteracy rates, Brazil joined Bangladesh, China, Egypt, India, Indonesia, Mexico, Nigeria, and Pakistan as the Summit of Nine, and international organizations promised to prioritize literacy efforts in the countries.

The expectations generated after 1988 were frustrated by the next decade. The *Educar* Foundation was abolished in March 1990 during the administration of the first directly elected president. The same year, the Ministry of Education developed the National Literacy and Citizenship Program, whose goals were as ambitious as its life was short. Victim of its own political and administrative inconsistency and discontinuity, the program disappeared in just a year, before President Collor de Mello's trial. Behind in fulfilling its international commitments agreed to at the World Declaration on Education for All and the Summit of Nine, in 1993 the Ministry of Education initiated a ten-year Plan of Education for All. The plan acknowledged the importance of basic education for youth and adults and developed the ambitious goal of teaching 3.7 million people to read and providing basic schooling for 4.6 million youth and adults with low educational levels. Developed at the end of the Collor de Mello administration, the plan was never approved by the legislature, and the next administration never embraced its goals. It is worth noting that currently, President Henrique Cardoso's wife, sociologist Ruth Cardoso, runs a Community Solidarity program. This program includes attention to literacy programs but does not explicitly mention or incorporate gender.

YOUTH AND ADULT EDUCATION IN BRAZIL'S CURRENT EDUCATIONAL REFORM

Since 1995 the federal government has implemented a series of legal, normative, and control measures whose extension and impact allow us to characterize them as education reform. These measures were parallel and simultaneous to the approval in 1996 of the new National Education Law and before the elaboration of a new National Plan for Education, which is still in the National Congress. The goal of the reform is to rationalize costs and increase internal efficiency in the basic education system in order to broaden coverage and improve the flow of students through the system by increasing learning levels. The major elements of the reform are financial and administrative decentralization of basic education to states and municipalities, with an emphasis on basic education for children and adolescents. Implementing these policies within the imperative of restricted public expenses imposed by the adopted structural adjustment model and by economic stabilization policies, the Brazilian federal government has reduced the priority given to the universalization and improvement of basic education for children and adolescents almost exclusively to the ages of seven through fourteen.

This strategy of educational reform resembles those adopted in other Latin American countries influenced or, rather, conditioned by World Bank advisors, whose policies concentrate public spending on basic education for children and adolescents, considered to be the level that provides greater individual and social economic returns. Given that primary education levels are currently high, and assuming that improving the flow of students in the system will solve other issues, measures are prioritized that promote improvements in teaching quality, decreases in desertion and repetition levels, and improvements in learning levels. This process narrows the concept of "satisfaction of the basic learning needs" that was established in Jomtien, and the notion of "education for all" is restricted to primary education for children and adolescents from the poorer social strata. Illiterate or poorly educated youth and adults are thus marginalized from educational policy priorities.

LEGAL AND CONCEPTUAL FRAMEWORK

The chapter of the new National Education Law dealing with basic education dedicates a brief and noninnovative section to youth and adult education, describing it as flexible and accelerated learning that evaluates and certifies knowledge acquired through out-of-school activities or that provides schooling that was not developed at "the appropriate age."

The law's language suggests the persistence of the compensatory idea that assigns to youth and adult education the function of replacing the education they did not have in their childhood and adolescence. This idea has been the subject of a broad critique in Latin American and international literature, and has been confronted by a broader paradigm of continuous lifelong education. By blaming illiteracy and low educational levels on the past, the argument defends the priority of investing in basic education for children and adolescents, and envisions the solution of the problem to be a "natural" process as new generations are educated at the basic level. This results in a sort of macabre educational genocide and "social Darwinism." On the other hand, by proposing to substitute for the missed childhood education, youth and adult education tends to reproduce the curricular and organizational models of formal school education, which is ineffective and reduces its potential as an important social and political investment. Furthermore, the idea of compensation ends up legitimizing psycho-pedagogic deficit theories that presuppose the existence of an appropriate age for learning, beyond which learning would be limited and results minimal. These theories foment age prejudices and ignore recent developments in the knowledge sciences. The persistence of the "compensation" concept makes it more difficult for society to envision the benefits of adult education and thus be willing to make investments, and this limits the building of a broad social consensus to justify continuous state policies to benefit this age group.

FINANCING

The 1988 Brazilian Constitution requires a minimal percentage of public tax resources to be linked to education development and maintenance: 18 percent at the federal level and 25 percent at the state and municipal levels. Because of this commitment, in 1993 total government spending in the education sector was 3.7 percent of the gross domestic product (GDP). Because it prioritized economic stability, the present federal government did not increase public investments in education (maintained at 1.3 percent of the GDP), choosing to optimize available financial resources.

The principal instrument of educational reform targeting decentralization of educational finance and emphasizing basic education for children and adolescents was the Fourteenth Constitutional Amendment, approved by the Congress in 1996. The Fourteenth Amendment canceled the article on Transitory Dispositions of the 1988 Constitution, which committed both society and government to eliminating illiteracy and universalizing basic education within ten years. The Fourteenth Amendment eliminated the government obligation to assign a minimum of 50 percent of education resources to literacy and basic education. In reality, the federal government never followed this constitutional obligation, and always spent most of the educational budget on federal universities. The amendment also created the Fund for the Development of Basic Education and Teacher Development (FUNDEF), an ingenious mechanism by which public resources linked to education are redistributed between state and municipal governments in proportion to the registered enrollments in basic education for children and adolescents. Given Brazil's fiscal and tributary structure, this mechanism leads to the municipalization of basic education and was implemented under the assumption that more effective investment of municipal resources in basic education would give more freedom to states to invest in secondary education and thus allow the federal government to invest in higher education.

This redistribution of educational duties among the different governmental levels implemented without increasing public resources for the sector causes significant concern. It is doubtful that public education can continue to expand in order to accommodate population growth as well as overcome current deficits in classroom space, while at the same time improving educational quality and teacher working conditions in order to reduce the dramatic rates of school desertion and repetition (repetition reached 27.4 percent of basic education enrollment in 1996).

By establishing the distribution model of municipal and state public resources to benefit basic education for children and adolescents, FUNDEF ignored two segments of basic education—early childhood education and youth and adult education. According to Brazilian legislation, municipalities are solely responsible for early childhood education, while the three governmental levels share responsibility for youth and adult education.

During most of its life as an independent republic, except when it implemented the MOBRAL Program, the three governmental levels have been giving infinitely small proportions of their budgets to youth and adult education. Federal participation in financing youth and adult education is supplementary, designed to resolve regional inequalities, and has remained at ridiculously low levels: While youth and adult students represented 5.85 percent of total national enrollment in basic education in 1997, the 1997 federal budget assigned adult education less than 0.5 percent of resources. The greatest responsibility for basic education funding for the population over fourteen years of age belongs to the states and municipalities, which have always invested poorly in that sector. The federal government prohibited the calculation of youth and adult education enrollments when it implemented FUNDEF in 1998, preventing the transfer of resources from the fund and discouraging the states and municipalities even more from investing in this age group. Youth and adult basic education thus had to compete for public resources with early childhood education at the municipal level and with secondary education at the state level. Given the spending deficit at those two levels for basic and secondary education and their greater explicit social demand, the expansion of funding for youth and adult basic education (a prerequisite to expand and improve quality) faces even greater challenges.

EDUCATIONAL ASSISTANCE

Due to the historic marginalization at the heart of educational policies, the persistence of the compensation idea, and the low levels of investment in resources, educational support of the Brazilian population over fourteen years old is quite limited. Less than 10 percent of the eligible population actually registers as students in regular or supplementary education, thus revealing the abyss that separates rights guaranteed by the law and the reality of access to compulsory education.

The majority of the school population over fifteen years old consists of young people who attend regular education but who are overage for their grade level, a result of repetition, desertion, and later returns to the school system. The funding explicitly targeted to the youth and adult population through Supplementary Education is even more limited: It covers only 3.3 percent of the potential demand for compulsory basic education. In addition to being severely limited, funding is also highly inequitable. Rather than progressive, privileging those at lower learning levels, supplementary education funding is distributed irregularly throughout the three levels of basic education without responding in relation to potential demand. Thus, the population with more relative schooling also has greater access to youth and adult educational programs. Educational opportunities are also unevenly distributed geographically, discriminating against rural populations and the country's poorest regions, precisely those with higher illiteracy and where the levels of instruction are lower. Only 4.6 percent of registered adult education students live in rural areas, but 41 percent of the illiterate population is rural; the Northeast region of the country, with 48.8 percent of the country's illiterate population, has less than 28 percent of total youth and adult enrollment in basic education.

TENDENCIES

The marginal inclusion of youth and adult education in Brazil's current educational reform reveals certain tendencies in the development of public policies directed toward this age group. The opportunity to be trained and educated continues to be extremely limited and unevenly distributed among youth and adults, and the fundamental tendencies of current government policies do not indicate an expansion of educational offerings for this age group. We are witnessing a progressive breaking down of the universal right to basic education and its shift to the field of assistance policies that use it to attenuate the perverse effects of social exclusion. In this shift, public responsibility for youth and adult basic education is being progressively transferred from the state to civil society, especially through contracts with social organizations.

At the same time, educational assistance is being divided into two hierarchical subsystems: one of them addressing the increasing needs for a qualified labor force by those sectors of the economy that underwent technological modernization; the other providing a social protection network for those social groups excluded from the labor and consumer markets. This tendency toward the segmentation of adult educational policies inhibits its potential for democratizing opportunities and training, and deepens social duality.

ILLITERACY AND WOMEN'S
ACCESS TO EDUCATION IN BRAZIL

Women make up the majority of Brazil's youth and adult population, and on average they are better educated than men (Table 2). Women are also a slight majority (51.8 percent) within the smaller group of almost twelve million Brazilians who attend youth and adult basic education.

Despite the relative advantage of the female population over the male population, absolute illiteracy rates among Brazilian youth and adults remain high. Among women, 13 percent have never been to school, just over 1 percent have less than one year of schooling, and over 17 percent have between one and three years of schooling. From this we can infer that more than 31 percent of Brazilian women are illiterate or functionally illiterate. Adding to this the third of women who have between four and seven years of schooling, 65 percent of Brazilian women have less education than mandated as a basic right of citizens under the 1988 Federal Constitution. Only 15.6 percent of Brazilian women completed mandatory basic education, 14.6 percent completed secondary education, and 4.6 percent completed higher education.

Table 2. Brazil: Population over Age Fifteen by Years of Schooling and Sex, 1996

Years of Schooling	Population in Thousands	%	Men (thousands)	%	Women (thousands)	%
No schooling or less than 1 year	15,245	14.2	7,442	14.2	7,803	14.1
Incomplete primary (1–7 years)	55,504	51.6	27,787	53.1	27,717	50.2
Complete primary (8 years)	10,174	9.5	4,945	9.5	5,230	9.5
Incomplete secondary (9–10 years)	6,233	5.8	2,857	5.5	3,377	6.1
Complete secondary (11 years)	12,197	11.3	5,328	10.2	6,780	12.3
Incomplete tertiary (12–14 years)	2,367	2.2	1,092	2.1	1,274	2.3
Complete tertiary (15 years or more)	4,992	4.6	2,444	4.7	2,548	4.6
Information not available	917	0.9	450	0.9	468	0.9
Total	107,541	100	52,345	48.7	551,196	51.3

Source: IBGE, 1996.

SOCIAL DISCRIMINATION FACTORS IN WOMEN'S ACCESS TO EDUCATION

The diagnosis of Brazilian women's educational situation worsens still more if we add to the equation other differentiation and social exclusion factors—income, region of residence, rural or urban location, race, and age. Those facing the greatest disadvantage are poor women living in the North and Northeast regions, in rural areas, who are black or indigenous, and are over age thirty-nine.

A person from a Brazilian family whose income is less than one-fourth of the minimum wage has twice as many possibilities of being illiterate as one whose income is above two minimum wages. Family income is the main factor explaining access to literacy in Brazil. It determines the observed differences among age groups, between rural and urban populations, and among regions. Gender and "race" act as relatively independent factors from the social and economic situation in determining educational opportunities.

The relative improvement of Brazilian women's schooling rates is directly a result of younger generations' schooling. Women are "behind" men only in that portion of youth and adults with one year or less of education; they are 51.2 percent of that population, in great part because of the educational exclusion of women over age forty, in particular those who live or come from rural zones. Differences in women's schooling among different age groups are very accentuated; while illiteracy among young women and women up to thirty-nine years of age is about 6 percent, this rate increases to 27.5 percent among women over age forty. While 36.7 percent of women up to thirty-nine years have four to seven years of schooling, only 27.9 percent of those who are forty or older are in the same situation. While in the fifteen-to-thirty-nine age group those women who have less than four years of education—strong candidates for functional illiteracy— are one-fifth of the total, among those who are over age forty this proportion is higher, almost half of the total. This evidence should lead to differential educational policies according to age groups, especially if we consider that in the case of young and adult women, age is related to the reproductive cycle and to motherhood, which under present conditions adds social responsibilities and limits access to work and training.

The problems of illiteracy and low schooling rates are heavily concentrated in the Northeast region, where absolute numbers and percentage rates are very high, even among younger groups; in this region, these phenomena are linked to extreme poverty and influence both rural and urban populations. On the other hand, the Southeast region—the most developed and urbanized region of the country—catches our attention due to the presence of a great number of illiterate or undereducated women, even if the rates are lower than the national average; in this case, illiteracy is linked to urban poverty, migration from the Northeast, and is concentrated in the suburbs of metropolitan regions and great cities.

Ethnic and racial characteristics are important factors in inequality of access to schooling for women, discriminating mostly against black and indigenous women.[4] While the average illiteracy rate is 19.7 percent, among black women this rate increases to 28.3 percent (see Table 3).

Historical data analysis indicates that gender differentiation in educational levels of Brazilian youth and adults has been inherited from the

Table 3. Brazil: Population Age Fifteen Years and Older by Literacy, Race, and Sex, 1991

Color	Population 15 Years and Older (thousands)				Women (thousands)			Men (thousands)		
	Total		Illiterate		Total	Illiterate		Total	Illiterate	
	No.	(%)	No.	(%)	No.	No.	(%)	No.	No.	(%)
Total	95,811	100	18,587	19.4	49,158	9,662	19.7	46,653	8,925	19.1
White	51,232	53.5	6,091	11.9	26,958	3,408	12.6	24,274	2,684	11.1
Black	5,133	5.3	1,615	31.5	2,531	829	32.7	2,601	786	30.2
Mulatto	38,471	40.1	10,709	27.8	19,174	5,332	27.8	19,297	5,377	27.9
Yellow/Asian	486	0.5	26	5.4	243	16	6.7	243	10	4.1
Indigenous	171	0.2	87	50.8	84	46	54.5	87	41	47.2
Undeclared	318	0.3	60	18.7	167	32	19.0	151	28	18.3

Source: IBGE, 1991.

past, and is gradually disappearing, while racial discrimination (a vestige of slavery) still contributes to educational exclusion in the present.[5] In fact, average schooling among the black population is lower than that of other ethnic and racial groups, and the gap is being closed very slowly. This differential has greater social consequences when combined with discrimination against blacks and women in the Brazilian labor market. Blacks and women both receive less education and get lower returns on that education, and black women suffer doubly.[6]

GENDER AND ACCESS TO EDUCATION

The tendency toward closing the gender gap in women's and men's schooling in Brazil began in the 1940s. Currently, girls are actually at a slight advantage in terms of access among younger age groups. Women have a slight relative advantage in schooling rates because younger age groups have more opportunities than boys to go to school, they remain for a longer period, and they get to higher grade levels, leading to fewer overage girls at each grade level. A series of hypotheses have been suggested to explain gender differences in access and achievement within Brazilian basic education:

- Male children and adolescents enter the labor market before girls and young women, and the incompatibility between their work and school attendance results in higher school desertion and repetition. Girls and young women manage to reconcile domestic tasks (assigned to them within the division of family labor) with school attendance.
- Families tolerate girls' and young women's presence in schools because they consider schools to be protected territory where social rules that control sexuality still prevail. On the other hand, girls and young women value school as a place where they enjoy greater freedom and possibilities for socialization compared to the domestic and family environment.
- Girls' superior performance in the initial years of basic education is attributed to the dominant models of human relations within elementary school. They are characterized, on the one hand, by hierarchical authority relationships that reproduce subordination patterns found in the patriarchal family, and on the other hand, by the values placed on passivity, obedience, and order—which are historically and culturally associated with femininity.

- Because women have less access to work and are paid less then men, young women are sent in search of greater schooling to compensate for discrimination and to compete with men in the labor market. Additionally, some of the spaces in the Brazilian labor market traditionally assigned to women—such as teaching, nursing, or secretarial activities—require a minimum technical degree.

SCHOOLING, WORK, AND INCOME

Despite the fact that official statistics underestimate women's labor levels by not calculating unpaid domestic labor, in 1995 women represented more than 40 percent of the economically active population with an activity index of more than 53 percent. Women's participation in the Brazilian labor market is closely correlated with schooling: Employed women are better educated than employed men, and as women are better educated, they participate more in the economy. Despite advances over the past decade, however, Brazilian workers have not been able to overcome occupational segregation and salary discrimination in the labor market. Women tend to have lower incomes, they make up the majority of the working population that does not receive any compensation for their work (due, fundamentally, to their participation in family agriculture), and they receive lower pay than men for identical work in all sectors of the economy (even in typically feminine occupations) even if they have the same or higher education levels as men.

Recently, the age profile of employed women has been changing, and this has significance for our discussion of adult education policies. Until the 1980s, the twenty-to-twenty-nine age group had the greatest participation in the labor market. While women's participation in the labor market increased across all age groups during the past decade, even among married women and heads of household (which grew an average of 11.2 percent) the thirty-to-fifty-nine age group registered the most significant increase in labor rates, over 17 percent. Several factors have contributed to this aging of the feminine work force, ranging from a broader definition of work in labor data collection to the change in the age profile of the Brazilian population as a whole. Other factors include women's greater attractiveness in the labor market because of their higher education levels, economic pressures to complement the family income, and shifts in reproductive behavior (late motherhood and decreased average number of children), in family relations, and in the construction of feminine identity.

For the purposes of our argument, we note that an increasing percentage of older women—precisely those who have less education—are joining the labor market, while continuing their family and maternal responsibilities. Men's sharing in the care and education of small children is not socially sanctioned, and women do not have greater possibilities for technical training. These two realities reinforce the tendency that women's insertion in the labor market continues to be subordinate to men and at a high personal cost.

SCHOOLING AND LITERACY

Given that Brazilian women have educational levels equal to or greater than men, we can posit that the learning and cognitive skills acquired in the schooling process could eventually lead to greater gender equity in other areas of social life. This assumption is based on the results of a study about functional illiteracy which, despite the caution that formal schooling is not the only factor that determines literacy levels of youth and adults, observes that certain educational minimums are necessary for individuals to have access to employment. These include social practices that favor the exercise of reading, writing, math, and of taking an interest in public debates, the enjoyment of cultural capital, and the seeking out of information and opportunities for more training. All of these are linked to the development and use of literacy in daily life. Meanwhile, given that a significant portion of women are presently subject to limiting cultural practices that restrict the social uses of learning and acquired skills, the benefits of greater education may not last or develop throughout time. This seems to be the most likely hypothesis to explain the results of research on literacy levels in youth and adults in São Paulo, where the performance of the women's subgroup who only engage in domestic work was lower than the subgroup that also engaged in paid work. The latter group, in turn, performed at levels similar to men; the women had a slight advantage in reading, and a slight disadvantage in mathematical tasks. Both results lead to the conclusion that although schooling and literacy are closely related phenomena, they are not the same, and that even though schooling is the best predictor of individual performance in situations that require abilities and competencies related to literate culture, this performance is also influenced by the quality and intensity with which the subjects make use of their reading, writing, and math skills in their everyday lives and especially at work.[7] Thus, it is not enough that women reach equality in schooling levels. They also need to overcome labor market discrimination, subordination within the family and other spaces, and sociocultural practices without which the advantages acquired through schooling do not offer possibilities for greater personal and social development.

LITERACY AND BASIC EDUCATION OF
ADULT WOMEN IN A GENDER PERSPECTIVE

In this chapter we have not identified the youth and adult basic education public policies that aim to eliminate inequality of opportunities based on gender. An exhaustive analysis of documents addressing 1985–1994 educational policies finds no reference to gender, and consequently there are no indications of positive discrimination strategies in favor of women.[8] More recent educational policy documents do not address the gender issue either, among them the legislative proposal of the National Education Plan[9] and the curricular orientations for teacher training.[10] This omission is even more significant when we consider the country's recent commitments before the international community in the various United Nations forums over the past decade.[11]

This policy and program analysis confirms the conclusion that, in Brazil, neither governmental nor nongovernmental adult literacy and basic education prioritizes women's education.[12] This does not mean, however, that the programs totally ignore gender issues. Recently, various public and nongovernment adult literacy and basic education programs have expressed growing concern about learners' self-esteem, about the sociocultural diversity of groups being targeted, and about the particularities of the construction of unique identities. This process has led to a more careful consideration of learners' rural/urban, ethnic-racial, age, gender, and religious backgrounds in the development of curriculum, methodologies, and didactic-pedagogic materials. Literacy and basic education programs that adopt this perspective are influenced by and benefit from pedagogic resources developed for popular communication or nonformal and extra-school modalities of education developed by movements and nongovernment organizations devoted to these issues.

Brazil's rich assortment of community associations and nongovernmental organizations has numerous educational programs where young people and women participate to overcome gender subordination. Among these, the following stand out: safe houses for girls, adolescents, and women victims of sexual exploitation, domestic violence, and other social risk situations; sex education programs that address reproductive health and the prevention of sexually transmitted diseases; day care, preschools, and community schools established and directed by women; popular educator training programs that include child education, community health, and defense of children's, adolescents', and women's rights; and training for income-generating projects. All these projects develop, more or less systematically, learning that expands participants' literacy levels. There are very few literacy or basic education programs specifically directed to women,[13] or that can be identified as both literacy and gender programs, and they deserve particular attention as part of an emerging phenomenon.

Based on a nonexhaustive revision of the existing literature on the subject, we were able to identify eight initiatives targeting women in eleven of the twenty-six Brazilian states, of which only half intentionally work to overcome gender subordination (see Table 4).

Women-focused literacy programs target those women who have problems participating in typical adult education programs. They tend to be older women or poor women who work in domestic tasks and the care of small children. The latter find it difficult or impossible to maintain strict schedules for evening shifts, and compulsory attendance is almost always incompatible with their maternal and domestic tasks. In addition, their husbands often object to their participation in coeducational programs. Women's literacy groups establish more flexible classroom schedules, but their participation still requires support and cooperation from all family members. When women do manage to accommodate domestic labor and child care with their studies, those with family responsibilities and reduced autonomy choose to attend programs close to home. They face transportation difficulties and fear the risks of violence in the poor residential areas.[14]

Another characteristic of these limited programs is that none of them emerged from public entities with the explicit intention of addressing women's educational needs. On the contrary, almost all of them grow out of the social initiative of feminist, women's, or community nongovernment organizations led by women who seek out public financial support to implement their activities autonomously. In most cases, literacy is not the only activity, but is combined with other training needs of women, such as legal and psychological assistance, sex education and information about reproductive rights, and professional training for income-generating projects.

Most of these initiatives are local and have only a few classes with a limited number of students. Those that manage to grow both geographically and in size also need to develop political skills to negotiate with

Table 4. Women-Focused Literacy/Training Programs

Program	Promoter	Location	Support	Characteristics
Women's Literacy Program	Women's Confederation of Brazil	Fortaleza (CE), Natal (RN), Recife (PE), Belo Horizonte (MG), São Paulo (SP), Rio de Janeiro (RJ), Curitiba (PR), Porto Alegre (RS), Goiânia (GO)	MEC, state and municipal education offices	Basic education classes geared toward professional training and income generation. Coordinators are strongly party-identified, some are members of Parliament.
Mato Grosso do Sul Women's Literacy Program	Women's Popular Movement of Mato Grosso do Sul	Campo Grande, Dourados, Fátima do Sul, Rio Brillante, Aquidauana, Três Lagoas (MS)	Mato Grosso do Sul state education office	One semester literacy program. Began in 1995 with goal of teaching 2,400 women to read in two years. Educators belong to Movement. They identify the goal of overcoming gender subordination. In 1996, there were 32 classes and 420 students.
Women's Literacy	Cabo Women's Center	Cabo de Santo Agostinho and other municipalities in the metropolitan region and the *Mata* zone (PE)	Contracts with municipal prefects	Literacy that aims to overcome gender subordination, focused on sex education, income generation, legal support, and defense of rights. It also includes public school teacher training on sex education. A pioneer organization, the founder is now a member of Congress.
Adult Women's Literacy	Women's Studies Group in Sertaneja, UFPB	Cajazeiras (PB)	German Technical and Social Cooperation Service	Begun in 1991, in 1996 it worked with 35 women in two literacy groups, whose pedagogic practice focuses on citizenship and feminism.

Program	Promoter	Location	Support	Characteristics
Professional training for child-care educators	FCC, AMEPPE, PMBH, IRHJP	Metropolitan region of Belo Horizonte (MG)	Vitae Foundation	Basic education focused on pedagogical training of approximately 100 preschool teachers from community preschool centers, set up between 1994 and 1998. One training module deals with gender.
The real joy of reading and writing	Themis and GEEMPA	Porto Alegre (RS)	MEC and UNICEF	Literacy in three months using didactic constructivism begun in 1997. The coordinator is a member of Parliament.
Women from Villa	Literacy Project of non-teaching employees of UFRJ	Rio de Janeiro (RJ)	UFRJ Union of Education Workers	Developed by the union and by Villa Residencial neighbors of non-teaching university employees. In 1991, there was one one class with 16 homemakers studying.
Youth and Adult Literacy Movement	Municipal Prefect and community associations	Angra dos Reis (RJ)	Municipal Education office	1995 records describe classes of black adolescents and women working as domestic laborers.
Bom Jesus da Lapa school	Private charity entity	Timbaúzinho, João Pessoa neighborhood (PB)	Municipal Prefect of João Pessoa	Literacy and professional preparation of domestic workers, documented in the 1980s.
Women's education	Women's ministry	Brasilândia, São Paulo (SP)		In process.
Women's literacy	Paulist Association to Support Women	São Paulo (SP)		In process.

governments and to access public resources. They find support in community movements, feminist and women's organizations, or in political parties.

In publicly sponsored educational programs, women learners do not intentionally meet to consider gender. Rather, they form groups based on other characteristics (geographic location, class schedule, or occupational category) and sometimes end up being predominantly women. In these cases, their awareness and/or discussion of the gender perspective depends on the pedagogic orientation and training of the educators.

Evaluations by promoters and educators committed to women's literacy projects have been extremely positive, but research by external observers puts this evaluation in perspective.[15] While the acquisition of reading, writing, and math abilities and the development of speaking skills, as well as the affective and social skills acquired through socialization in the educational center, are factors that improve women's self-esteem and broaden their possibilities for greater autonomy and mobility in the urban environment, the available studies did not observe that literacy has also led to significant changes in gender relations within the family, in the domestic division of labor, in professional advancement, in income and living conditions, or in women's political involvement.

FINAL NOTES

The relative advantage that young and adult Brazilian women as a whole have reached slightly higher levels of schooling than men does not guarantee them equal access to the labor market, equal returns to their labor, or other opportunities for personal and social development. Illiterate women continue to be a large group, the majority of Brazilian women possess limited schooling, and discrimination persists in terms of educational access for the subgroups of low-income women, and especially black women over age forty who live in rural areas and the North and Northeast regions of the country.

Current educational policies remain silent about these inequalities and offer no direction or policy to address the biases of the school system that favor the reproduction of gender subordination in the labor market, in society, and in families. On the contrary, analysis of Brazil's current educational reform reveals that the priority placed on basic education for children and adolescents, as well as restrictions on public spending on education, deepens the preexisting asymmetries. By marginalizing basic adult education within educational policies, current reforms erect additional obstacles for lower-income and illiterate or poorly educated women by restricting their access to training. Women have full responsibility for the care of the small children, further limiting their access to paid and quality work.

Scant and incipient, social literacy and basic education initiatives for young and adult women with a gender equity perspective sketch a modest picture of hope. Their existence may signify progress, if they are able to resist the current state logic that transfers social tasks to civil society when the state cannot provide sufficient resources, and if they know how to anticipate responses and model social policies that favor women's awareness and organization to combat educational and cultural inequalities in Brazilian society.

NOTES

[1]Nelly P. Stromquist, "Woman and Illiteracy: The Interplay of Gender Subordination and Poverty," *Comparative Education Review* vol. 34, no. 1 (1990): 95–111; Nelly P. Stromquist, "Woman and Literacy in Latin America," in Nelly P. Stromquist (ed.), *Woman and Education in Latin America: Knowledge, Power and Change* (Boulder, Colo.: Lynne Rienner Publishers, 1992); Nelly P. Stromquist, *Literacy for Citizenship: Gender and Grassroots Dimensions in Brazil* (Albany: State University of New York Press, 1997); Fúlvia Rosemberg, "Instrução, rendimento, discriminação racial e de gênero," *Revista Brasileira de Estudos Pedagógicos*, vol. 68, no. 159 (1987): 324–355; Fúlvia Rosemberg, "Education, Democratization, and Inequality in Brazil," in Nelly P. Stromquist (ed.), *Woman and Education in Latin America: Knowledge, Power and Change* (Boulder, Colo.: Lynne Rienner Publishers, 1992), pp. 33–46; Fúlvia Rosemberg, "Subordinação de gênero e alfabetização no Brasil," in Fundâo para o Desenvolvimento da Educacao (ed.), *Alfabetização: passado, presente, futuro.* (São Paulo: FDE, 1993), pp. 125–148; Fúlvia Rosemberg and Edith Piva, "Analfabetismo, gênero e raça no Brasil," in Lucia Bogus and Paulino Yara (eds.), *Políticas de emprego, políticas de população e dereitos sociais* (São Paulo: Educ, 1997), pp. 115–142.

[2]The law uses the term *supletivo,* which has no direct translation in English. It could be considered similar to "complementary," because its goal is to offer primary or secondary education to youth and adults who could not go to formal school.

[3]The Brazilian system established in the 1988 Constitution and the 1996 National Education Law (9394) is divided into basic and higher education. Basic education has three levels: early childhood education (targeting children from 0 to 6 years), basic education (8 years, meant to include an additional year of preschool), and secondary education (3 years). Professional education can be

concurrent with basic and secondary education or can be postsecondary. Youth and adult education—or supplementary education—has curricular and pedagogical flexibility and offers accelerated timetables.

[4]We designate as black the population of African origin or resulting from intermarriage; this population is identified in the census as black and mulatto. See Rosemberg, *op. cit.*, 1987; Rosemberg, *op. cit.*, 1993; Rosemberg and Piva, *op. cit.*, 1997.

[5]Rosemberg and Piva, *op. cit.*, p. 126.

[6]Rosemberg, *op. cit.*, 1987; Rosemberg, *op. cit.*, 1992; Fúlvia Rosemberg et al., *Mulher e educação formal no Brasil: Estado da arte e bibliografia* (Brasília: INEP, 1990).

[7]Sérgio Haddad (ed.), *Alfabetismo funcional no Município de São Paulo* (São Paulo: Açao Educativa, 1997), Vera M. Ribeiro, *Alfabetismo e atitudes: Pesquisa junto a jovens e adultos paulistanos* (São Paulo: Tesis de doctorado, Pontificia Universidad Católica de São Paulo, 1998).

[8]Sérgio Haddad Maria Clara Di Pierro, *Diretrizes de Política Educacional de Educação de Jovens e Adultos: Consolidação de documentos 1985–1994* (São Paulo: CEDI, 1994); Rosemberg, *op. cit.*, 1993.

[9]MEC, *Sinopse Estatística da Educação Básica: Censo Escolar 97* (Brasília: MEC/NEP, 1998).

[10]MEC, *Referencial pedagógico-curricular para a formação de professores da educação infantil e séries iniciais do ensino fundamental: Documento preliminar* (Brasília: MEC/SEF/DPEF/CGEP, 1997).

[11]Sônia Correa (ed.), *La educación en movimiento: Acuerdos sobre educación y género en las conferencias mundiales de los '90* (Montevideo: REPEM, 1996); UNESCO/CEAAL/CREFAL/INEA, *Hacia una educación sin exclusiones: Nuevos compromisos para la educación con personas jóvenes y adultas en América Latina y el Caribe* (Santiago: UNESCO/OREALC, 1998); Atila Roque and Sonia Correa (eds.), *Observatório da Cidadania. Vol. 2* (Montevideo: Instituto del Tercer Mundo, 1998).

[12]Rosemberg, *op. cit.*, 1993.

[13]Marcela Ballara, "Perspectivas de género en la alfabetización y educación básica de personas adultas," *La Piragua* 10 (1995): 72–78.

[14]Stromquist, *op. cit.*, 1992; Stromquist, *op. cit.*, 1997

[15]Paulo Barbosa, *Quando Maria aprende a ler Maria: A fala de um grupo de mulheres do Morro do Borel e da Favela Indiana, a respeito da alfabetização* (Rio de Janeiro: disertacion de maestria, Universidad Federal de Rio de Janeiro, 1994); Nelly P. Stromquist, *Mulher e marginalização social: alfabetização de adultos em São Paulo* (São Paulo: CEDI, 1992); Nelly P. Stromquist, *A mulher e os programas de alfabetização: avanços, obstáculos e paradoxos* (São Paulo: CEDI, 1994); Nelly P. Stromquist, "Access, Content, and Vision Gender Issues in Education in Latin America." Paper presented at the XX LASA International Congress, Guadalajara, 17–19 April 1997.

REFERENCES

Anderson, Jeanine. *Sistemas de gênero, redes de atores e uma proposta de formação.* Brazil: CEAAL/REPEM, 1997.

Andrade, Tereza Gally de. *Célestin Freinet em uma experiência educacional com domésticas analfabetas.* João Pessoa: Master's thesis, Universidad Federal de Paraíba, 1983.

APEOESP. "Pesquisa aponta soluções para segurança e discute gênero." *Jornal da APEOESP* no. 235 (1998).

Ballara, Marcela. "Perspectivas de género en la alfabetización y educación básica de personas adultas." *La Piragua* no. 10 (1995): 72–78.

Barbosa, Paulo. *Quando Maria aprende a ler Maria: A fala de um grupo de mulheres do Morro do Borel e da Favela Indiana, a respeito da alfabetização.* Rio de Janeiro: Master's thesis, Universidad Federal de Rio de Janeiro, 1994.

Brazil. "Mulher: Educar para participar." *CMB* vol. 6, no. 6. (1994).

Brazil. *Programa Alfabetização Solidária. Relatório final: Segundo semestre de 1997.* Brasilia: Conselho da Comunidade Solidária, 1998.

Brazil. *Programa Nacional de Capacitação do Trabalhador. Avaliação Gerencial. 2o. Ano do Triênio: Resultados até 31/12/97.* Brasilia: MTb/SEFOR, 1998.

Bruschini, Maria Cristina.*Trabalho das mulheres no Brasil: Continuidades e mudanças no período 1985–1995.* São Paulo: Fundação Carlos Chagas, 1998.

Cardoso, Mona Lisa F. "Em busca do tempo perdido." *Cadernos do CEDES* vol. 38. (1996): 32–40.

Conferencia Mundial de Educação para Todos. *Declaração Mundial sobre Educação Para Todos e Plano de Ação Para Satisfazer as Necessidades Básicas de Aprendizagem.* Brasília: UNICEF, 1990.

Congresso Nacional de Educação, 2o. *Plano Nacional de Educação: Proposta da Sociedade Brasileira.* Belo Horizonte: CNE, 1997.

Correa, Sônia (ed.). *La educación en movimiento: Acuerdos sobre educación y género en las conferencias mundiales de los '90.* Montevideo: REPEM, 1996.

De Tomassi, L., M.J. Warde, and S. Haddad (eds.). *O Banco Mundial e as políticas educacionais.* São Paulo: Cortez/PUCSP/Ação Educativa, 1996.

Federegui, Paolo. "Lo nuevo y lo viejo del 'lifelong learning' en Europa." *Revista d'Informació i Investigació Socials Fòrum* vol. 6 (1996): 116–124.

Gomes, Cândido Alberto. "Os caminhos e descaminhos dos recursos financeiros em educação." *Revista Brasileira de Estudos Pedagógicos* vol. 75, nos. 179–181 (1994): 9–32.

Gonçalves, Aparecida. "PALMAS para a cidadania: Programa de Alfabetização de Mulheres Adultas em Mato Grosso do Sul." *RAAAB, Alfabetização e Cidadania* vol. 4 (1996): 41–46.

70 Gender Equity in Education Policy

Haddad, Sérgio (ed.). *Alfabetismo funcional no Município de São Paulo.* São Paulo: Ação Educativa, 1997.

Haddad, Sérgio and Maria Clara Di Pierro. *Diretrizes de Política Educacional de Educação de Jovens e Adultos: Consolidação de documentos 1985–1994.* São Paulo: CEDI, 1994.

IPEA. *Relatoria sobre o desenvolvimento humano no Brasil.* Rio de Janeiro: IPEA y PNUD, 1996.

Latapi, Pablo. *Una aproximación teórica para el análisis de las políticas de educación de adultos.* Mexico, mimeo, 1986.

Madeira, Felícia R., et al. Recado dos jovens: Mais qualificação. En Commissao Nacional de População e Desenvolvimento (ed.), *Jovens acontecendo na trilha das políticas públicas. Vol. 2,* pp. 427–498. Brasilia: CNPD, 1998.

MEC. *Plano Nacional de Educação.* Brasilia: MEC, 1997a.

MEC. *Referencial pedagógico-curricular para a formação de professores da educação infantil e séries iniciais do ensino fundamental: documento preliminar.* Brasilia: MEC/SEF/DPEF/CGEP, 1997b.

MEC/INEP. *Sinopse Estatística da Educação Básica: Censo Escolar 97.* Brasilia: MEC/NEP, 1998.

"Nós, aqui!" (3) Porto Alegre: GEEMPA, Themis, December 1997.

"Quem ensina nossos filhos: Estudo traça perfil dos professores e mostra que é hora de investir na qualidade." *Veja* vol. 31, no. 32 (1998): 96–101.

Ramos, Lauro and Soares Ana Lúcia. *Participação da mulher na força de trabalho e pobreza no Brasil.* Brasilia: IPEA, 1994.

Ribeiro, Vera M. *Alfabetismo e atitudes: Pesquisa junto a jovens e adultos paulistanos.* São Paulo: Doctoral dissertation, Pontifícia Universidad Católica de São Paulo, 1998.

Roque, Átila and Sonia Correa (eds.). *Observatório da Cidadania. Vol. 2.* Montevideo: Instituto del Tercer Mundo, 1998.

Rosemberg, Fúlvia. "Education, Democratization, and Inequality in Brazil." In Nelly P. Stromquist (ed.), *Woman and Education in Latin America: Knowledge, Power and Change,* pp. 33–46. Boulder: Lynne Rienner Publishers, 1992.

Rosemberg, Fúlvia. "Instrução, rendimento, discriminação racial e de gênero." *Revista Brasileira de Estudos Pedagógicos* vol. 68, no. 159 (1987): 324–355.

Rosemberg, Fúlvia. "Subordinação de gênero e alfabetização no Brasil." In Fundação para o Desenvolvimento da Educação (ed.), *Alfabetização: passado, presente, futuro,* pp. 125–148. São Paulo: FDE, 1993.

Rosemberg, Fúlvia and Edith Piza. "Analfabetismo, gênero e raça no Brasil." In Lucia Bogus and Paulino Yara (eds.), *Políticas de emprego, políticas de população e dereitos sociais,* pp. 115–142. São Paulo: Educ, 1997.

Rosemberg, Fúlvia, et al. *Mulher e educação formal no Brasil: Estado da arte e bibliografia.* Brasilia: INEP, 1990.

Schmelkes, Sylvia. "La investigación latinoamericana: Algunos resultados." *Educación de Adultos y Desarrollo* no. 45 (1995): 149–156.

Stromquist, Nelly P. "Woman and Illiteracy: The Interplay of Gender Subordination and Poverty." *Comparative Education Review* vol 34, no. 1 (1990): 95–111.

Stromquist, Nelly P. *Mulher e marginalização social: Alfabetização de adultos em São Paulo.* São Paulo: CEDI, 1992a.

Stromquist, Nelly P. "Woman and Literacy in Latin America." In Nelly P. Stromquist (ed.), *Woman and Education in Latin America: Knowledge, Power and Change.* Boulder: Lynne Rienner Publishers, 1992b.

Stromquist, Nelly P. *A mulher e os programas de alfabetização: Avanços, obstáculos e paradoxos.* São Paulo: CEDI, 1994.

Stromquist, Nelly P. *Literacy for Citizenship: Gender and Grassroots Dimensions in Brazil.* Albany: State University of New York Press, 1997a.

Stromquist, Nelly P. "Access, Content, and Vision Gender Issues in Education in Latin America." Paper presented at the XX LASA International Congress, Guadalajara, 17–19 April 1997b.

Torres, Carlos Alberto. "Adult Education Policy, Capitalist Development and Class Alliance: Latin America." *International Journal of Political Education* no. 6 (1986): 157–173.

Turma da Vila. *Mulheres da Vila.* Rio de Janeiro: SINDUFERJ, 1995.

UNESCO/CEAAL/CREFAL/INEA. *Hacia una educación sin exclusiones: Nuevos compromisos para la educación con personas jóvenes y adultas en América Latina y el Caribe.* Santiago: UNESCO/OREALC, 1998.

Vilgovino, M.D., et al. *A educação de adultos numa perspectiva feminista.* Ponencia presentada en Seminario Internacional Educacao e Escolarizacao de Jovens e Adultos: Experiências brasileiras. Brasília: MEC/IBEAC, vol. 2 (1997): 26–31.

"Viva a Edileusa!" *Veja* vol. 31, no. 32 (1998).

PART II

Nongovernmental Organizations and the Education of Adult Women

Learning for the Construction of a Feminist Agenda within Organizations in Civil Society

NELLY P. STROMQUIST

INTRODUCTION

The construction and diffusion of feminist ideas are closely linked to the women's movement, which is crystallized in women-led nongovernmental organizations (NGOs). These kinds of NGOs exist in all countries, even those experiencing strong religious repression. There are numerous women-led NGOs in Latin America; diverse in form, size, and objectives, these nongovernmental organizations have experienced rapid growth in the past fifteen years.[1]

Political and sociological literature has recognized the emergence of women's or feminist movements since the 1970s as part of the new social movements, which seek not only to satisfy material needs but also to build a new social order. As Maxine Molyneux affirms: "one of feminism's more significant contributions has been the development of a new perspective of social and political life, a new perspective that not only reveals its deep inequalities and its generic character but that also requires a reformulation of the priorities of the state as well as of the normativity of the social order."[2]

Feminist perspectives share a double impact with other social movements. Movements both awaken in their members a critical awareness of their surroundings, and also influence public decisions, especially on issues regarding national development in third world countries. NGOs have sought both vindication—demanding political rights equal to men—and liberation—creating new social identities. The character of both these tasks is eminently educational.

Though formal education is not the highest priority within the feminist movement in Latin America[3] nor in other regions of the world, fundamental learning takes place in women's groups, whether they are constituted as nongovernmental organizations, grassroots groups, or as protest movements based on feminist demands.[4]

Adult women learn through nonformal education (defined as education outside of the school setting but whose explicit purpose is the transference of knowledge) in frequent workshops sponsored by women's groups, but even more through informal education (which occurs through social and political engagement), such as participation in movement actions, in preparations for national or world encounters and in participation in these forums. Informal education has only recently begun to receive scholarly attention.

The wide variety of knowledge transmitted through the women's movement has not been systematically ordered, and thus little is known about its range, variation, and achievements. This chapter offers a brief summary of the NGOs that have worked with women and gender in Latin America and examines their contribution to the educational field through their actions in formal, informal, and nonformal education.

THE WOMEN'S MOVEMENT
AS A SOURCE OF KNOWLEDGE

There is general agreement among sociologists that the women's movement should be classified with the so-called new social movements. If traditional social movements centered on the class struggle, the new social movements function in the cultural arena. Touraine defines the new social movements as "conflictive actions that seek to change the social relations of power in the decisive cultural areas, such as production, science and ethical values."[5] Broadening this definition, Dalton and Kuecher indicate that these movements generally include "a significant sector of the population which develops incompatible interests with the existing political and social order and pursues them through non-institutionalized means, invoking the use of physical force or coercion."[6]

According to Touraine, it is necessary to frame the analysis of these movements so that their actions are not seen as a response to a given social situation, but on the contrary, the given social situations are seen to result from conflict propitiated by the social movement.[7] This inversion of causes is fundamental because it helps us understand how these social movements redefine the social order and thus determine the "historicity" of many societies.

Social movements introduce a new conception of the individual and thus always proceed based on a certain level of consciousness. But, as Touraine makes clear, political conscience is not enough to create a political organization.[8] Women's movements have not led to direct political organization, as have other social movements (particularly the ecological movement). Women's movements tend to act through multiple organizations and events. It is also important to observe that though other movements have used threats, demonstrations, and even violence, women's movements have been characterized by nonviolent strategies and patience, and only recently have they exhibited a willingness to make use of political power. Not surprisingly, these postures have influenced the educational programs that women's groups offer as well as the lessons derived from the mobilizing practice of these institutions and groups. Touraine affirms that Latin America has always experienced excessive political expression and a deficit of social actors.[9] In this sense, women-led NGOs in the region are creating political arenas of great vitality that surpass gender dimensions.

Molyneux notes that literature on women's movements generally identifies two types: feminist groups in collective action on an international level and the struggles of poor women to improve their basic consumption and to protest against social injustice.[10] A third and incipient group, according to Molyneux, is constituted by the mobilization of women under fundamentalist social regimes, such as Iran's revolution. Molyneux maintains that studies about women's movements have generally been descriptive, centered on the historic, social, and institutional facts that accompany women's activism and the way in which gender appears in collective identity, although there have also been attempts to develop taxonomies of these movements and their relationship to issues of democracy.

Molyneux suggests a taxonomy of women's movements centered around autonomy, and distinguishes three ideal types:

1. *Independent movements.* In these movements, women participate autonomously, but the movements are not formulated in terms of gender issues, even if their objectives are universal. These movements' actions are generally linked to the country's independence and its development, such as women's participation in struggles against colonialism and protest movements against the

high cost of living. Molyneux notes that these movements generally operate within the limits of the formal exercise of power and can be based on conventional authority models where there are no democratic relations between participants and their leaders. In the case of Latin America, many of the rural NGOs in Mexico where women organize around a productive activity or access to credit but without a gender perspective can also be placed in this category.[11]

2. *Movements with associative links.* These are organizations of independent women with individual objectives and institutional autonomy. They generally form alliances with other organizations based on limited agreements. Power and authority are constantly negotiated. Molyneux considers that this type escapes the dilemma of "autonomy and integration." Also according to Molyneux, these movements have the potential to move in the field of public political reforms, though she believes that this can also lead to alliances with institutions whose different objectives might dilute the feminist agenda.

3. *Movements based on direct mobilization where initiative for action comes from external and greater institutional authority, such as political parties or the government.* These movements, which according to Molyneux represent "the antithesis of independent organizations of women,"[12] are the most common. Examples of these movements include the mobilization of women to participate in the internal guerilla struggles of Bolivia and Peru, or the struggle to improve women's condition within existing political parties or mobilizations initiated by the government to defend the logic of the current system (e.g., the racist system in Nazi Germany or the political posture of Iran after the shah was overthrown).

This typology is useful to acknowledge that gender is not always the principal motivating force for women's action and that women do not always mobilize to change the social order of gender. Obviously, groups with different objectives produce different types of knowledge. In the following discussion, I will focus exclusively on the second group, women's movements "with associative links," because I seek to recover the liberating and political efforts to build a new social order. This labor has been essentially carried out by women-led NGOs either in order to improve women's situation in the short term or to initiate major social transformations.

THE EVOLUTION AND TRAJECTORY OF NGOS LINKED TO WOMEN'S MOVEMENTS IN LATIN AMERICA

Systematic analysis of women's objectives indicate that multiple interests have led and continue to lead women toward action. Thus, women's interests are neither transparent nor ordinary and gender identity is not their sole identity.[13] What we call women's movements actually represent very heterogeneous forms of participation. Frequently, different tendencies join together around basic needs, without central coordination, without a single agenda, and with multiple strategies, revealing a diffuse agency with no center. In addition, since poor women are a critical sector in these movements and they face critical issues of economic survival, relatively few women are able to participate in and address self-awareness.

I consider three factors to have affected the evolution and thus the learning that takes place within the feminist movement. First, feminists face the question of whether they seek equality or difference between the sexes. Second, feminist analysis has probed the differing concepts of "women and development" and "gender and development," which seek to reformulate feminist analysis and actions. Finally, the feminist movement has widened its scope, it has moved from limiting itself to dealing exclusively with women's condition, to encompassing a broader vision of citizenship that embraces other marginalized groups.

Between Equality and Difference

Two major feminist schools—feminism of equality and feminism of difference—must be reevaluated in light of the objective of working for a new social order. The first school struggles for a society where differences between men and women are minimized, while the second stresses women's place in society through the acceptance of certain attributes particular to women. These visions about equality or difference lead to different political strategies or at least to great ambiguity in the selection of solutions.

Feminism of equality—the most common—struggles for equal conditions and human rights for men and women. Feminism of difference opens up at least four positions: (1) the most radical argues that women are fundamentally more ethical, solidary, and pacifist than men and thus seeks a separate society, if not from men then at least from the state; (2) a second struggles for the legal and social recognition and acceptance of women's unique characteristics, such as right to maternity leave, labor protection laws against difficult jobs, and early retirement of the labor force; (3) the third accepts that women, perhaps due to socialization more than to genetic reasons, have attributes that make them useful social subjects (for example, that motherhood offers a more human and altruist vision of the world) and that these attributes (being emotive and empathic) should be recognized and even imitated by men; and (4) the position that argues that strong differences exist between women depending on their ethnic background, social class, or sexual orientation.

The problem of equality and difference in the women's movement has not been solved. Further, some groups who identify themselves with feminism of equality work for objectives that seem to fit better within the notion of difference, such as differential labor laws or social legislation by sex. In my opinion, ambiguity toward equality or difference constrains the development of a more unified women's movement, because instead of facing this contradiction, many women avoid it.

Women or Gender?

With the initiation of contemporary feminism in the third world, between 1975 and 1985, women's situation and position in society and, subsequently, in development projects was identified under the term "women in development," or WID. Later the term was modified to "gender and development," or GAD, to indicate that women's situation has to be conceptualized as the result of interaction with men and thus as a constant political and social construction. Although GAD promises a more complete analysis, in practice the new perspective has not brought significant changes. After a detailed discussion of the health sector in Latin America, Diaz and Spicehandler[14] conclude that there have been greater achievements in GAD's definition than in its implementation. Stromquist[15] presents a similar conclusion after analyzing educational projects supported by several international agencies.

One of the unintentional consequences of the gender concept is that it is often used to criticize the work of certain women-led NGOs, concluding that they are not complex enough to respond to the problem of asymmetrical power or women's subordination. There have also been contrasts between WID and GAD that undervalue women's struggles to better their economic situation and even ridicule past efforts of many NGOs. At times, this has created divisions between the more academic feminist movement and the popular women's movement.

FROM WOMEN'S RIGHTS TO CITIZENSHIP RIGHTS

Women initiated their actions through demands to improve their condition as women, frequently focusing on their important role as mothers and wives, responsible for the well-being of the family. But as some of these demands were expressed and some achievements gained it became clear that the debate was shifting away from a mere improvement of "women's condition." With the many international forums, especially the 1995 Second Conference on Population and Development in Cairo and the 1995 Fourth World Conference on Women in Beijing, the discourse has moved toward "full citizenship," "social justice," and toward women's rights as "human rights." This broadened vision is clearly reflected in DAWN's declaration[16] that upholds the need to fight not only against those gender-based power relations but also those based on "religious, caste and sexually-oriented differences as well as any other that limits the development and expression of points of view and cultural values of subordinated groups."[17] This new perspective drives the women's movement to look beyond the question of gender.

The feminist movement has learned many lessons over the past twenty-five years, all of them with consequences for contemporary and future educational practices. These lessons include: better understanding regarding participation and organization, more acceptance of power, an incursion in formal political areas, and greater comprehension of informal education. I will now consider several actions that fall within three modalities: formal education, nonformal education, and informal education.

FORMAL EDUCATION

Although formal educational systems can provide the necessary knowledge for the development of a critical gender awareness, many times the school actually acts as a mechanism to transmit dominant ideologies, not only regarding gender oppression but also regarding the subordination of ethnic and "racial" minorities. Moved by egalitarian tides, the feminist movement has emphasized women's access to schools and universities, minimizing efforts to question the knowledge obtained in the formal system.

In this section, I will not consider activities that attempt to change formal education from within, but will focus on how the feminist movement is acting from outside the school system to improve the contents and curricular experiences of the formal sector. These interventions, distressingly small in number, range from the pioneer efforts of Bonder and Schmukler[18] in the mid-1980s to change the pedagogical practices of teachers in primary school or to promote democratization on a family level and between school and community, to more recent examples like that of Valenzuela. Valenzuela offers a concrete example of preschool education in Mexico City, where feminists, aware of education's role in gender identity construction, created a program for teachers and mothers that offered a broader understanding of gender, of sexist and sexed practices within family and school, and of the importance of working toward a nonsexist education. This program has involved participants from different levels in the school and community, and the local government has responded favorably to disseminating the training and curricular design components more broadly.

Unfortunately, there are very few cases of alliances between women's groups and the state education sector. Projects generally emerge from outside the system, they tend to be small and of minimal duration, and they have few effects on the rest of the system. Three exceptions of great importance are Bolivia, where gender issues have been included in the current educational reform, Argentina, which experienced significant change from 1991 to 1995 until the offensive by the Catholic Church, and the very successful instance of Uruguay, which is implementing a very complete overhaul in the gender nature of its educational system. These experiences represent examples of comprehensive reforms that include curriculum, training, and the role of the community. These initiatives prove the importance of carrying out multiple actions at the same time; given that changes in gender relations imply changes in power relations, there is a need for constant struggle to legitimize those changes.

Another important event involves the increasing incorporation of the gender issue within the activities of CEAAL, a broad-reaching adult education network. This incorporation has significance because of its role in civil society, and more specifically the women's movement. Although some feminist groups consider that CEAAL's receptivity has not been as far-reaching as it could be, it has taken initiatives that it would not have previously, such as: calling on governments to incorporate gender analysis in educational project evaluations; to include gender issues more often in teacher training; to promote gender justice in educational reforms, especially at the secondary level; to study masculinity in schools; and to promote sexual and reproductive education in schools. CEAAL has been trying to create a pedagogic movement with teacher participation in favor of a nonsexist education since 1998. It has also promoted more symbolic measures such as the creation of a day—June 21—for nonsexist education.[19]

One of the educational interventions with greatest impact has been carried out by REPEM (the Women's Popular Education Network in Latin America and the Caribbean), which initiated a campaign for nonsexist education in 1994 that allowed various NGOs to give gender training in public schools, especially in urban areas. It ought to be mentioned, however, that despite great enthusiasm to intervene in formal education and to develop a regional project, little is known about the results of the efforts to promote a nonsexist education. In part because of the extremely small support by donor agencies, NGOs and participating schools were not able to participate in a sustained fashion.

In any case, the question emerges of why such critical interventions to change the gender perspective in schools come from outside, and in particular from feminist NGOs. There is not high demand within the formal system because many teachers are themselves the product of a patriarchal ideology, and they do not perceive the considerable gender problems in their everyday practices.[20] On the other hand, Latin American teachers are extremely focused on labor demands and seldom examine their own function critically. Because their relationship with the state has been one of subordination and great tension, they do not define themselves as professionals willing to work together on common problems.

ACTIONS INVOLVING NONFORMAL EDUCATION

Women's groups have organized nonformal education through a broad spectrum of workshops in areas considered fundamental to resolve everyday pressures in women's lives, both to guarantee survival needs and to lead a life with more gender justice.

The small training workshops began by dealing with issues like health, sexuality, self-esteem, income generation, literacy, legal training, and domestic violence as a personal and health problem. As time passed and women gained a deeper understanding of the gender system, workshops on domestic violence began to address the issue as a human rights violation, and focused on empowerment, leadership, and training for citizenship and counseling. Over the years, the spectrum of topics has expanded, and now ranges from topics that try to solve personal problems and crises, to issues that address broader social situations beyond the question of women.

Literacy programs are a key area within nonformal education. Although illiteracy among women is a significant problem, especially in rural areas and among the indigenous and peoples of African origins, governments do not offer enough literacy programs for these populations and they do not design them taking into account the practical and strategic needs of women as a subordinate group. In Brazil, Di Pierro (this volume) shows the extremely meager attention states give to literacy programs and to the fact that women participate in these programs. Di Pierro identifies several efforts made by women's organizations to work in this area and finds that the majority of programs do not develop an explicit theoretical approach on gender, although they combine literacy classes with other skills and knowledge dissemination useful to women, such as reproductive rights, legal assistance, and training for income-generating projects.

The workshops offered by women's NGOs seem to target women with a certain educational level, and they try to provide these women with skills to be less silent and submissive in both the public and private spheres. It ought to be mentioned that evaluations of these programs have been merely anecdotal, but they indicate that the workshops have led to substantial changes in participants' gender identity. Through nonformal education—educational interventions outside school with no link to the formal system—women's movements have addressed issues previously ignored or considered taboo in society, such as the right to control one's body and knowledge about our own sexuality.

Women's organizations implement activities that take into account identity rights, citizenship, the right to peace and a life free of violence, sexual and reproductive rights, and the right to national development and environmental rights. While the notion of citizenship can have different meanings, a common one is women's participation in all spheres of the nation's public and political life. The groups also work with reproductive rights, which are defined as "rights to a free and informed reproductive life and to exercise voluntary and safe control of fertility, free from discrimination, violence and coercion as well as the right to enjoy the highest levels of sexual and reproductive health including access to legal and safe abortions."[21]

Although there are few documents about educational programs run by women's organizations, the majority of them carry out activities of technical, pedagogic, and organizational support in many areas at the same time. The most important areas are: health, violence, human rights, and theoretical discussions about gender, especially in the case of Mexico.[22] Two examples of this work are presented below.

CIPAF (*Centro de Investigación para la Acción Femenina;* Research Center for Feminine Action), in the Dominican Republic, initiated workshops in 1986. With pedagogic methodologies that favor participatory learning, the use of personal experience, and group work, CIPAF has offered courses targeted at leaders in organization and democratic participation. It has offered workshops for community-level political agents and for women representatives at the municipal and congressional level. Other courses have addressed issues like health, reproductive health, work, women's sexuality, women in history, and feminism—workshops always linked to a new concept of women and their protagonist role in society. CIPAF has not only made significant contributions in nonformal education, but has also worked in formal education through teacher training courses in nonsexist education, and it was the motivating force behind the provision of the women's studies courses at the Santo Domingo Autonomous University.

The *Casa de la Mujer* in Santa Cruz, Bolivia, another women-led NGO, was founded in 1990 in order to "improve the quality of life of women from popular sectors in particular, and to seek more equal gender relations for women in general, through training and offering direct services and through strengthening their organizations to achieve structural changes."[23] Its work is typical of other women-led NGOs and its mission emphasizes women's sexuality and reproductive health. *La Casa* treats women of all ages through medical appointments in the health program but also offers workshops to address issues of lack of power over one's body, domestic violence, distorted sexual experiences, depressed lives, lack of legal protection, and unemployment as causal factors of many diseases.[24] The workshops also address issues of pleasure and sexuality. Health training includes educational games and participatory skits in neighborhood health workshops, with mothers in child-care centers, with housewives and in schools. The workshops use modules that follow a single content which trainers adjust to the participants. *La Casa* provides other services, including legal support for domestic violence and family assistance, as well as psychological support especially with housewives and women from poor neighborhoods. The workshops also deal with environmental issues like garbage, the use of detergents, toxic matter, and ways to control insects. *La Casa* encourages husbands to attend, but they generally do not. It is a small organization; in 1994–1995 it was attended by only 910 women as health patients.[25] *La Casa* has been successfully involved in legal actions to pass anti–domestic violence laws, laws to protect domestic workers, and forestry protection laws.

Whether large or small, long-standing or recently formed, there are common threads that run through the workshops offered by women-led and women-targeted NGOs.

LEARNING THROUGH INFORMAL EDUCATION

The work of informal education has just started to be acknowledged and systematized in an analytical fashion.[26] It has gotten a late start because activists are not accustomed to documenting their experiences, and when they do, their accounts and analysis do not capture the richness and complexity of those experiences. On the other hand, only in the past ten years has discourse analysis gained strength within the social sciences, especially with Foucault's contributions and that of educators who work in critical pedagogy.[27] These analyses help us understand how ideas and the formation of ideologies within discourse are linked to power and domination strategies; they also show how being conscious of discursive practices helps create counter-hegemonic discourses that produce new identities and lead to different realities. In addition, as feminist theories develop, one can perceive that gender social change encompasses a socioeconomic improvement together with the creation of a new feminist culture, one that brings about the social recognition and respect for women[28] and particularly "the public expression of dissent and the affirmative enunciation of alternatives" by themselves.[29]

Feminist and women's NGOs have played a fundamental role in the creation of international forums that address women's issues. Initially, NGOs from the north pressured their governments and development agencies. The latter, reflecting domestic pressures, influenced United Nations agencies and third world governments receiving aid from the development agencies to address the gender issue.

Without doubt it has been the NGOs that have achieved almost a global consensus on issues of poverty, health, violence, armed conflicts, the economy, decision making, human rights, media, the environment, education, and the condition of girls. These issues, and in particular their implementation, have produced knowledge regarding political mobilization, deepened understanding of the existence and mechanisms of gender ideologies, and the incipient development of broader political projects.

Presenting the perspective of REPEM serves to rescue the voice of women-led NGOs in this learning process. According to its leaders, REPEM acquired significant knowledge during the preparations for world summits on population, women, and adult education. As described by Eccher in detail,[30] these experiences cover numerous areas of action: the use of language in the formation of demands; the recognition of political allies; the importance and the art of lobbying; the exploitation of electronic communications; micro and macro relations; and the possible links among state, civil society, and international cooperation organizations.

REPEM has also learned to work with productive enterprises as effective mechanisms to achieve women's empowerment. Conscious of the scant publicity given to these efforts, many of which have been successful, REPEM has promoted a Latin American competition so that some of these projects can publicize their achievements, failures, and challenges, as a way to gather and distribute knowledge about successful strategies and experiences.

Political protest movements have been the source of significant learning experiences. Participation, mobilization, and the development of arguments to define and reformulate problems from a given perspective serve as powerful tools to gain knowledge. Though the processes are highly complex and sometimes contradictory, participants unlearn old ways of perceiving the world, leave aside old understandings as if they were mere ideology, and learn a different discourse. Through the participation process itself, they learn to control their fear, to have more self-confidence, and to observe contradictions, complexities, and ambiguities.

Although the learning spheres are often part of women's daily activities, the lessons do not lose their legitimacy for being "ordinary." For example, even in ostensible social groups like mothers' clubs, opportunities arise to reformulate concerns and translate them into demands made of political representatives. These opportunities for discussion sometimes lead to the delineation of more complex strategies and to the need to interact with government agencies. This consciousness raising is linked to issues that spring from women's everyday experiences and emerges through sharing, in situations of strong collective support, the worries and needs that concern a great number of families and people in the community or neighborhood. As Alvarez argues, these needs are not necessarily defined in terms of the economic and political system nor related to a theoretical or ideological understanding of the system,[31] but the fact that they are articulated in a dialogic way favors the development of a collective consciousness that then addresses areas which were previously taboo and that later, linking situations together, builds a more complex and profound schemata of daily problems.

Lagarde raises a key point; she maintains that feminism implies a "feminist acculturation" where women make certain connections within themselves and with other women.[32] These include the internal and subjective process of building an individual and daily feminist awareness, communication of feminist discourse and alternatives by women and their organizations to civil society, personal communication between women and specific movements, interactive communication between social spaces (whether mixed, just women, or feminist), communication with "men allies," and finally, communication between men of feminist discourses and alternatives.[33] Discourse is critical in this process of acculturation, that is, the adoption and creation of a new culture, given that the women's movement has not been characterized by violent practices and large political demonstrations. Thus, continuous dialogue and the creation of a new subjectivity constitute critical tools for creating change in social gender relations.

The analysis presented by Alvarez[34] of discursive processes within the micro-politics of women's movements is of fundamental importance to detect informal education occurring in these places. Based on Alvarez' original contributions, Foley identifies several principles that contribute to political apprenticeship of social movements. Foley argues that critical knowledge is gained informally, through experience—acting and reflecting over action—more than through formal educational courses.[35] I now present some of these principles within a gender perspective context:

1. The use of spoken and written language should be analyzed as a linguistic process as well as a sociological phenomenon.[36] On the one hand, women's interests are constructed in a political and discursive way.[37] On the other hand, as assessed by Foucault, discourses deal not only with what can be said and thought but also about who can talk, when, and with what authority.[38] Women develop a collective and public discourse through participation in women's movements or feminist organizations.

2. Consciousness formation fluctuates between a moment of incoherence, breaking with old languages and postures, and moments of new formulations, often temporary and tentative.[39] Mediation by institutions that allow dialogue between their members, as do NGOs, make possible the emergence of new forms of self-awareness.

3. Every critical learning process involves making private experiences previously thought to be an idiosyncratic part of the public domain, broadening understandings and opening possibilities of action and changes in the structure and frame of the experience.[40] The process of critical learning requires that people ponder their own experience and look at it with a certain distance to reorder it using concepts like power, conflict, structure, values, and autonomous choice.

4. In increasing self-awareness in general and around gender issues in particular, oppositional discourse plays a fundamental role in relation to issues like human rights, social justice, equality, and freedom.[41] These are learning experiences that make the women's

movement a mechanism for social and political demands as well as a source of social and cultural freedom. This type of informal learning is taking place in women-led NGOs and NGOs that target women. This newly learned knowledge helps promote the development and strengthening of new identities and visions of gender. Although the work of feminist NGOs can only reach out to a few women, these changes are gradually passed on to the entire society.

As we reconsider learning in the framework of informal education carried out by women, we can delineate five categories: about what is not known, about one's self and others (gender identity), about the state, about possible allies, and about efficient strategies.

About One's Self

Leadership experiences have taught women both as individuals and as social actors. Problems related to the creation of a different and democratic leadership, the use of power without repeating old patterns of domination, the practice of leadership both at the local and job level rather than in formal politics are being reexamined. These lessons also include the recognition of issues of representation, that is, to what extent leaders know and defend other women's desires. Vanguards are limited by definition, and in situations of great oppression and thus little awareness, no regular processes of formal representation take place. For this reason it has been difficult to respond to the criticism that certain NGOs do not "represent" some groups of women. Another important lesson has been the acknowledgment of conflicts that women leaders have found in other social roles women play, from consumers to patients.[42]

An important aspect of this knowledge includes women's transformations to a condition of individuality, that is, to seeing themselves as subjects, and not only as mediating social agents between family and society.[43] Another important aspect is that women not feel guilty for taking on leadership and being more decisive and even more aggressive at certain times.

Finally, the challenge remains of how to link women's demands to national measures and not only to local or family-related solutions. This challenge is intimately related to the problem of how to go beyond poor and marginal women's situation and make them an intrinsic part of civil society.

About the State

There have been numerous concrete lessons about how the state's machinery works, especially the different bureaucratic agencies. These include acknowledging that it is not always bureaucratic conspiracy against women, but also institutional inertia, that blocks progress. There is also greater understanding of the symbolic, as opposed to substantive, answers from the state. In many important projects, the state offers an official affirmative answer or gives moral support, but does not accompany the support with a budget distribution for the projects.[44] Many NGOs also realize that in many cases the state has been giving significant roles to NGOs, but within a framework that can be considered "domesticated citizenship" in the sense that local participation is seen as the culmination of citizenship and actions are limited to distribution of food or work in popular dining halls. The NGOs are not engaged in more significant areas like access to land, credit, or employment. At the international forums, women-led and feminist NGOs have learned from each other through the distribution of national reports describing women's conditions and achievements. In certain cases, as in Argentina, when preparing for the Beijing conference, the women learned to question the official version and produced alternative national reports.

Women-led and feminist NGOs are much more conscious of the importance of economic factors and of how weak economies are not capable of managing favorable conditions for gender change. With globalization, economic development no longer guarantees more jobs or an end to poverty,[45] and also implies less resources to conceive of or experiment with a new social order.

Certain feminist NGOs, among them DAWN (Development Alternatives with Women for a New Era), demand that states intervene more in the social sector to benefit the majority. They want the state to redirect the market and to assume a major social responsibility to restructure institutions and thus build a stronger civil society that would offer the women's movement a larger space.[46] Concrete demands formulated by DAWN, which were undoubtedly discussed within the NGOs that are part of this network, include national and international measures: reduction of military spending, placing taxes on speculative financial transactions, negotiation of the foreign debt, the formation of structures that gather more sensible taxes, and the adoption of a rural reform, among other things.[47] These demands reflect a deep and perceptive understanding of the way politics and economics function. They also indicate a clear position of the role the state should play within society.

Not only do NGOs learn about the state, but they also address what they perceive that the state learns about women or about gender. For example, in an analysis of the progress made since the Cairo declarations about population and development, DAWN observes that the most evident expression of progress has been the "semantic revolution" or "the transformation of language in policies and of those who make political decisions." Even when sexual and reproductive rights are officially addressed, women's autonomy and self-determination are given little attention. While the rhetoric has improved, often it has not been accompanied by actions; DAWN notes that in many cases the old "family planning" has been renamed "reproductive health and sexual rights" without great changes in contents and programs. Even though the public discourse refers to gender equality and condemns the problem of domestic violence, the implementation of these concepts in terms of broad coverage and quality service offerings have lagged behind.[48]

About Possible Allies

While the experiences of mobilizations and alliances with different institutions have contributed significant knowledge, they have also created division within the women's movement. Even though many priests within the Catholic Church, especially those linked to Liberation Theology, accept women's struggle to change the social order, the higher levels of the Catholic Church hierarchy oppose the essential principles of women's liberation, such as abortion rights or women's right to control their own bodies. Though there has been some conceptual improvement, some issues, like abortion rights, have experienced an increase in legal limitations; abortions are illegal in more countries today than in the recent past.

Collaboration with political parties to support women candidates and resource allocation to support gender policies has proved that these alliances are possible, but are also fragile and have clear limits. Stronger NGOs with greater national political visibility and global organizations like DAWN believe that more support from international agencies is needed to have a more sustained dialogue with the respective governments and to broaden the public debate. On the other hand, many small NGOs that defend the interests of lesbian women oppose alliances with the government and international cooperation agencies. They argue that external funding limits autonomy and thus commitment to supporters at the base is lost. The conflict between "dependent" and "autonomous" NGOs divided the Sixth Latin American Feminist Encounter and limited its impact. These differences continue unresolved. As Krawcyk notes,[49]

NGOs in Latin America currently face a challenging period as they deal with multiple issues: representativity, capacity to attract supporters, the debate about autonomy of thinking and funding, and the ability to establish links with the state.

While there are progressive international agencies that support women and the changes they demand, there are also many that operate within the narrow terms of the states that benefit from agency support. Gradually, women-led NGOs have accepted that international meetings support the institutionalization of responses to gender problems but that the responses are often limited to acknowledging their legitimacy rather than seeking concrete solutions.

About Effective Strategies

These are the lessons that the women's movement has learned from their incursion into political actions. Many of them are related to their participation in world forums and subsequent efforts to implement the agreements in every country that signed.

The lessons collected by REPEM are of great importance due to their position as a leader in Latin America. REPEM has learned that lobbying is fundamental for success in the political arena, and has produced a "Proactive Lobby Manual."[50] REPEM also learned that while it is necessary to work for laws that improve or change women's condition, it is also necessary to build a strong movement because "without correlation of forces there is no political pressure."

Access to electronic mail and the use of electronic networks has allowed the movement to have immediate communication between its members and to put pressure on political authorities. Recently, REPEM has used the Internet to hold virtual seminars. Electronic mail has been a critical technological tool for the global feminist movement.

About What Is Not Known

Many NGOs have realized that economics must be understood in greater depth and detail. They argue that more feminist economists are needed for this, as well as people who understand public budgets and who can identify excessive spending and corruption in order to reassign funds. Part of this economic knowledge will tell us that low-cost investments do not necessarily create low-cost programs, because they can generate high social costs for certain groups, especially those officially meant to benefit from the programs.[51]

It is also worth noting that there have been few evaluative studies of the educational role of social movements at the formal, nonformal, and informal levels. This is partly due to the almost nonexistent budget for research, and thus for reflection. In particular, we know very little about educational initiatives and feminist action that takes place within labor unions and peasant federations.

EMERGING CHALLENGES AND DILEMMAS

Every learning process creates new questions and helps to identify dilemmas. Greater action and reflection about experiences leads to greater recognition of the complexities and multiple factors involved. I will now point out some of these challenges and dilemmas.

1. As feminist NGOs professionalize, they handle a more so-phisticated discourse with greater impact on the state and on international cooperation agencies. At the same time, the profes-sionalization creates a greater distance between them and women from marginal sectors.
2. The introduction of gender as an analytical framework has pro-duced interest and progress in the academic world. Work within universities has moved toward a growing recognition of the importance of discourse, the fluidity of identity, and the relative role of gender in the social world. NGOs also recognize the ten-sion that is created between fighting for women and against oppression, but they are aware of the danger of creating, as many academics suggest, a single subject. There is still a clear division between "academics" and "activists." In large cities, like Sao Paulo and Mexico City, there are signs that the feminist move-ment is separating from the academics.[52]
3. The unsolved tension between equality and difference in the women's movement creates contradictions in various actions that must be resolved. The movement faces the related challenge to uncover and deconstruct the meaning and nature of the differ-entiation between genders in a society marked by social, cul-tural, spatial, and temporal complexities.
4. Many achievements have come through small victories. These victories have shown that the state rejects the most radical pro-posals regarding abortion or sexuality; they have also shown that even the less radical reforms, like those that increase women's access to better social services, are frequently poorly financed,

hindering them from actually improving the women's condition on a broad scale, and even less from producing changes in cultural practices. Given this reality, what are the implications of cooperating with the state? In which situations are mutual benefits achieved?

5. Various practical challenges merge in the area of education: The education sector receives limited funds, and NGOs educating adult women receive even less. It is clear that the state does not recognize women's strategic needs. The economic situation drives women to fight for survival, as individuals or in organizations, and this limits the transformative possibilities of the educational work. Global financial and market forces favor competition over solidarity.

6. In the field of alliances, the women's movement has identified men and institutions run by men that are receptive to feminist ideas. How should women's groups cooperate with them without being coopted? This is a question that many women-led NGOs ask themselves. Some groups think that the time has come to work with progressive men. Others consider that this strategy is still premature and could dilute feminist demands, especially in Latin America where the intellectuals (predominantly men) perceive social inequalities mainly within the context of socioeconomic status or class.

7. In Latin America, perhaps more than in other regions of the third world, there is talk of a redemocratization process, with the growing existence of governments formally elected by their citizens. However, this region, like others, faces serious challenges in the forces of economic globalization and political neoliberalism, which demand a state with reduced interests in equity and other forms of social justice. In this context, the Latin American feminist movement faces serious problems linking progress at the micro level, through constructing a women's identity as an alternative to the current model, to support at the macro level, such as public policies in favor of gender equity.

WOMEN-LED NGOS AND EDUCATION

Women-led NGOs and their networks continue to play a central role in social learning through multiple functions: as agents that respond to and solve problems on a local level, as important mediators between the state and society, and as articulators of a new social worldview that includes full citizenship.

In this chapter, I sought to recapture the multiple educational tasks that are carried out within the women's movement and to prove that many significant changes in the conceptualization of women's issues in contemporary society come from the practical struggles of women-led and feminist NGOs. Table 1 presents the various types of learning in a schematic form.

Education is clearly intertwined in many ways with the actions of the women's movement. It is difficult and even artificial to try to separate political objectives from practices with an educational content and their consequent lessons.

The women's movement in Latin America has given relatively little emphasis to the transformation of formal education. There is little acknowledgment of the ideological role of formal education, and demands are often limited to improving young women's access to schools in rural areas or to improving access for indigenous or black girls and women. With the exception of efforts to design a nonsexist education, there have not been strong strategies linked to schools.

Despite this blind spot, the women's movement has made strong contributions to nonformal and informal education. The holistic conception of education within many NGOs has led them to design workshops that address extremely important areas for women both personally and politically. These workshops have given women greater confidence and spirit for struggle and leadership. The intense involvement of these groups in the formulation of national, regional, and global strategies has led to a broader understanding of women's reality, of possibilities for social and cultural change, and of the need to see gender issues as both cultural and economic. There is also an understanding of the possibility of weak alliances with institutions run by men. By successfully uniting with global networks, the women's movement has managed to introduce a social development agenda with a human focus that therefore represents an expanded vision of what individual and collective progress for human beings means.

Much still remains to be done to systematize the educational experience of feminist groups working in NGOs. Without resources for evaluation or for research, these lessons remain undocumented and live only in the memory of the members who still work with the respective institution. Even though formal educational activities remain in the shadows, this does not diminish the valuable task of political and cultural lessons that are carried out within women-led NGOs.

Table 1. Typology of Educational Processes within Women's Movements

Type of education	Content of New Knowledge and Current Learning Processes
Formal Education	Demands made to the state to expand educational offerings, including workshops on gender and society and on gender and education for teachers to improve their educational practices.
	The promotion of models with more community participation in educational offerings with a gender perspective.
Nonformal Education	Supplying educational services that are not offered by the state in sufficient amounts, for example, reproductive health, environmental health, and literacy.
	Offering workshops on topics that the state does not cover or chooses not to cover. For example, domestic violence, women's control of their own bodies, and knowledge about family and labor legislation.
Informal Education	Experiences that increase knowledge and skills about organization and mobilization.
	Experiences that increase knowledge and skills about democratic forms of participation and leadership.
	Experiences that increase the capacity to identify and analyze social and gender issues.
	Developing capacities to critically analyze the surrounding reality.
	Developing capacities to create counter-hegemonic discourses and alternative sociocultural views.

The chapters that make up the second part of this book contribute to efforts to better understand the work of women-led NGOs. Valenzuela's work on the conceptual expansion of preschool in Mexico unifies the school and community in the tasks of nonsexist education. The mutual and continuous support between the university and NGOs in terms of gender and development training is amply illustrated in the chapter by

Anderson and Mendoza, in which they point out comparative advantages of both institutions. Di Pierro analyzes state efforts around women's literacy, and finds the policies and programs to be lacking in terms of gender formation. Finally, the chapter by Bonino and Eccher demonstrates the growth of political awareness that pushes women to work for and monitor public policies linked to popular and adult education.

These educational examples, though they represent cases that are difficult to generalize, point out conceptual and strategic advances that have been made by the women's movement. They also indicate the initiation of a new stage in the understanding and use of education as a tool for social change.

NOTES

[1]Rosario, Aguirre and Virginia Guzmán, *El género en el quehacer institucional de las ONGs afiliadas al CEAAL* (Santiago, Consejo de Educación de Adultos de América Latina, September 1995).

[2]Maxine Molyneux, *Analyzing Women's Movements, Development and Change,* vol. 29 (1998): p. 242.

[3]Celia Eccher, "La educación como dimensión estratégica en el ejercicio de la ciudadanía de las mujeres," presented at the annual meeting of LASA, 21–22 September 1998; Nelly P. Stromquist, "Gender Delusions and Exclusions in Latin America," *Comparative Education Review* vol. 40, no. 4 (1996).

[4]Nelly P. Stromquist, "Sex-Equality Legislation in Education: The State as Promoter of Women's Rights," *Review of Educational Research* vol. 63, no. 4 (1993).

[5]Alain Touraine, "Social Movements: Special Area or Central Problem in Sociological Analysis?" *Thesis Eleven* no. 9 (1984): 5.

[6]Quoted in Boaventura de Sousa Santos, *Pela Mão de Alice* (São Paulo: Cortez Editora, 1997), p. 257.

[7]Touraine, *op. cit.,* p. 7.

[8]Touraine, *op. cit.,* p. 9.

[9]Alain Touraine, *Palavra e Sangue. Politica e Sociedade na America Latina* (Campinas: Trajetoria Cultural, 1989), p. 538.

[10]Molyneux, *op. cit.,* pp. 220–221.

[11]Molyneux, *op. cit.*

[12]Molyneux, *op. cit.* p. 231.

[13]Molyneux, *op. cit.* p. 231.

[14]Margarita Díaz and Joanne Spicehandler, Foro Latinoamericano, *La incorporación del enfoque de género en la capacitación, implementación, investigación y evaluación en los programas de salud sexual y reproductiva* (Washington D.C.: International Center for Research on Women and Population Council, October 1997).

[15]Stromquist, Nelly P., "Gender Issues in Educational Cooperation," in Kim Forss, Basil Cracknell, and Nelly P. Stromquist, *Organizational Learning in Development Cooperation. Stockholm: How Knowledge is Generated and Used.* (Stockholm: Swedish Ministry of Foreign Affairs, 1998).

[16]DAWN, Development Alternatives with Women for a New Era, is undoubtedly the NGO that best represents the global feminist movement.

[17]DAWN, "Rethinking Social Development: DAWN's Vision," *World Development* vol. 23, no. 11 (1995): 2002.

[18]Gloria Bonder, "Altering Sexual Stereotypes through Teacher Training," in Nelly P. Stromquist (ed.), *Women and Education in Latin America, Knowledge, Power and Change* (Boulder: Lyne Reinner, 1992); Beatriz Schmukler, "Women and the Micro-social Democratization of Everyday Life," in Nelly P. Stromquist (ed.), *op. cit.*

[19]Eccher, *op. cit.*

[20]The teaching force is heavily dominated by women, especially at the elementary school level. According to studies that address teacher professionalization, family duties and their primary self-definition as mothers and wives limit the creation of more substantive concerns from a pedagogical perspective. See Regina Cortina, "Gender and Power in the Teachers' Union of Mexico," in Nelly P. Stromquist (ed.), *Women and Education in Latin America. Knowledge, Power, and Change* (Boulder: Lynne Reinner, 1992), pp. 107–124; Marilia Carvalho, "Between Home and School. Tensions in the Professional Identity of Teachers," in Nelly P. Stromquist (ed.), *Gender Dimensions in Education in Latin America* (Washington, D.C.: Organization of American States, 1996), pp. 73–94.

[21]Margarita Percovich, "Sin las mujeres los derechos no son humanos," *Ciudad Abierta* no. 12, Montevideo (December 1998).

[22]See María Luisa Tarrés, "The Role of Women's Organizations in Mexican Political Life," in Victoria Rodríguez (ed.), *Women's Participation in Mexican Political Life* (Boulder: Westview Press, 1998).

[23]Casa de la Mujer, *La salud física y mental de las mujeres de los barrios* (Santa Cruz, Equipo de Salud, Casa de la Mujer, 1992).

[24]S. Paulson, M.E. Gisbert, and M. Quiton, *Innovaciones en la atención de la salud sexual y de la reproducción: dos experiencias en Bolivia* (Santa Cruz: Centro de Información y Desarrollo de la Mujer, 1996).

[25]Centro de Información y Desarrollo de la Mujer, *Plan Trienal, CIDEM, 1995–1997* (Santa Cruz: CIDEM, 1995).

[26]A recent exception is represented by a study of twenty women who work with NGOs in reproductive health and in public health clinics in Rio de Janeiro (de Sousa, 1998). This study found that the two most important factors in developing gender awareness were informal education from events linked to work (especially the process of knowing other women's daily reality) and political activism.

[27]Michel Foucault, *Discipline and Punish: The Birth of the Prison* (London: Allen Lane, 1997).

[28]Nancy Fraser, *Justice Interruptus. Critical Reflections on the "Postsocialist" Condition* (New York: Routledge, 1997).

[29]Marcela Lagarde, "Aculturación Feminista," in Eliana Largo (ed.), *Género en el estado. Estado del género* (Santiago: ISIS Internacional, 1998), pp. 135.

[30]Eccher, *op. cit.*

[31]Sonia Alvarez, *Engendering Democracy in Brazil: Women's Movement in Transition Politics* (Princeton: Princeton University Press, 1990), p. 88.

[32]Lagarde, *op. cit,* p. 136.

[33]Lagarde, *op. cit,* p. 136.

[34]Alvarez, *op. cit.*

[35]Griff Foley, *Learning in Social Action* (London: Zed Books, 1999).

[36]N. Fairclough, *Discourses and Social Change* (Cambridge: Polity Press, 1992).

[37]Molyneux, *op. cit.*

[38]Steven Ball (ed.), *Foucault in Education* (London: Routledge, 1990).

[39]Foley, *op. cit.*

[40]Mechthild Hart, *Working and Education for Life: Feminist and International Perspectives on Adult Education* (San Francisco: Jossey Bass, 1992), p. 55.

[41]Foley, *op. cit.*

[42]Alejandra Valdés, in this volume.

[43]Valdés, *op. cit.*

[44]Only three Latin American countries have their own budget for organizations focused on women's issues: Argentina, Chile, and Costa Rica. The majority of these units depend on the contributions of international development agencies. See Miriam Krawcyk, *Algunos elementos para la agenda: mujeres en América Latina y el Caribe a fines de los noventa.* Mimeo (Santiago: Comisión Económica para América Latina y el Caribe, Septiembre 1998).

[45]DAWN, *op. cit.,* p. 2003.

[46]DAWN *op. cit.,* pp. 2003–2004.

[47]DAWN, "Seguimiento Cairo + 5," *La Red Va,* Montevideo, REPEM, No. 56 (1998): 2–6.

[48]NGOs that receive funding from the state or from international agencies are sometimes called "project feminism." In my opinion this attack is counterproductive, for women cannot work without any financial aid. Receiving funding does not automatically imply that the original view is lost.

[49]Krawcyk, *op. cit.*

[50]Bonino & Eccher (this volume).

[51]Rosemberg (this volume).

[52]This rupture can also be seen on a national level. The last national feminist gathering in Brazil (in 1997) had almost no representatives from the academic world. Certainly, university professors did not accept the invitation to participate in planning the event.

REFERENCES

Aguirre, Rosario and Virginia Guzmán. *El Género en el quehacer institucional de las ONGs afiliadas al CEAAL.* Santiago: Consejo de Educación de Adultos de América Latina, Septiembre 1995.

Alvarez, Sonia. *Engendering Democracy in Brazil: Women's Movement in Transition Politics.* Princeton: Princeton University Press, 1990.

Ball, Steven (ed.). *Foucault and Education.* London: Routledge, 1990.

Bonder, Gloria. "Altering Sexual Stereotypes through Teacher Training." In Nelly P. Stromquist (ed.), *Women and Education in Latin America. Knowledge, Power, and Change,* pp. 229–249. Boulder: Lynne Rienner, 1992.

Carvalho, Marilia. "Between Home and School. Tensions in the Professional Identity of Teachers." In Nelly P. Stromquist (ed.), *Gender Dimensions in Education in Latin America,* pp. 73–94. Washington, D.C.: Organization of American States, 1996.

Casa de la Mujer. *La salud física y mental de la mujeres de los barrios.* Santa Cruz: Equipo de Salud, Casa de la Mujer, 1992.

CIDEM. *Plan Trienal CIDEM 1995–1997.* Santa Cruz: Centro de Información y Desarollo de la Mujer, 1995.

CIPAF. *Informe Programas Educativos.* Santo Domingo: Centro de Investigación para la Acción Femenina, 1999, mimeo.

Cortina, Regina. "Gender and Power in the Teachers' Union of Mexico." In Nelly P. Stromquist (ed.), *Women and Education in Latin America. Knowledge, Power, and Change,* pp. 107–124. Boulder, Colo.: Lynne Rienner, 1992.

DAWN. "Rethinking Social Development: DAWN's Vision." *World Development* vol. 23, no. 11 (1995): 2001–2004.

DAWN. "Seguimiento Cairo+5." *La Red Va.* Montevideo; REPEM, No. 56. (1998): 2–6.

de Sousa, Isabela. "The Educational Background of Women Working for Women in Rio de Janeiro." *Convergence* vol. 31, no. 3 (1998): 30–37.

Díaz, Margarita and Joanne Spicehandler. *Foro latinoamericano. La incorporación del enfoque de género en la capacitación, implementación, investigación y evaluación en los programas de salud sexual y reproductiva.* Washington, D.C.: International Center for Research on Women and Population Council, October 1997.

Eccher, Celia. "La educación como dimensión estratégica en el ejercicio de la ciudadanía de las mujeres." Paper presented at the 1998 Pre-LASA Conference, September 21–22, 1998.

Fairclough, N. *Discourse and Social Change.* Cambridge: Polity Press, 1992.

Foley, Griff. *Learning in Social Action.* London: Zed Books, 1999.

Forss, Kim, Basil Cracknell, and Nelly P. Stromquist. *Organizational Learning in Development Cooperation. Stockholm: How Knowledge Is Generated and Used.* Stockholm: Swedish Ministry of Foreign Affairs, 1998.

Foucault, Michel. *Discipline and Punish: The Birth of the Prison.* London: Allen Lane, 1977.

Fraser, Nancy. *Justice Interruptus. Critical Reflections on the "Postsocialist" Condition.* New York: Routledge, 1997.

Hart, Mechthild. *Working and Education for Life: Feminist and International Perspectives on Adult Education.* San Francisco: Jossey-Bass, 1992.

Krawczyk, Miriam. *Algunos elementos para la agenda: Mujeres en America Latina y el Caribe a fines de los noventa* (mimeo). Santiago: Comisión Económica para América Latina y el Caribe, September 1998.

Lagarde, Marcela. "Aculturación feminista." In Eliana Largo (ed.), *Género en el estado. Estado del género,* pp. 135–149. Santiago: ISIS Internacional, 1998.

Molyneux, Maxine. "Analysing Women's Movements." *Development and Change* vol. 29 (1998): 219–245.

Paulson, S., M.E. Gisbert, and M. Quiton. *Innovaciones en la atención de la salud sexual y de la reproducción: Dos experiencias en Bolivia.* Santa Cruz: Centro de Información y Desarrollo de la Mujer, 1996.

Percovich, Margarita. "Sin las mujeres los derechos no son humanos." *Montevideo Ciudad Abierta* no. 12, December 1998.

Santos, Boaventura de Sousa. *Pela Mao de Alice.* Sao Paulo: Cortez Editora, 1997.

Schmukler, Beatriz. "Women and the Microsocial Democratization of Everyday Life." In Nelly P. Stromquist (ed.), *Women and Education in Latin America. Knowledge, Power, and Change,* pp. 251–276. Boulder: Lynne Rienner, 1992.

Stromquist, Nelly P. "Gender Delusions and Exclusions in Latin America." *Comparative Education Review* vol. 40, no. 4 (1996): 404–425.

Stromquist, Nelly P. "Organizational Learning in International Development Agencies: The Case of Girls' Education." Paper presented at the Annual Conference of the Comparative and International Education Society. Toronto, April 1999.

Stromquist, Nelly P. "Sex-Equity Legislation in Education: The State as Promoter of Women's Rights." *Review of Educational Research* vol. 63, no. 4 (1993): 379–407.

Tarrés, María Luisa. "The Role of Women's Nongovernmental Organizations in Mexican Public Life." In Victoria Rodríguez (ed.), *Women's Participation in Mexican Political Life,* pp. 131–145. Boulder: Westview Press, 1998.

Touraine, Alain. *Palavra e Sangue. Política e Sociedade na América Latina.* Campinas: Trajetoria Cultural, 1989.

Touraine, Alain. "Social Movements: Special Area or Central Problem in Sociological Analysis." *Thesis Eleven* no. 9 (1984): 5–15.

Valdés, Alejandra, in this volume.

Other Ways to Be Teachers, Mothers, and Fathers

An Alternative Education for Gender Equity for Girls and Boys in Preschool

MALÚ VALENZUELA Y GÓMEZ GALLARDO

INTRODUCTION

The educational experience related in this paper is the result of an alternative education project that seeks to eradicate gender inequities between boys and girls within the Mexican public education system.

Despite constitutional changes, reforms, and modifications of the educational modernization framework that began in 1992, as well as the ratification by the Mexican government of accords and recommendations emanating from international forums and summits to eliminate sexist tendencies and to promote equal educational opportunities for women and men, to date the necessary regulations are not in place to fulfill these commitments, nor are there explicit programs to promote their implementation. Given this situation, we participated actively in 1997 in the "Other Ways to Be Teachers, Fathers and Mothers" project promoted by the Training Program for Women Workers of the *Grupo de Educación Popular con Mujeres* (Grassroots Women's Education Group), which has worked for almost ten years with different basic education teachers in Mexico City.

This project saw itself as a pilot alternative education project to analyze and explore other ways of being with, teaching, and caring for girls and boys that would be more gender fair and equitable, accepting this perspective as the shared responsibility of different agents involved in child education. The project took concrete form in the pilot project for preschool education with the participation of an independent group of teachers and was later replicated in two schools in Mexico City. It has now been extended to a three-year project, during which time it will be extended to more schools in order to consolidate it as a regular program within preschool education.

This experience is just the first step along the path of looking at, experimenting with, and analyzing proposals that address gender within preschool education. Many personal and collective reflections about the daily issues that teachers face in the workplace have contributed to our understanding. This chapter looks at the intentions, the development, and some of the results from this pilot project, which hopes to become a viable alternative response to the multiplicity of issues facing personnel and teachers in preschools and in their relationships with parents.

THE ISSUES

Given that in the educational sector we construct, day by day, the present and the future for new generations, we are concerned about the transmission and reproduction of values, attitudes, and behaviors that devalue girls. Within the public education context, despite efforts by the Secretariat of Public Education beginning with the 1992 legal modifications to broaden coverage and improve quality under the banners of modernity and world competitiveness, there are no concrete policies nor specific programs to eliminate the large gender inequities between men and women, boys and girls, which limit the full development of their skills and capabilities.

In quantitative terms, according to the 1995–2000 Educational Development Program, school attendance in the five-to-eleven age range was similar between girls and boys, but in the twelve-to-fourteen age range, 1.22 girls did not attend school for every boy that did not attend. This is an improvement at the national level.[1] However, that is precisely the age (5–11 years) at which children learn and internalize different stereotypes of sexism, codes of conduct, and attitudes without modifying them in response to our country's new social realities.

It may seem exaggerated to speak of sexism, given that schools are now mixed and both genders have equal access to school programs. However, the fact that girls and young women have greater educational opportunities does not mean that there is gender equity. Rather, it means that the discrimination takes more subtle, less evident forms, and that there are different manifestations of sexism that must be exposed.[2] Some of the manifestations that we can point out include: the unequal attention and treatment that boys and girls receive during school and extracurricular activities, the differentiation made by children between male and female teachers, and the discriminatory use of language or even the exclusion of girls, women teachers, and mothers by not naming them in documents, speeches, brochures, educational materials, and textbooks, despite the importance of building positive feminine models.[3]

Teachers at school find behavior and learning differences between boys and girls to be almost imperceptible. Some examples from our own experiences serve to illustrate those differences by observing boys as they move around the school spaces; they express their right to talk, they interrupt and make themselves heard, they participate confidently in the classroom, and even use violence to solve problems. In contrast, girls speak in low voices, they wait their turn to participate in different activities, they take care of their appearance as well as of the classroom, they ask the teacher for help in resolving problems, they run and play in more collective ways. We believe without a doubt that these differences affect learning and the way that girls and boys access knowledge, as well as the construction of stereotyped behaviors that they will later exhibit as adults.[4]

In addition to these observations, the issue of sexism within schools must be addressed, particularly because boys and girls are taught almost exclusively by women teachers. It is evident that historically in Mexico, as well as in other countries, women are the majority of the teaching profession at the basic level. Thus in Mexico City, according to the Ministry of Public Education, 81 percent of the 35,951 preschool and primary teachers are women.

It is very common to hear from educational authorities, teachers, and parents themselves that the school is children's second home and that teachers are their second mothers.[5] This is accompanied by the interpretation that it is women's "natural" condition to prioritize early, preschool, and primary education, because women are "in charge of" raising children, all of which have gender implications. This reinforces the vision that women have been educated to take care of others, whether children, parents, husbands, students, and so on.[6] By considering women's majority presence in primary schools to be "natural," their work is maternalized and takes on an important affective and emotional charge. This prevents teachers from establishing limits so that they themselves can identify their work as professional, requiring theoretical and empirical preparation and development and multiple didactic and pedagogical strategies.[7]

Current educational demands imply abandoning beliefs stemming from the end of the nineteenth century and the beginning of the twentieth that defined women's primary task, with minimal training, to lovingly care for girls and boys in the centers that would later become schools.[8] While in recent years, because of educational modernization, teachers have had access to greater professionalization, their work continues to be devalued and stereotyped by society as just a women's job. In this sense, it is worth pointing out that despite the reforms in teacher training, a vision of gender has not been incorporated in the normal schools and ongoing teacher training institutes, nor have teachers been provided with the indispensable elements to address the multiple manifestations of sexism in teaching and the teaching profession.

It is worth considering how gender identities and the learning of gender roles of both girls and boys are preponderantly influenced by mothers and fathers, as well as by personnel at school. Thus, it is critical to link school, families, and the community. However, this insistence can be little more than rhetoric when there are no formal educational programs that include parents' opinions in relation to their children's education and school goals and objectives.[9] On the contrary, links between school and families become more difficult when parental participation is limited to their contribution to school maintenance.

In recent years women as a percentage of the economically active population has increased to 35 percent, with no change in patterns of responsibilities in the care of families.[10] Today, according to documented research, women are now the heads of 25 percent of all Mexican households. At the same time, many men face great difficulties because they have lost their jobs, and when they do have jobs, the salaries have diminished earning power. This new economic reality affects boys and girls in an alarming way, in many instances forcing them to drop out of school and work at a very young age.

It is thus very important to generate concrete alternatives that can raise awareness and offer pertinent educational and didactic tools to promote equal opportunity and gender equity within the educational community, particularly for women and girls.

TOWARD A NONDISCRIMINATORY EDUCATION

There have been numerous world forums and summits in recent years committing participating countries and governments to promote programs, corrective measures, and alternatives for a non-gender discriminatory education. Such is the case of the World Declaration on Education for All that took place in Jomtien, Thailand, in March 1990, as well as the IV World Conference on Women in Beijing in 1995 and the Fifth International Conference on Adult Education (CONFINTEA) that took place in Hamburg in 1997, which identified the following objectives:

- Guarantee, as an urgent priority, access to and improvement of the quality of education for girls and women, and overcome any obstacles that prevent their active participation. All sex stereotypes should be eliminated from education.
- Guarantee girls' universal access to primary and secondary education before 2015, adopting measures such as increasing scholarships for girls.
- Elaborate study plans and textbooks free of stereotypes at all levels of learning, including teacher training.
- Eliminate all barriers that prevent pregnant teens and teen mothers from attending school, including offering child-care facilities.
- Adopt positive measures to increase the number of women who participate in decisions around educational materials, especially teachers.
- Eradicate illiteracy among girls and women.[11]

The 1992 reform of Article 3 of the Mexican Constitution resulted in the development of regulations for the General Education Law. The rationale for the law emphasizes the state's obligation to provide preschool education because of its developmental importance in stimulating the learning cycle. Current increases in programs for four- and five-year-olds, notes the legal document, reveals the growing tendency among private and public entities to cover preschool education needs, as well as the accelerated process of incorporating women in productive activities.

The regulation notes not only the state's obligation to offer preschool education services, but also the parents' responsibility to send their children to educational centers. The extension of preschool education coverage tends to eliminate inequalities and generate an important advance in the offerings of educational opportunities to the child population. This idea is strongly identified in the 1995–2000 Educational Development Program, which establishes the following goals for 2000: Sixty-five percent of four-year-olds will attend preschool, and only 10 percent of five-year-olds will not attend. Although it is desirable to expand attention to greater coverage of four- and even three-year-olds, the priority is that all children will have at least one year of preschool education before entering primary school.[12]

The Preschool Education Program recognizes that early childhood development is a complex process that includes affective, intellectual, social, and physical dimensions, and also that particular needs, desires, and conduct of individual children vary according to age. Among its objectives, the program establishes the development of a child's personal autonomy and identity, and considers the links between the school and the home environments.

> Every child, according to the program, by interacting with other people, interiorizes his or her own image, structures his or her uncon-scious, learns his or her aptitudes and limitations, likes and dislikes, recognizes him- or herself as different from others and, at the same time, as part of a gender group (by age, social and cultural aspects, etc.). That is, children build their identity; an identity with both posi-tive and negative connotations, agreeable or problematic constructs, that will be their self-presentation to others and that, added to later experiences, will build a sensation of control, security, competence, failure, or inability.[13]

The implications of this statement to offer an integral development to boys and girls must be reviewed from a gender perspective. Without ignoring recent efforts to address equity of access issues for boys and girls, it also must be recognized that Mexico still faces major economic, social, and cultural issues that prevent women and men from attaining the same educational levels.

In response to these needs, the Women Workers Program of the Women's Popular Education Group,[14] based on its mission and objec-tives to work in favor of women in the popular sectors, proposed promot-ing this project in order to make education into an effective instrument for equity, relevance, and quality for all Mexicans.

PROPOSAL AND OBJECTIVES

Based on the above, this project's general objective is to design and implement an educational alternative that includes active participation by teachers, mothers, and fathers, in order to create new forms of early childhood care and education that are more equitable and just between the genders, and that share responsibility among all people involved in the educational process.

Three specific objectives were identified:

• Analyze the distinct dimensions of the educational phenomenon from the gender perspective, recognizing the construction of preschool teachers' identities as women and the importance of their work in the schools, as well as the implications of the relationships they establish with parents.

- Within the framework of the educational program in the preschool education centers, analyze with the educators some pedagogical and didactic proposals to promote new ways for boys and girls to treat each other and to relate to each other that promote the integral development of capacities and abilities.
- Offer reflection and awareness tools for mothers and fathers to develop positive attitudes of equity toward their daughters and sons, in order to eliminate gender obstacles that limit their psychic and social growth.

DESCRIPTION OF THE EXPERIENCE

We initially planned to implement this project in two schools, and so we sent the preschool education authorities the proposal to be read and subsequently approved. We requested appointments and we knocked on doors, we met innumerable times in an attempt to have our project accepted, but we could not get an immediate response. That is why we decided to implement the project independently; twenty-five preschool teachers, directors, and supervisors participated.

The experience consisted of a training course from March 15 to July 12, 1997, a total of twenty-four hours divided into five educational sessions. The course content was divided into the following themes:

First Module:
- Introduction to gender.
- Construction of sex and gender identities (psychic and social dimensions).
- Role of education in transmission of sex and gender roles in society and its political, social, and economic implications.
- Training and identity of preschool education teachers.
- Role of teachers' maternal identity in the teaching profession.

Second Module:
- Evolution and current reality of Mexican families. Social, psychological, economic, and legal characteristics.
- Diagnosis of student socioeconomic situations.
- Situation of child care while parents work.

- Community, family, and school relationships.
- Alternatives to modify discriminatory attitudes and behaviors both in the home and in the school environment, as a shared responsibility.

Third Module:
- Nonsexist education.
- The importance of nondiscriminatory oral and written language in educational processes.
- The design and testing of alternatives to promote gender equity in schools: games, songs, and activities related to socio-affective and cognitive development.
- Design and testing of nonsexist materials.

The selection of this content responds to methodologies used by the Women's Popular Education Group[15] in its educational work. The methodology, which has been in use for years, emphasizes the importance of initiating the analysis of sex and gender identity construction of men and women at the social level, from there moving to the development of proposals to transform inequitable relationships between men and women. The contents are based on the assumption that "when I analyze and reflect on my identity as a teacher and as a woman, then I can generate a change of perception and attitude within my students." This change offers, at the same time, the development of multiple didactic alternatives, under the gender perspective, that can generate greater equity in treatment and opportunities for learning between girls and boys.

In this project, the teachers came from schools in different zones, and so it was impossible to promote direct educational work with mothers and fathers, but each of the participants implemented different activities with parents according to their possibilities.

Given the results of this experience, we received approval from the Preschool Education Office to replicate it in the two schools initially selected. Thus, after some adjustments and refinements based on the previous experience, the project was implemented from September to December of 1998 in the Bartolomé de Medina School in the Alvaro Obregón district and the Tenochtitlán school in the Benito Juárez district.

The teachers' course included seven educational sessions, and we also held three sessions with the parents. Each weekly session lasted four hours, and took place during school hours. The Preschool Education Office and especially the Technical Support Unit not only approved the project, but they offered their collaboration in the reproduction of necessary materials and they offered eight educators from the Office to take over the classrooms while the teachers participated in the course. We also had the opportunity to evaluate this experience with the authorities and to receive their comments and observations. All of the teaching personnel from the two schools participated in the whole project. There were a total of twelve teachers, two directors, two supervisors, and on some occasions the sector chiefs participated. One hundred and fifty mothers and one hundred fathers also participated in the working sessions.

In order to have the greatest possible participation in the educational sessions for the course for mothers and fathers, and because we did not have the appropriate conditions at the schools to receive all of them, we designed one session just for fathers and one just for mothers, finishing with a third that included both fathers and mothers.

The following themes were addressed in the parent sessions:

- Paternity: myths, realities, and proposals about family and educational and economic responsibilities.
- Maternity and motherhood: social value versus shared loneliness.
- Proposals and alternatives to modify discriminatory attitudes and behaviors within the families.

At the first session, psychological specialists worked with the fathers, from the perspective of masculinity, to address the difficulties they face with their paternal responsibility. Specialists also participated with the mothers in the second session, addressing issues related to maternity in the face of new social and economic realities, and in the last session each teacher worked in an open class together with fathers, mothers, and students. The goal was to promote, both in the school and at home, measures that would tend to guarantee gender equity between girls and boys.

RESULTS OF THE EXPERIENCE

As rich, innovative, and interesting as is daily work with girls and boys, we argue that a primordial element in raising educational quality in Mexico is incorporating the gender dimension in the entire educational system, promoting respect and tolerance for differences, whether class, ethnicity, or gender, and opening the door to the integral development of each individual's abilities. We can say specifically that the results of this pilot phase of the project were very successful for the following reasons:

1. We noted the absence of frameworks to orient reflection and modification of sexist practices in public education and especially preschool education. We also recognize, however, that some authorities do have conviction and understanding and are open and interested in dealing with the value put on sexual and gender differences in education, and their particular manifestation in all school and extracurricular activities.

   To continue in this vein, we think it is necessary to continue educating officials and society in general, through the dissemination of information about work that has taken place, so that issues of gender inequities in education will be recognized and so that specific measures and programs will be established to address them. We also propose, based on this experience, that much investigation remains to be done, and there is a particular need for deeper understanding in order to open new alternatives to address this complex issue understood as gender inequity in education, particularly in Mexico, which faces the reality of poverty among the children who attend public schools.

2. We carefully analyzed the situation facing preschool teachers, considering the maternal functions they fulfill as part of their professional work.

   We consider that the teaching profession, before it was raised to university degree level, was chosen by many because it required fewer years of study and offered immediate benefits of working in a school, at the same time as it represented a "women's career" and could be useful to women in their future lives as mothers and wives. Despite educational modernization, these connotations about the teaching profession continue to prevail.

   Even though the teaching profession should be highly valued, because teachers are forming the new generations, in practice it is devalued. Pejorative expressions abound, including "nannies with degrees," or "if you know how to sing and play with kids, that's all you need to be a teacher." While these statements have been changing since university titles have been required for preschool teachers, and while there are now greater benefits and options for professionalization, society's low view of preschool teachers has still not been changed. On diverse occasions, though we do not have data to back it up, it was mentioned that the teaching career is devalued in social and salary terms because most teachers are women, and if they were men they would be earning better salaries. A number of people recounted how when a man began to work in a preschool, he was given preference, greater opportunities for promotions, and better treatment.

Another aspect reiterated around identity analysis and the role of educators was the maternal work that they carry out daily as they deal with boys and girls. This was one of the main points of interest and personal reflection by the teachers during the educational sessions, and we learned that while boys and girls need objective and subjective conditions to learn, teachers are not their mothers, and they cannot resolve the multiple problems that children face. We are referring to problems like child abuse, malnutrition, the absence of affective support (neglect), behavior alterations, learning delays, and so on. In this sense, it is and will continue to be the state's responsibility, and not that of particular teachers, to deal with issues of poverty and the lack of objective conditions that guarantee children's learning, as well as to guarantee quality education.

All of the above led us to the conviction that we should promote teachers' professional identity both in their personal and professional lives, as well as continue to promote their interest in further study, especially about issues related to the gender perspective, and to be more proscriptive with school administrators about proposing and developing alternatives to improve teachers' current situation.

3. Changes in language, activities, and some teaching materials were reviewed and analyzed, in terms of images and content picturing women's subordination. This included stories, songs, games, and physical education.

It was very interesting to see from the inside how schools reproduce gender differentiation in the development of skills and talents, including fine and gross motor skills, oral expression, identity construction, and care for the classroom, the school, and the environment. We perceived, among many other things, that boys are more active and assertive than girls, girls are not encouraged to participate as much, and that since girls wear skirts, they cannot run and jump as freely as the boys. We noted that boys tend to be first in line, and that girls are usually asked to do the domestic tasks like keeping the classroom clean.

We realized that when we began to use more inclusive language with the children, girls began to participate more in different activities. We also noted that five- and six-year-old children demonstrate greater respect for sexual differences than do younger children. These and many other reflections must be investigated in depth in order to change our attitudes about gender equity in preschool education.

4. We do not want to neglect to mention that we were also able to sensitize mothers and fathers to the importance of modifying attitudes and values that undervalue the feminine gender in families. We are sure that the fathers' education session, which analyzed the father's role in their children's education from the masculine perspective, opened many alternatives for communication, because it addressed problems like the following: the use of force and power within which men have been educated in terms of the way they treat their wives, sons, and especially daughters, as well as the lack of spaces and conditions for fathers to express their feelings and even their weaknesses, especially when faced with the loss of work and economic difficulties. Many fathers were made aware of the need to change their attitudes given the many ways they discriminate and foster gender inequity in their wives and daughters.

   With mothers, we looked more carefully at the difficulties they face because they have to solve their family's economic needs and they also have to care for their children, as well as the issue of violence and mistreatment many of them experience from their husbands. With the mothers, we also found that they became more open to looking at how they treat their sons and daughters, and to eliminating sexist tendencies and discriminatory behavior.

5. Finally, another major achievement was that we had the support of the Preschool Education Department to implement the program in the schools, as well as to analyze together the progress and evaluation of this educational experience.

FINAL REFLECTIONS

Given the progress this project initiated around an innovative issue in Mexico, we consider that it is important to continue extending the program's benefits as part of a broader strategy to eliminate the inequitable features of the educational system and to fit within the 1995–2000 Educational Development Program, as well as with the objectives and corrective measures emerging from international forums and conferences in favor of nondiscriminatory education, to promote tolerance and respect for individuals. This project emphasizes pro-children proposals, but in an integral way that overcomes obstacles and takes advantage of those who work both in the home and the school. In the next three years, we will be consolidating this project (see Appendix A), in order to put gender on the public agenda and make it part of the regular program promoted by the Preschool Education Office in Mexico City.

Appendix A

Below is a description of the major activities that will be implemented in the next three years of the project:

First Year:

1. *Formation of a promoter group.* To promote the school program that gives the teachers pedagogical and didactic tools from the gender perspective and at the same time make parents aware of the need to promote greater gender equity within families, we will form a promoter group of twenty-five teachers, who will receive a six-month training course. This course will help the group to collectively acquire the necessary preparation to use a gender perspective in preschools.

2. *Application of the work program in schools.* The promoter group, once its training has finished, will work in preschools to develop a training program for both teachers and parents. The many experiences obtained from the application of the program will be registered and catalogued in order to generate didactic alternatives and proposals, to elaborate new materials, to modify activities, and to develop new pedagogical practices linked to project goals. Evaluation and follow-up of the work will be done monthly by the promoter group, as long as the work in the schools continues (three months), in order to receive consultations and to make pertinent adjustments to the program.

3. *Evaluation and follow-up.* Once the work has finished in the schools, there will be a final evaluation of the experience to consider progress, obstacles, and achievements. This evaluation will serve as the basis for the project's continuation in the second and third years.

Second Year: During the second year, the promoter group will grow as participation increases, and new members will also receive training. While the twenty-five new teachers are being trained, the initial group will do follow-up work with their own teaching, as well as doing follow-up in the schools where they worked, in order to understand the obstacles and achievements of the program.

After the new group has been trained, all fifty teachers will meet so that they can work in new schools, taking into account the adjustments and modifications based on the previous year's experience. Records will also be kept of these experiences and the monthly evaluation and follow-up meetings.

As part of the promotion activities, in the second year there will be a national workshop with participation of preschool teachers in order to publicize the project's experience. Teachers from the promoter group will play an important role in the workshop by their sharing of their school experiences.

The evaluation of this second year will be substantive, and the results will influence whether the project will be expanded to all preschools in Mexico City.

Third Year: During the third and final year of the project, the program will have been consolidated through the write-up and cataloguing of recommendations, activities, materials, and documents that orient teachers in the classrooms, as well as directors, supervisory personnel, mothers, and fathers, all around giving more equitable and just treatment to girls and boys from the gender perspective.

These recommendations will be given to the authorities throughout the duration of the project, and the promoter group will assume responsibility to consolidate the program in the schools where they work. At the same time, in the third year and as part of the project's final activities, there will be a national forum open to all, which will discuss, analyze, and publicize the issue and possible concrete alternatives dealing with the incorporation of the gender dimension in preschool education.

NOTES

[1]Poder Ejecutivo Federal, *Programa de Desarrollo de Educación 1995–2000* (Mexico, 1996).

[2]Marina Subirats and Cristina Brullet, *Rosa y azul. La transmisión de los géneros en la escuela mixta* (Madrid: Instituto de la Mujer, 1992).

[3]Marina Subirats and Amparo Tomé, *Pautas de observación del sexismo en el ámbito educativo* (Barcelona: Instituto de Ciencias de la Educación, 1992); Monserrat Moreno, *Cómo se enseña a ser niña. El sexismo en la escuela* (Barcelona: ICARIA, 1986); Eulalia Lledó, *El sexismo y el androcentrismo en la lengua. Análisis y propuestas de cambio* (Barcelona: Instituto de Ciencias de la Educación, 1992).

[4]Beatriz Fainholc, *Hacia una escuela no sexista* (Buenos Aires: Aique, 1994).

[5]Malú Valenzuela, "Apuntes para la reflexión sobre el hecho de ser maestras," *Revista Huaxyacac,* July 1998.

[6]GEM, *Mitos, realidades y propuestas de la maternidad* (México: Grupo de Educación Popular con Mujeres, 1994).

[7]Aurora Huerta, "La maestra, una madre, pura, bella y afectuosa," in Patricia Corres (ed.), *La verdad del mito* (Guadalajara: Universidad de Guadalajara, 1994).

[8]Graciela Hierro, *De la domesticación a la educación de las mexicanas* (México: Editorial Fuego Nuevo, 1994).

[9]Benno de Keijzer, "Paternidad y transición de género," in Beatriz Schmukler (ed.), *Familias y relaciones de género en transformación* (México: EDAMEX, 1998).

[10]Brígida García, *El trabajo extradoméstico de las mexicanas* (México: CONAPO, 1995).

[11]In the most recent world conferences, there has been an emphasis on raising the educational levels of girls and women throughout the world, especially those girls and women who are poor and marginalized. This is clearly demonstrated in the Action Platform of the Fourth Conference on Women, which took place in Beijing in 1995, and in the Action Plan for the Future from the International Adult Education Conference (CONFINTEA V), which was held in Hamburg in 1997.

[12]Poder Ejecutivo Federal, *op. cit.*

[13]Subsecretaría de Servicios Educativos para el Distrito Federal, *Guía para la planeación docente 1998–1999* (México: Coordinación Sectorial de Educación Preescolar, 1998).

[14]GEM, *op. cit.*

[15]GEM, *op. cit.*

REFERENCES

de Keijzer, Benno. "Paternidad y transición de género." In Beatriz Schmukler (ed.), *Familias y relaciones de género en transformación*. México: EDAMEX, 1998.

Fainholc, Beatriz. *Hacia una escuela no sexista*. Buenos Aires: Aique, 1994.

Garcia, Brígida. *El trabajo extradoméstico de las mexicanas*. México: CONAPO, 1995.

GEM. *Mitos, realidades y propuestas de la maternidad.* México: Grupo de Educación Popular con Mujeres, 1994.

Hierro, Graciela. *De la domesticación a la educación de las mexicanas.* México: Editorial Fuego Nuevo, 1994.

Huerta, Aurora. "La maestra, una madre, pura, bella y afectuosa." In Patricia Corres (ed.), *La verdad del mito.* Guadalajara: Universidad de Guadalajara, 1994.

Lledó, Eulalia. *El sexismo y el androcentrismo en la lengua. Análisis y propuestas de cambio.* Barcelona: Instituto de Ciencias de la Educación, 1992.

Moreno, Monserrat. *Cómo se enseña a ser niña. El sexismo en la escuela.* Barcelona: ICARIA, 1986.

Poder Ejecutivo Federal. *Programa de Desarrollo de Educación 1995–2000.* México: Poder Ejecutivo Federal, 1996.

Subirats, Marina and Cristina Brullet. *Rosa y azul. La transmisión de los géneros en la escuela mixta.* Madrid: Instituto de la Mujer, 1992.

Subirats, Marina and Amparo Tomé. *Pautas de observación del sexismo en el ámbito educativo.* Barcelona: Instituto de Ciencias de la Educación, 1992.

Subsecretaría de Servicios Educativos para el Distrito Federal. *Guía para la planeación docente 1998–1999.* México: Coordinación Sectorial de Educación Preescolar, 1998.

Valenzuela, Malú. "Apuntes para la reflexión sobre el hecho de ser maestras." *Revista Huaxyacac.* Oaxaca, México, July 1998.

Educating about Gender
A Comparison of Two Institutional Contexts

JEANINE ANDERSON AND ROSA MENDOZA

One of the central challenges involved in bringing about greater gender justice in the real world is disseminating new understandings of gender and gender relations among persons who are not necessarily convinced of the need for such change. These are people for whom the categories, concepts, and associations that are a routine part of a "gender analysis" are not obvious and often are simply wrong, even willfully wrong. This is the challenge of education about gender and gender justice in "foreign" institutional settings—that is, outside the feminist and gender-sensitive community.

This chapter is concerned with the transmission of gender concepts in two institutional arenas. One is development organizations, governmental and nongovernmental organizations whose mandate is to plan and execute projects for economic and social development in less privileged countries and regions. The other is postsecondary institutions, especially colleges and universities. The chapter compares and contrasts various strategies for responding to the need for education about gender in these settings in Peru (in the case of the academic audience) and in Peru and Latin America more broadly in the case of development organizations.

In the world of international development, education about gender goes under the name of "gender training." The name alludes to the typical format used for such education in this context. This is the short course, intended to be introductory and, above all, motivational. In the development world, there are well-established "packaged courses" that have been in circulation for over a decade. Several of these have been widely used in Latin America, translated and adapted, to different degrees, for different countries and client groups.

In the academic world, on the other hand, there are apparently few or no precedents (so far as we have been able to determine) for gender education that seeks to influence the way college teaching is conducted. Gender studies programs exist in numerous Latin American colleges and universities. Some have extension programs that include gender training in some form (or they advise or evaluate such educational projects), but their focus is the world outside the university, not the university itself.

In comparing development organizations and institutions of higher education as contexts and publics for gender education, the central questions we want to address are the following:

1. What kind of gender education presently takes place in these two institutional arenas?
2. What are the assumptions and "philosophy" that lie behind gender education strategies, curricula, and methodologies in the two settings?
3. What are the achievements of gender education as currently practiced, both at the level of the individuals who participate and in relation to processes of institutional change? What are the problems and failures?
4. How might gender education projects be reformulated and improved, particularly in ways that would increase their capacity for productive, two-way dialogue with contemporary gender theory?

To advance our understanding of these questions, we will draw heavily on our own personal experience, in addition to bibliographic materials. Anderson is an anthropologist based in a university; Mendoza is an educator based in a private development organization that offers an evolving menu of short courses designed to raise the level of technical and planning skills of the Peruvian NGO community. The "academic" part of our chapter relies on our recent shared experience of developing a long-distance education course for Peruvian college professors on "Gender in University Teaching." The "development organizations" side of our analysis and arguments relies on Mendoza's experience as an instructor and planner in the development of courses and other activities of the *Escuela para el Desarrollo*. Anderson has also been involved in planning gender education strategies for governmental and nongovernmental organizations. In recent years, this has been primarily through the regional program of the *Red de Educación Popular Entre Mujeres de América Latina* (REPEM) and the Latin American Adult Education Network (CEAAL; *Consejo de Educación de Adultos de América Latina*).

Latin America functions as a single region for many purposes related to development questions. Many development projects are regional or subregional (Central America, Caribbean, Andean countries, Southern Cone, Mercosur, and Amazon Basin being some of the possible "cuts" for subregions). Many education and training activities have involved regional audiences, particularly when high-cost, standardized, prepackaged courses are being used. In addition, there is a recognizable pool of "gender trainers" and "gender consultants" that travel from one country to another. Courses and course contents are disseminated from one country to another through these kinds of mechanisms.

Latin American institutions of higher education, by contrast, are weakly linked. Some coordinating bodies exist, such as an association of university presidents, but these tend to be formal, to meet infrequently if ever, and to have little impact on the day-to-day life of any college or university. Most public colleges and universities in Latin America are seriously underfunded. They have difficulty putting books in the library; much less can they afford cultivating intensive exchanges with their institutional peers. This means that initiatives for reaching new understandings about gender in higher education will probably spread slowly and may even involve some duplication of effort that has largely been avoided in the densely interconnected development world.

With this background in mind, we turn to the questions that organize this chapter.

WHAT KIND OF GENDER EDUCATION TAKES PLACE?

To explicate the kind of teaching and learning about gender that occurs in the two settings of our interest, we need to examine two sets of issues: who the audiences are and what is being offered them in terms of courses and curriculum. Because they are different and, to a large extent, separated socially and institutionally (although we will suggest some points of contact later on), we will look at our two "worlds" of development and higher education in turn.

The Development World

Gender education in the world of institutions involved in development projects has fundamentally to do with bringing to awareness previously hidden dimensions of reality (multiple inequities in gender relations) so that development policies and projects can take them into account. At the same time, because development activities involve encounters among human beings where much depends on the example, sincerity, identification, and spirit of respectful cooperation that development agents project, gender training must create the conditions for an emotional conviction to occur on the part of the trainees. This conviction revolves around the injustice of many situations affecting women (and some affecting men) in the present state of the world (or a corner of it) and the compelling logical and ethical demands of transforming these situations.

The development community of public and nongovernmental institutions is large and complex. At least three different groups can be distinguished as possible candidates for gender education. There are (1) top-level policy makers, (2) program directors and operators, and (3) the leaders of grassroots organizations involved in development projects. In addition, gender training courses are used in many international cooperation agencies to bring their own staff up to current standards for gender-sensitive grant-making and technical support. To date, however, most gender training courses have probably been designed with the second group in mind.

International development cooperation agencies increasingly condition their aid on proof that the recipient organization is aware of the arguments about gender equity, operates programs that pay special attention to women's needs, and uses indicators and evaluations that assess impacts in reducing gender inequalities in the groups the organization works with. Thus, the international cooperation agencies are partly responsible for having created the demand for the gender training courses that circulate among Latin American NGOs, government offices, and organizations. Sometimes what is required is little more than knowing enough "gender talk" (key words, key concepts woven together in a plausible discourse) to permit the organization to present itself as competent in this arena. The demand for gender education is also strongly driven by earlier successes within development organizations. The existence of one or more projects focused on women creates a need for greater expertise. The existence of a group of specialists assigned to those projects creates a lobby within the organization that can pressure for further training or for a course tailored to the organization's program and needs.

Let us take the case of Peru to examine more closely the place that gender training currently occupies in the development world. The development community in Peru has a history of nearly forty years. The first large development-oriented NGOs were founded in the 1960s and early 1970s in a context of modernizing governments that included professionals and technocrats, many educated overseas in countries with an active nongovernmental and philanthropic tradition. The first women's NGOs date to 1979. The Peruvian NGO sector is broadly representative of that of other Latin America countries, although there have been periods when Peru stood out because of the very large number of development organizations it had relative to its population as the South American continent's fifth largest nation. In Peru, the legal restrictions on forming such organizations are few and the costs of public registry are low, a situation that probably encouraged multiplication and a certain fragmentation.

In the early years, development was understood to be a question of deep moral conviction rather than technique and expert knowledge. Well-intentioned people who chose to stand with the poor and oppressed would simply "get it right" by instinct, perhaps aided by earlier experiences of political training that honed their strategic capabilities. The shortcomings of this approach to development projects—not to mention policies—quickly became apparent, and a demand was created for the services of an institution like the *Escuela para el Desarrollo*. It was established in 1991, after a two-year period working as a program of DESCO, another Peruvian NGO. The *Escuela* defines its role as promoting institutional consolidation and providing in-service training and capacity building in the NGO sector. This it accomplished through a broad range of training courses, seminars, and public education activities, and through providing consulting services to individual organizations in the government and NGO sector.

Table 1 presents a comparison in the number of events between participants that registered in the overall training activities and those in the Gender Program. Regarding the overall training activities, the initial four years reveal a consistent increase in the supply and demand of training activities. However, from 1994 the data show a less stable pattern. This situation reflects in part a demographic reality: A number of small organizations are disappearing because of shrinking funds from international cooperation and because of their weak competitive position in relation to large, multifaceted NGOs and private business such as social survey and marketing firms and banks that are increasingly entering the field of micro-credit. There may also have been a certain "saturation" of the market for courses in the theory and practice of development, with many practitioners having already gone through the full sequence of topics locally available. Finally, it is likely that colleges and universities are

Table 1. Events and Enrollments in the Training Activities of
Escuela para el Desarrollo. **Overall Training and Gender**
Program, 1990–1998

Year	Number of Events		Enrollment	
	Overall Training	Gender Program	Overall Training	Gender Program
1990	7	1	109	19
1991	14	4	199	68
1992	20	5	332	96
1993	30	7	722	202
1994	25	5	492	85
1995	23	6	446	118
1996	36	12	601	192
1997	43	14	881	301
1998	32	12	541	190

Source: Melgar, 1998.

taking up part of the demand as they experiment with more practice-oriented "special diploma" and master's programs.

The Gender Program has been an element of continuity, within the overall training activities over these years. In 1991, it was the leader in the growth of the training events and participants. Until 1994, the growth rate of the gender program courses and participants lagged somewhat behind the rate of overall growth. From 1995 until now, it maintains a consistent one-third of the enrollment and events of the *Escuela's* courses. An element in the success of the Program is the development of a set of sequential courses. These courses have diversified both the topics they cover and the methodologies they use. By 1999, few if any Peruvian NGOs remained completely outside the circle of gender training in some form. Part of the growth derives from the demand for hand-tailored courses to meet specific needs of development organizations.

However, during the past two years there has been a shift in the priorities given to the training demands. Courses designed to respond to concrete demands of planning, monitoring, and evaluation are leading the demand for both the regular and hand-tailored courses. The percep-

tion of the directors of Peruvian development organizations lags behind
the reality of this shifting scene. Table 2 reports the results of a survey
carried out by the *Escuela para el Desarrollo* on the demand for courses
and topics as of 1996. The respondents—directors of NGOs—were
asked to distinguish among what they believed to be needs for further
training for four different categories of personnel in the organizations
they directed: field workers in direct contact with the target populations
of development projects, technical assistants, researchers, and managers.
The question allowed them to identify as many training options as they
considered pertinent for each type of personnel on a wide variety of topics. Planning, monitoring, and evaluation were clearly the more consistent demands for all categories of personnel, while gender received little
priority in all cases.

Regardless of personnel category, gender training is fourth or fifth
in level of perceived priority: highest for field workers and lowest for

**Table 2. Training Priorities for NGO Personnel as Perceived by
Directors, 1996**

Priority	Field Workers %	Technical Staff %	Researchers %	Managers %
Planning, monitoring, and project evaluation	61.7	42.0	18.7	57.6
Organizational management	20.5	32.3	0.0	94.0
Training methods and tools	29.4	9.7	6.3	0.0
Research methods	8.8	3.2	87.5	0.0
Gender approaches	17.6	9.7	6.3	2.9
Local development	17.6	6.5	0.0	0.0
Information management	11.8	9.7	31.2	11.8
Work and employment generation	11.8	19.4	0.0	0.0
Other	17.6	41.9	3.1	5.9

Source: Melgar, 1996.

managers. It seems that, in the directors' perceived needs for training, the gender approach deserves little attention from the top and middle-level managers, although it may nonetheless be of interest for the field workers. This assumption runs counter to the general understanding of the experts and trainers in gender, who consider that without a clear commitment from the top level, few changes can be truly successful in the long-run practice of the NGOs. The data base of the *Escuela para el Desarrollo* training area shows that the actual participation of different levels of NGO staff was consistent with the directors' perceptions. Between 1995 and 1997, around two-thirds of the participants in the gender courses came from the field level. However, the remaining one-third came from the intermediate and managerial levels, participants who by virtue of their position have more room to influence the overall institutional practices.

An interesting issue is why gender training remains an important topic for NGOs despite the little priority given by the directors to it. The survey asked the directors about who makes the decision to send a staff member to a training course. In one-third of the cases, the director decided. In another third, the decision was made jointly by the area of department head and the director of the organization. In 20 percent of the cases, the decision was made by the area of department head, and in 5 percent of the cases, by the actual participant. In most instances, the field and intermediate staff take the initiative in proposing that they attend a course, and the decision then moves up through the organization. Judging from their actual participation in relevant courses offered by the *Escuela,* probably the need for broadening knowledge and capacities in gender issues is clearer to many middle-level NGO project directors, planners, and field promoters than to the directors of their institutions.

The *Escuela para el Desarrollo* is fundamentally interested in organizational development and change, and accordingly, it markets its courses to organizations. Consistent with this, the initial offer in the gender field was gender education designed for individuals who were leaders in their organizations, either because of their formal position or because of their personal qualities. They were expected to be professionals at intermediate-level positions. For them, the *Escuela* designed a special program that contains a sequence of courses—a structured learning experience leading to a Certificate of Gender Specialization.

At the same time, the *Escuela* encourages the participation of individuals who can demonstrate that they have, if not the sponsorship of their organizations, at least some limited support (for example, released time) in the hope that they will become a link back. This opens the door to individual participants who, though they may not be connected to a development organization at the moment, are interested in gaining skills and knowledge that can give them a competitive edge and permit them to negotiate a new position in an NGO. Such a person usually decides to participate in the certificate program, but they can, as an alternative, enroll in a single specialized course. The decision to enroll may spring from a change in the individual's professional interests or the search for new challenges.

This ideal scheme—emphasizing institutional change as a necessary condition for gender to permeate the development sector—has broken down in the face of economic realities in Peru in recent years. One of the most dramatic changes has been the near elimination of long-term work contracts, including those in development organizations whose programs (ironically) may involve the promotion of labor unions and the defense of workers' rights. A large cohort of workers in development NGOs are now hired on short-term contracts as promoters or consultants. This ensures high mobility among personnel and puts limitations on teamwork. Both factors reduce the organization's willingness to make an investment in training or educational activities, since it is pointless to devote time and money to people who may not have a further opportunity to apply their knowledge in that organization or share it with other members and employees. Under the new conditions, a small, high-level group tends to remain as the only permanent staff. For this group there are high levels of expectation of both academic training and technical knowledge. Many NGO directors have advanced degrees and specialized studies outside the country and the region.

The *Escuela para el Desarrollo* has attempted to respond flexibly in the new context with a program for developing individual professional careers. This involves increasing the participants' knowledge and capacities in a variety of fields and suggesting how to make use of them in a variety of organizational contexts.

Teresa's (pseudonym) experience shows the kind of bargaining that goes on within NGO development organizations in relation to participating in a training activity. The idea can be enthusiastically accepted by a staff member, but if the organization does not give him or her the necessary support, it is very difficult to continue. We summarize her experience below:

> Teresa was recently hired by a development organization to work in a rural development project incorporating a gender perspective. A year before, the organization contracted with the Escuela para el Desarrollo for technical assistance. An output of the consultancy was a strategy that

> *recommended the incorporation of at least two women in the project. As a first step in applying this strategy, the NGO sent Teresa to her first gender course in the Escuela. Later, she had to negotiate with her organization in order to participate in the second course leading to the Certificate of Gender Specialization. She took some vacation days and paid for her own ticket to travel from her provincial base to Lima. The organization paid for the course but made it clear this was the last time. Teresa became highly motivated to continue with all the courses in the certificate program. She believes that it would be useful to her current work as well as help her in her professional career. However, because she could not get a consensus within her NGO, Teresa could not continue the specialization program.*

In some fortunate cases, a participant's individual interest coincides with an organizational need. Typically, the organization detects a problem in a project, program, or institutional process. Often the solution implies group training that may include follow-up activities to evaluate the results. This is the case for the following governmental agency:

> *A Peruvian governmental organization was required to change its institutional mission in order to occupy a new position in the overall structure of the executive branch. From being an agency concerned with providing community infrastructure, its mandate now focused on the promotion of women. In response, the managerial and professional personnel needed training in basic concepts of gender and development. The Escuela para el Desarrollo prepared a course to fit in the timetable provided by the organization.*

Smaller organizations may prefer to send a block of participants to one of the regular courses of the *Escuela* rather than requesting a tailor-made package, as in the case of the following NGO:

> *Lucía is a Catholic missionary who returned to Peru after ten years. Her congregation designated her to create an NGO whose purpose would be to improve the quality of the work the congregation does in poor urban neighborhoods. The nuns wished to move from a social assistance program to a project for real development. Between May 1997 and June 1998, Lucía completed the Certificate of Gender Specialization and has almost finished a second Certificate in Development. She is trying to design her organization on the basis of the ideas she developed in the courses. Another member of her staff is now participating in the gender courses.*

Both individual courses and the certificate programs rely on a carefully planned, logical sequence intended to facilitate the appropriation of skills and selected, updated information. These two elements are essential to improving the quality of the work the participants later do. Nevertheless, they are not sufficient to guarantee changes in the organizations they come from or will work in at some future time. The experience of the *Escuela para el Desarrollo* clearly suggests that institutional change depends upon the power the participants wield within their organizations and on the will to change of the organizations in question. And those are not guaranteed by the simple fact of involving some staff in gender training courses.

The Higher Education Community

The faculty, students, and administrators of Latin American institutions of higher education are more difficult to characterize as a community than the development community. The higher education sector is undergoing a transition in many respects. Governments are less willing to underwrite the massive public universities that formerly dominated higher education. Small, highly competitive private universities are springing up and offering an array of technical careers. In this context, gender "arrived" as a topic alongside environmental issues, globalization, "cultural studies" in various forms, communications, computer engineering, and the business and financial specialties of the present decade.

The current transition also involves a demographic turnover from a generation of older academics—almost exclusively male—to a new generation, many of whose members have M.A. and Ph.D. degrees from Europe and North America. The two cohorts contrast notably in teaching styles, the way they do research and writing, their relationship with students, and probably even in the way they understand the objectives of higher education. The new generation of college professors continues to be predominantly men, but the proportion of women is growing, including women in nontraditional fields such as mathematics, science, architecture, and engineering. Despite the change, the male ethos of the university continues to be very strong, and most college presidents and top administrators are men.

The academic community has the leavening of a sprinkling of gender specialists. Nearly all of them are women and most are social scientists, but a few men and specialists in other areas might consider themselves part of the new wave. Many gender specialists have come into the universities specifically hired to staff gender studies programs, programs that now exist in numerous Latin American colleges and universities.

University-based gender studies programs in Latin America vary widely in their dimensions, quality, objectives, and level of consolidation. Most are quite young and still experimental. A handful of programs lead to an M.A. degree, while most lead to "special diplomas" or are designed to offer courses that enrich and complement the normal course offerings in the humanities and social sciences. The programs also vary widely with respect to the level of engagement they seek with social problems and processes in their immediate environment. Some have an academic orientation, others are practice-oriented, and others lie in between. Some, while academically oriented, experiment with practical projects when special demands and opportunities present themselves. That would be a fair description of the Catholic University of Peru's program, for example. Those toward the "practice" end of the scale may be involved in extension activities that often include education about gender outside the university walls. Thus, the National University of Colombia has worked with feminist groups in sponsoring gender training courses and in providing training to nongovernmental development organizations and to government officials.

University-based gender studies programs are both a symptom of and a further stimulus to a process that is moving research and theory-building around gender away from women's NGOs, where it was centered for almost two decades, to the academe. Throughout the 1970s and the 1980s, most of the funds available for research on women in Latin America (leaving aside for the moment a large amount of research done by expatriates) were channeled to nongovernmental women's organizations that combined research with a program of local development projects focused on women. Often feminist militancy was added to these other two as a third line of activity. The research that was done tended to be small-scale (a few women, a few families, an urban neighborhood, a rural community) and tended to be designed to have rather direct applications in the development projects of the organization.

To some extent, the new gender studies programs have been able to break the pattern of isolation of universities and the absence of networks and exchange. They have organized several meetings among themselves and promoted some short-term faculty exchanges. Bibliography and resources such as course syllabi are circulated. Occasionally, there has been shared sponsorship of a visiting academic from outside the region.

These initiatives have almost invariably been assisted with funds and logistical support from development cooperation agencies, which suggests a certain separation and even vulnerability of the programs in relation to mainline university budgetary commitments.

Despite what would probably be its wishes, the higher education community is not a compact community exclusively dedicated to teaching and research. With low salaries and poor working conditions, many college faculty members carry on a double life. Often they are simultaneously active and influential members of development NGOs. Many academic social scientists founded such organizations in the 1970s and 1980s, and many continue to direct them or to direct development projects within such organizations. Faculty members in branches of business administration or engineering are likely to be heavily involved in the private sector. They may own private businesses or work part time for business organizations. Academics in general are consultants to governments, to international cooperation agencies, and to a wide range of private organizations and initiatives. All of this makes it impossible to draw a very clear line between the "development" and the "academic" communities we initially separated for purposes of analysis.

The existence of such interconnections raises the question of how much transfer there may be between the academic world and the development community, with respect to new ideas and understandings about gender. In Peru, it is rather easy to identify a segment of both men and women academics who have brought back to the university the benefits of gender courses and seminars they attended under their NGO hats. Overall, it seems clear that the development world is out in front of the higher education sector with respect to the exposure of its staff to gender concepts. Whatever the volume of expertise that flows from one community to the other, the direction of the flow is likely to be from the development world toward the higher education world.

The limited experience of academics with gender education has another explanation, and that is the extremely limited opportunities for further education available to college faculty members in whatever specialty or topic. In impoverished colleges and universities, especially those outside the capital cities, it cannot be presumed that serious academics are constantly renewing their knowledge as a matter of independent reading, study, research, and participation in academic events. Some new perspectives on gender relations and some of the current literature on gender in society should have "trickled down" through those channels. Yet this is where *multiempleo* (multiple jobs) takes its principal toll at the level of individual faculty members and where underfunding of universities takes its toll at the institutional level. Surfing on the Internet has become an important strategy used by some of the younger and more motivated professors to refresh their bibliographic resources and gain access to new ideas.

In the higher education world, the principal beneficiaries of education about gender should undoubtedly be faculty members. They can rework, reproduce, and transmit new concepts to students and colleagues. There are also arguments for involving administrative staff and planning directors, however. For all, gender education should motivate the discovery of how their society's gender system works through their own institution and should help them to see the equity and equal opportunity issues that are at stake.

Over the past two years, the gender studies program of the Catholic University of Peru[1] has been developing a long-distance education module, "Gender in University Teaching" (*Género en la docencia universitaria*). To the best of our knowledge, this is the first such course to have been developed in a South American country. Anderson acted as principal author of the module, and Mendoza, besides participating in the conceptualization and writing of the material, was primarily responsible for giving it pedagogical form. In the end, the course is the product of suggestions and contributions from many colleagues and friends. A series of group discussions with professors from the Catholic University and from three other colleges and universities around the country provided fundamental inputs.

The course contains eleven units addressing different substantive issues. The first unit is an introduction to some basic concepts in gender theory (for example, the concept of "gender system"). The second unit lays out the arguments in favor of a conscious effort to create opportunities for women in higher education and to end patterns of discrimination. The next unit is a review of how gender inequality is constructed as children proceed through their years of basic education. The three following units deal with basic tasks that college professors perform: planning courses, designing a syllabus, selecting readings and supporting material, and planning and presenting classes. One unit is devoted to the issues surrounding the teaching of science and engineering, careers where women are drastically underrepresented and where biological explanations are often brought forward as justification. The next unit discusses problems of self-esteem as they play out in the classroom and in the relations among faculty and students. Next is a unit devoted to questions of men's and women's performance and the fairness of the standards by which students are evaluated. The subsequent unit raises the thorny problem of sexual harassment and abuse. The module ends with a unit that discusses the labor market that college graduates face and the risk of "self-fulfilling prophecies," whereby faculty fail to stimulate male and female students to aspire to certain jobs and careers because they do not correspond to conventional gender roles.

The "Gender in University Teaching" course was launched in a pilot version in the second semester of 1998 in three public institutions in the Andean sierra region of Peru. Two are well-established universities and one is a very young, technically oriented college. The gender studies program hired an outside consultant to guide the experience and to produce a report with recommendations. When this article was being written, one of the groups had completed the eleven units and two others were near the end. The consultant's report is available in a preliminary version. Overall the experience was highly successful: The participants felt they learned a great deal from using their own institution as a laboratory for observation and exercises, and they considered that their own practice had changed.

The course is designed with approximately equal emphasis on individual reading and reflection, discussions in a group of five to eight faculty members who agree to take the course together, and group tasks such as gathering statistics on the rates of admission of male and female students in different departments and programs. With very little outside assistance, the mixed groups that formed in the three pilot universities and colleges guided themselves through the module. One of their recommendations was that the experience be extended to non-teaching university staff, since their decisions (for example, reducing the required class load of a pregnant student or young mother) may affect questions of gender equity fully as much as the decisions and behavior of the faculty.

WHAT ASSUMPTIONS AND "PHILOSOPHY" LIE BEHIND GENDER EDUCATION STRATEGIES AND ACTIVITIES?

Education about gender is polemical, particularly when it is intended to have practical consequences in the type of work the participants do afterward and the processes of institutional change they engage in. Almost inevitably there is a moment of "position taking." The field of gender studies is itself rife with controversies ("essentialists" versus constructionists, emphasis on material conditions versus subjective experience—to name two of the lines of division). This section of the chapter analyzes some of the dominant assumptions and conceptual frameworks that underlie gender education in the two settings that concern us.

The Development Community

One of the most systematic efforts to understand the issues surrounding gender education in development organizations in Latin America was undertaken by CEAAL in 1995. Two researchers, Rosario Aguirre and Virginia Guzmán (1996), conducted a survey of the nongovernmental organizations affiliated with CEAAL. The sample included eighty-seven NGOs with mixed membership (defined as comprising both men and women as leaders and beneficiaries) and fifteen women's NGOs (defined as having an almost entirely female leadership and implementing programs and/or projects concerned with women and gender equity). Sixty percent of the mixed NGOs, however, had women's departments or women's projects, and many had accumulated a relatively long experience in educational programs for women (literacy training, for example).

Several of the CEAAL-affiliated organizations, both mixed and women NGOs, had experience with gender training workshops. Some had carried out workshops or courses internally, while others had sponsored one or more of their members to attend gender seminars. Some had done both. The report by Aguirre and Guzmán reviews some of the demands and needs for knowledge about gender that are recognized by the respondents to the survey, that is, directors and heads of women's divisions or projects within the organizations. In general, the results document the very high expectations that are raised by gender training and the relatively poor match between many of the courses currently offered and the programs that the organizations were trying to move forward.

Aguirre and Guzmán asked the NGO respondents to identify the topics they considered most important for education and training in gender. Table 3 shows the responses of the directors of mixed NGOs and the responses of the directors of women's NGOs and the heads of women's departments within the mixed NGOs.

The directors of mixed NGOs identified priority issues in explicitly political arenas such as: machinery for gender equality at the governmental level, political participation by women, the response of the political system, and tool kits for advocacy and lobbying. Leaders of women's NGOs and women's departments in mixed organizations agree with the importance of these issues but add a set of concerns about social relations and social policies. In assigning high priority to feminist theory as

Table 3. Topics Preferred for Programs in Gender Education by CEAAL-Affiliated NGOs, 1995 (Preferences Expressed in Percentages)*

Topic	Mixed Organizations	Women NGOs and Women's Divisions of Mixed NGOs
Equality of opportunity, policies, and programs	95	93
Citizenship, democracy, women's political participation	83	76
Feminist theory	53	72
Development theory and trends from a perspective of gender justice	84	94
Social policy and planning	62	76
Project monitoring and evaluation	66	79
Methodologies for advocacy, political action, and lobbying	72	74

* Informants could select more than one topic.
Source: Aguirre and Guzmán, 1996, p. 30.

one component of gender education, the women seem to be expressing the need to take up a broad range of subjective and identity questions, as well as (probably) a more critical stance in relation to fundamental issues of gender justice.

Despite some differences, the consensus of the NGOs is that gender education should be oriented to disseminating information about the theory of democracy and the meaning of citizenship and to explicating the ways women and men relate to the political system. In addition, it should contain instruction about strategies and tactics for influencing the political machinery. The inference to be drawn is that, in the analysis (explicit or tacit) of both mixed and women's NGOs, the political process should and will resolve outstanding issues of gender equity and injustice.

Meanwhile, the "gender" projects actually being carried out by the CEAAL-affiliated NGOs concentrate on two areas. One is time use: the sexual division of labor and proposals for making housework more efficient and less time-consuming, new technologies for household tasks, and/or a more equitable division of housework among family members. The other is income generation and micro business formation for women.

The authors of the CEAAL report point out that it is the women's NGOs that are more likely to address directly women's experience of subordination and the unjust distribution of power and resources. These organizations sponsor activities such as sharing women's life testimonies, and analyzing time use, and projects such as providing legal services, health clinics, services for women victims of domestic and other types of violence, and child care and related systems of support. In the mixed NGOs, the assimilation of a discourse about equality of opportunities and the redistribution of resources between women and men is more recent and less profound. It has not yet materialized in projects and activities, certainly none that are visible and important (and therefore worth mentioning in the survey) from the point of view of the directors of the organizations.

From this brief report on a sample of Latin American NGOs, the high ambitions of much gender training shine forth. By contrast, the *Escuela's* survey of NGO directors mentioned earlier shows a demand for more practice-oriented courses. In fact, in the format of a short course, with an audience that may or may not have chosen to be there, gender trainers move from one extreme to other: either seeking to construct a complex understanding of a wide range of topics or simplifying basic gender concepts in a handbook style, with the risk of underestimating the true complexity of contemporary discussions of gender. In the first option, the topics covered are theoretical and general, while the projects to which the training is later to be applied are specific and specialized. In the second option, participants go back to their organizations with a set of tools that they tend to apply mechanically, without establishing connections to the theoretical discussion. Moreover, they operate in many different institutional contexts, from community organizations to commercial banks. The participants in the training are expected to discover the relevance of what they learn to their own projects and roles in their organizations. The question becomes, then, whether the training gives them sufficient help in doing that. High expectations may lead to great frustration, a point we will return to at the end of this section.

The Higher Education Community

In looking at the assumptions behind efforts to educate about gender in the higher education community, we will once again (in the absence of similar experiments in other countries) rely on the case of the Catholic University's correspondence course. The philosophy and approach of the course were greatly enriched by a series of group discussions with faculty members of colleges and universities from around Peru, during the process of designing the module. The professors that participated came from a wide range of disciplines, including architecture, archaeology, engineering, chemistry, mathematics, nursing, social work, linguistics, sociology, and history. All felt that education about gender should be linked to other projects for modernizing, democratizing, and improving the quality and effectiveness of Peruvian higher education.

Thus, in the opinion of the Peruvian college professors, more equal relations among men and women faculty members and male and female students can and should be framed in an overall proposal for the democratization of higher education. This goes against a long tradition where knowledge, science, and "culture" have been seen as monopolies not only of males, but specifically of white and mestizo males, as opposed to Andean and "Indian" males. At the same time, projects for radical improvement in the quality of higher education (a priority few would dispute in Peru and probably most other Latin American countries) could be tied to proposals for new classroom methods and standards for professors' conduct and competence. Such ideas can readily be linked to proposals for greater use of discussion and participation by all students, women and men, and a requirement that faculty be up-to-date on the gender literature as they should be in other emerging fields. Improving quality is linked to propitiating a more horizontal, less authoritarian relationship between faculty and students of both genders.

At the same time, the Peruvian college professors have transmitted a vision of the university as a hierarchical institution seriously constrained by the weight of tradition. Compared to the NGO community and the development world, higher education appears as a less open environment and a somewhat less auspicious arena for promoting change in gender relations. In response, the professors, similar in this respect to the directors of the CEAAL sample of NGOs, mentioned a range of political strategies and political skills necessary to further gender justice in institutions of higher education. One is creating a critical mass. Another is strengthening the hand of isolated figures with gender sensitivity that are already present (for example, faculty grouped in gender studies programs). Another involves gaining the support of the administration and persons in positions of authority in the academic hierarchy.

The same groups of Peruvian faculty considered the mobilization of emotions and moral commitment to be an essential part of education about gender, even in that paragon of rational discourse and thought—the university. For the Peruvian professors, there are many valid arguments for promoting gender equity that connect logically to convictions they already hold about disadvantaged students. Particularly in provincial public universities, faculty members identify closely with students and know them individually. Many are the daughters and sons of shopkeepers and struggling farming families in rural towns. They often make enormous sacrifices to go to college, something that many of the professors also did when they were students.

The professors portray themselves as tolerant and understanding in relation to students who have to work and study at the same time, in conditions in which "work" might translate into daily ten-hour shifts as a waiter, welder in a shop, or even a domestic servant. Their empathy takes in, without hesitation, the situation of women with one or two young children and a husband to care for in addition to attending classes and keeping up with assignments. The professors, particularly those teaching in provincial colleges, have seen many students, many times, fail to show up for class because they lacked the busfare, and fail a course because they could not buy, rent, or photocopy the necessary books. Under these conditions, identifying with women college students as "underdogs" comes easily. Faculty in provincial colleges feel themselves to be the "underdogs," with enormous disadvantages, in relation to more fortunate colleagues teaching at colleges and universities in the capital city.

At the same time, the discussions among professors from a range of specialties made it clear that, to many of them, gender inequality is somehow inevitable. It can be reduced but not eliminated, they seemed to say. They attributed this inevitability to two different sources. The first was biology and the "natural" differences between women and men. This explained why the high investment of time and emotional energy in home and caring work on the part of married women students was recognized as a reality but not questioned as a fact of current social arrangements. The second set of factors that seemed to make gender inequality inevitable, in the minds of most of the Peruvian professors, was the inertial force of school experience leading directly to a labor market that finished the work of channeling men and women into gender-stereotyped occupations and, indeed, lives.

Building on these and other suggestions of the participants in the faculty discussion groups, the "Gender in University Teaching" course organizes almost its entire contents around the university as a community of individuals who occupy a diversity of positions and roles, and as an institution with formal and informal "agendas" or "curricula" simultaneously in play. The course seeks to lead participants through a series of settings in college life that reveal the operation of the gender system. In this sense, the methodological strategy is almost entirely inductive. The examples and exercises speak directly about the positions and relations of women and men in the context of each participant's institution. The professors who enroll in the course are asked to observe themselves: their teaching styles and classroom behavior, their selection of topics and bibliography as they plan their courses, and the kind of relations they establish with colleagues and students of both genders. Then they are asked to analyze critically the implications of their own actions—in and out of the classroom—on the question of gender justice in the university.

In comparing the suppositions underlying gender education in the development world and in colleges and universities, at first sight it could seem almost ironic that the strategies being developed for institutions of higher education rely more strongly on examples and analysis of concrete reality than would appear to be the case in the NGOs. The image we usually have of these two institutional settings leads us to expect exactly the opposite situation. Higher education and college professors seem to be engaged in abstract thought and analysis long removed from everyday life, while development organizations seem to be engaged with the dense details of projects and programs firmly tied to social reality. Yet the way education about gender plays out in the two settings produces a curious reversal of identities. The reason this is so helps us to understand some of the problems with gender education as it is practiced nowadays.

Gender education in the development world began almost a decade ago. At the same time, the effort was to foster sensitivity through concrete examples of the surrounding reality where the NGOs worked. However, the demand for a more in-depth background led in some of the cases to a search for theories and ongoing discussion, which are still in initial stages of development. At the same time, after ten years of working on the topic, the process in the development world shows some constraints, related to the internal organizational forces whose power is affected as the process of gender-related changes unfolds and matures. In our efforts within the academic world, the process is still very young and the current responses of college faculty give us hope because they tend to center on the issue of academic freedom and its classic space: the classroom. Opening the possibility for exploring a new way of designing their syllabi, improving teaching methodologies, and enhancing ways of relating to students gives the faculty room to maneuver and improve the quality of their work. However, this approach has yet to challenge the university system.

Nonetheless, the overly broad scope of most of the gender education that takes place in and for development organizations seems to be another key to explaining the paradox we just identified. Although colleges and universities may differ dramatically within Peru and certainly within Latin America as a region, they have a similar basic structure, mandate, and history as institutions of higher learning. They have faculties, an administration, students, classes, curricula, libraries, and extracurricular programs. There are important similarities in the rules and procedures such institutions recognize and apply.

Development projects, in contrast, range over a large number of substantive problems and institutional settings. A key and, we believe, mistaken assumption of gender education in development organizations is that a few general principles can be applied with minor adjustments in development projects concerned with vastly different types of problems and operating in vastly different institutional contexts. The result is what we observe in most gender education: a general framework of analysis set out at a high level of abstraction and, in counterpoint, a plethora of vignettes or case studies of specific development projects that have been implemented in some part of the world. What is lacking is a middle range, precisely where ought to lie the specific institutional analysis that proves so useful a teaching tool in the case of higher education. In this middle range as well would lie the analysis of process, especially political process, which the CEAAL survey respondents judge to be of such critical importance in efforts to move development institutions and projects toward greater gender equity.

WHAT HAS BEEN ACHIEVED? WHAT ARE THE CONTINUING PROBLEMS IN CURRENT STRATEGIES AND ACTIVITIES OF GENDER EDUCATION?

Beyond the CEAAL study, no serious, large-scale, independent, comparative evaluation of the effectiveness of gender education or training "packages" and strategies has yet been done in Latin America. We do not really know what are the separate or cumulative effects of the courses, seminars, workshops, and programs that seek to equip development organizations and their members for doing a better job of promoting gender justice in their projects and programs. Given the large investments of money, time, and intellectual resources in such activities, this state of affairs is surprising.

The scarcity of evaluations may be related to the fact that many training "packages" have been commissioned by large development agencies

(USAID, CIDA, Oxfam, GTZ, FAO, among others). This has three possible consequences. First, partial evaluations may exist but have not circulated beyond the agencies themselves. Second, the agencies may not
recognize their responsibility for a large family of adaptations of their
"package" and these adaptations remain unevaluated. Third, interagency
rivalries may have discouraged high-quality comparative evaluations.

Even scarcer are evaluations of gender education activities in colleges and universities *as directed to changing gender arrangements
within the institution itself.* There have certainly been evaluations of
women's studies and gender studies programs that have sought to measure their success in providing a grounding in gender theory and its
implications to students not enrolled in a degree program. Probably—as
we know to be the case in such evaluations applied to the Catholic University of Peru's own gender studies program—these reports make some
reference to the program's internal impact. In the Peruvian case, this has
involved citing the number of seminars and other events that have drawn
in persons other than gender specialists or, in general, produced demonstrations of interest and commitment on the part of faculty and administrators of the university.

With this background in mind, let us look at what we do know about
the achievements of gender education in our two sectors of interest and at
what some of the persistent problems seem to be.

The Development Community

In the NGO and development community, the clearest, most unequivocal
impacts of gender education are at the level of individual conviction and
capacities. The importance of this is evident in the vignette about Teresa,
presented in our first section. The men and women who go through the
courses usually emerge with a sense of orientation in relation to the conceptual debates around gender. They "learn the language" of gender; in
fact, many training courses provide glossaries of terms as a handout.
They acquire new skills and a palette of technical resources for working
with women (and, increasingly, men) in addressing gender identities and
gender inequities. Frequently, the participants come away feeling that
they can deal more constructively with issues of gender in their own
lives: relations with partners, parent-child relations, and relations with
coworkers of both genders. This must all be counted as a very important
product of gender training.

The graduates of gender education courses often feel that they have made little progress toward clarifying—much less resolving in practical terms—the issues of gender equity and justice in the projects and programs they are assigned to work on. This result seems to hark back to the problem we signaled in question 2 at the beginning of the article: the highly abstract nature of much of the material and many of the concepts that are reviewed, interspersed with examples and cases that never quite coincide with the project one is involved with. Given the current underdevelopment of middle-level theories, this may be an inevitable situation, since gender education was never meant or conceived to be a matter of recipes, but it does prove frustrating for many participants, especially men.

The most desired result of gender education in development organizations would be actually bringing about lasting institutional change. What is wanted is for the organizations to redirect their projects and activities toward gender justice and equity, and for them to recognize the relevance of such goals in the broad scope of their development agenda. Institutional change might involve new kinds of programs, new internal structures, leadership roles for women, and the assimilation of men in program areas traditionally reserved for women. Unfortunately, experience shows that the awareness of injustice, inputs for conceptualizing gender systems and relations, the ability to use new analytical tools, practice in preparing gender-sensitive projects, and instruments for monitoring and evaluating projects, while taking full account of their impact on gender relations, are rarely sufficient to produce a shift in the dynamics of development organizations with a long tradition built on very different assumptions.

The *Escuela para el Desarrollo* has begun looking at the constraints within organizations that prevent them from advancing more effectively toward these goals. Some new proposals attach first importance to changes at the structural level (the organizational chart, recruitment policies, selection and promotion of personnel, and so on) with the hope that from new structures will emerge a new organizational culture. Undoubtedly, some change is possible, but the effectiveness of a proposal for transforming structures alone has not yet been demonstrated. Institutional cultures remain a crucial sticking point.

One way of looking at organizational culture identifies three operational levels: artifacts, values, and assumptions.[2] Artifacts are visible: They include job titles, formal written policies of the organization, ceremonies, dress, rules, language, and how space and equipment is allocated. Values may be more difficult to access, but they often are made explicit in the principles, philosophy, vision, and mission of the organization. Assumptions are the hardest of all to access, partly because they have become so habitual that the directors and members of the institution are not aware of their existence.

Power and privilege are involved at all these levels. It may be that gender education has made the inroads it has in the Peruvian NGO community in part because of a turnover of generations in the old leadership. Nearly all the founding generation of mixed development organizations were men. Many of them have moved on to careers in journalism, academia, business, and politics. Some have been replaced in their posts by women. Old relations of power may not be so easy to disrupt, however. At the *Escuela para el Desarrollo,* Mendoza is initiating a research project that seeks to establish whether there is a gendered conception and practice of power in Peruvian NGOs that forms part of their organizational culture. This study will be exploring a possible relationship between styles of using power and the opportunities for organizations to assimilate, as part of their culture and programs, a gender justice perspective.

Meanwhile, educating about gender can occur in many ways, under many natural conditions and in many natural settings. "Gender training" as practiced in the development world seeks to speed up the clock and foreshorten what may otherwise be a long process of gradually coming to see the realities of men's and women's situations and relations. There is usually also an implication of control by the trainers over the outcome of the process. Yet one of the most important lessons of the past decades may be that educational processes take a rather long time and that training courses must be reinforced by lived experience in the real world.

The overall cultural change that has taken place in urban Peru (and rural Peru to a surprising extent) has involved processes of urbanization, globalization, international migration, the informalization of work, the market economy, ruptures in the traditional social bonds of family and close local communities, secularization, the dissemination of women's rights and roles through the mass media, and new models of public participation. All this may have contributed in important ways to the results of explicit educational activities focused on changing gender roles and understandings. Separating out the strands would be a major challenge.

The Higher Education Community

Evaluating the effects of gender education in university settings is even more difficult than in the case of development organizations. Because of its pilot nature, we can no longer be guided by the Catholic University's

"Gender in University Teaching" course. The participants in the groups that completed the trial run of the course in three Peruvian colleges considered that it would have an effect on the way they organized their courses and classes, and on the way they dealt with male and female students. We cannot be sure that will happen, however, until the module has been used by many more faculty and until there is an independent evaluation of its actual impact.

Our strategy in this section, therefore, will be to point to some of the areas and dimensions where an evaluation could take place to educate about gender and to change gender arrangements in the higher education sector.

A first point to be made concerns the special characteristics of universities as labor markets. In Latin America as in other regions, academic jobs are buttressed by a number of protective mechanisms. Enshrined by tradition, these are alleged to be necessary for ensuring academic freedom and the opportunity for research and writing that has no short-term payoff. They have the side effect, however, of making turnover in academic posts a very slow process and, meanwhile, of excluding talented young colleagues because there simply are no available positions at the top. This phenomenon has made it very difficult to change institutions of higher education even in countries such as Sweden and Germany that have been leaders in the gender equity struggles in other institutional arenas. The competition for teaching and research positions is fierce, making it difficult not only to increase the overall proportion of women faculty in the university system but also to promote women academics to positions as full professors and chairs of powerful committees. In this connection, the world of higher education contrasts markedly with the world of development organizations, which can—as long as money can be found to support projects—expand and multiply themselves almost indefinitely.

Under these conditions, the most likely arena for real change in higher education is in the classroom itself. Under the principle of *libertad de cátedra* (academic freedom), college faculty in Latin America have a wide degree of freedom in the way they present their material and conduct their classes. Junior faculty members may have more contact with students than senior professors and thus be particularly important in efforts to restructure gender relations in the classroom. While a senior faculty member may set the overall framework for a course, instructors and teaching assistants can do much to change the climate in the classroom and vary the emphasis on different readings and discussion materials. They can do much to encourage women students to take active part, to consider career options that may have seemed impossible, to explore lines of thought, and to make common cause with other women.

At the same time, higher education has a centuries-long accumulation of rituals and customary procedures that penetrate almost all areas of academic life. These discourage head-on confrontation. They also tend to displace debates from the immediate present to the distant past and far-off future. To a large extent, the norms of the academe require both students and faculty to behave like disembodied, impersonal inquirers after universal, enduring truths that tend to cast immediate personal problems—such as managing family and academic life simultaneously—in a light of insignificance. In such a climate, the personal involvement that many Peruvian professors have with their students, especially those based in provincial colleges and universities, could easily disappear as these colleges become more professional, "modern," and mainstream.

The faculty discussion groups that were part of the preparation for the distance course on "Gender in University Teaching" revealed a number of details about how some women students take advantage of certain dubious "privileges" they are offered under the unspoken norms of the academe. They told of how male students in physics and engineering laboratories, for example, may consider it a gentlemanly duty to "help" a female student to avoid dirtying her hands, lifting heavy objects, or pulling her own weight in work groups. Sometimes, women students with family responsibilities ask professors to lower standards of evaluation instead of exploring with them more positive solutions to their problems. For example, one male professor called both husband and wife into his office and reviewed with them the division of labor in the household; he later followed up to make sure the young husband was meeting his agreement to share the work at home. An evaluation of the efficacy of gender education in institutions of higher education would have to find ways to measure the reduction in practices that, while they appear to favor women students, in reality affirm their lesser competence and deny them equal treatment with men students.

Next, if gender equity in higher education institutions is tied to raising the quality of teaching in those institutions, an evaluation of the success of gender education would have to examine the risks and benefits of making one contingent on the other. The privacy and respect for each professor's right to control his or her own courses and teaching methods may be a double-edged sword. For many old-style faculty, the lack of standards of good pedagogical practice has meant that they can repeat the same lessons from the same class notes, year after year. Few courses or books are available to college faculty that want to improve their teaching skills. Here, then, colleges and universities would have to advance on both fronts simultaneously: organizing for teaching about gender and developing means in and outside the classroom to improve pedagogy.

Finally, evaluating the progress of efforts to educate about gender in higher education would require monitoring the course of what we found to be a high level of pessimism about the possibility of changing gender arrangements outside the protected walls of the university. Again we refer to the discussion groups of Peruvian faculty from a variety of colleges and universities in different parts of the country. They were unanimous in blaming a large part of the gender inequalities observed in higher education on the earlier experience of students (and, in their time, professors) in the school system. They were also nearly unanimous in their perception that gender discrimination in labor markets for college graduates was almost impossible to change or obviate. Such attitudes suggest that gender education within the university might be accepted in a spirit of experimenting with an alternative world, with faculty members believing that it is futile to try to affect the outside world from the base of the university. This would not be the result we would expect in education about gender, tied not only to a project for improving the quality of college teaching but also to a project of democratization and modernization of the broader society.

HOW MIGHT GENDER EDUCATION BE REFORMULATED IN THE LIGHT OF CONTEMPORARY GENDER THEORY? HOW MIGHT IT BETTER SERVE THE CONSTRUCTION OF GENDER THEORY?

Education about gender—at least, as practiced in developing countries such as Peru and most of the rest of Latin America—involves three domains that are independent but partially intersecting. The first is the *feminist action* domain. It poses questions such as: Who are "we" (women, feminists, a subordinate gender, a segment of women)? What do we want? What political means are available to better the lot of women and to encourage gender justice? Who are our allies? Who and where is the enemy or opposition? The second is the *academic* domain. Here, the questions posed are: What is the origin of gender inequality? What forms does inequality take, here and cross-culturally? What are the social contexts that encourage or discourage practical action for resolving gender discrimination and inequality? The third is the *development* domain. The questions that are posed here are: What can be done? What actions are possible in the real-world conditions of our local and national environments? How can we measure the effectiveness of different strategies for action? What are the institutional resources that can be brought to bear (those of our own institutions and those of others that become involved through our influence; those of institutions that were prior actors on the field)? What are the forces of opposition, and what institutional resources do they deploy?

The activities that happen in these three domains ought, in theory, to be mutually reinforcing. Academic research ought to feed into feminist thought and mobilization. Both ought, in principle, to contribute to development projects and to a vision of gender justice adequate to the complexities of subaltern countries undergoing processes of industrialization and urbanization in conditions of an increasingly globalized world economy and cultural system. Yet it would be difficult to show just how this happens and just how the model plays itself out in reality. The points of overlap of these three domains are seldom studied in detail as the subject of empirical research. They are vastly undertheorized.

One point of overlap involves the risks of backlash, both in gender education activities and in development projects with a strong element of women's promotion and promotion of new relations between the genders. In the development community, one might expect opposition to come from the perceived difficulties of realizing projects that accent women and gender equity, or from the perception on the part of NGO staff of the high liabilities of undertaking such projects for other actors, for example, traditional adult male political authorities in rural communities of the Andes. The opposition is likely to be clothed in discourses of "not pushing change too fast" or that point to the need for protecting the interests of other vulnerable sectors of the population. From the academic community, one might expect opposition to spring from what is perceived as the danger of destabilizing intellectual schemes adopted years ago and the displacement of more traditional academics from positions of power. The opposition is likely to be disguised by reasoned arguments, for example, about men's and women's inherent "natures" and "natural" roles.

In both the development world and the academe, the fear of change and the desire to preserve existing power relations can be expected to be important ingredients. In both, there may be an element of what Hola and Todaro found to be, among Chilean business executives, a sort of bottom-line expression of resistance to change toward greater gender equity in that particular institutional context: Having run out of arguments, many confessed that they simply "did not like" sharing their working groups with women. And "feminism" is a much maligned and misunderstood term in both of the settings that have been our focus in this chapter.[3]

One of the major contributions to gender theory in past years is Amartya Sen's application of the concept of "cooperative conflict"[4] to relations between the genders, particularly in day-to-day interaction and face-to-face groups such as couples, families, and work groups. Sen's theory sits well with a growing tendency in gender theory to focus on dynamic relations of exchange and bargaining between the genders rather than static notions of gender roles and apparently inflexible hierarchies of power. The problem, for our present purposes, is that development projects are consensus oriented, and consensus is probably also one of the strong institutional norms of the university.

The concept of "cooperative conflict," in addition to legitimating difference and discrepancy as an inherent part of gender relations, also clearly captures an orientation to process rather than end-states. And here too difficulties arise when this vision of gender is translated to the development world and to the world of higher education. Both are far more accustomed to thinking about end-states than ongoing processes. In the case of development organizations, these end-states are the changed situations that development projects seek to bring to reality. They are measured by indicators and expressed in the objectives and goals of logical frameworks and other technical supports. In the case of the academe, the end-states have to do with notions of truth and proof.

This presents a challenge for feminist theory. Educating about gender requires openness to the open-endedness of gender arrangements. So far, very few proposals for gender training deal adequately with questions of ongoing processes of negotiation of gender relations, values, and understandings. Few even recognize the importance of procedural rules and their effects on gender equity. Meanwhile, the demand for quick fixes, certain answers, and unambiguous guides to action is very strong, not only in the development world but also (we have argued) in the academe. Yet gender education strategies that deny the importance of "cooperative conflict" and that skirt the issues of procedural justice are simply out of step with the best of contemporary gender theorizing.

A further challenge is keeping ahead of changes that occur in society. Gender roles, the linchpin of much education about gender over many years, are a case in point. Much of the writing about gender roles even ten years ago, in college textbooks but also in the materials used by

NGOs, seems irremediably dated. The danger is that the images of gender that development organizations and college teaching project lag behind the real world, and that these two institutions may be promoting hegemonic "ideal types" that have already been left far behind by social reality.

In closing, we want to recall the important suggestion put forward by Irene Tinker almost a decade ago. In her introductory chapter to her edited book *Persistent Inequalities,* Tinker argued that the literature on development projects is a vastly underused resource for constructing gender theory. Whether they willed it or not, all development projects have instigated change in the gender systems of the societies they affected. In that sense, development projects—particularly those that were least self-conscious about the kinds of changes they wished to bring about in gender relations and identities—represent "natural experiments" on gender systems. Yet the development literature in general is not usually considered a legitimate source of knowledge as a basis for college teaching and academic discourse.

Tinker correctly demands that we rethink this situation. For good teaching about gender to occur, the knowledge base must expand. For good gender theory to be constructed, the focus of theorizing must be on the dynamics of flux and change. Here, not only is the practice of development organizations a critical input, but the processes of institutional change—in colleges and universities and in development organizations—are just such an input as well.

NOTES

[1]The Catholic University of Peru is a private, nonprofit institution of higher education. It maintains links with other Catholic universities and include representatives of the Peruvian Catholic Church on its board of directors. The university has repeatedly affirmed its adherence to the principles of academic freedom and inquiry, and its practice reflects such principles.

[2]Carole Pemberton, "Organizational Culture and Equalities Work," in Jenny Shaw and Diane Persons (eds.), *Making Gender Work. Making Equal Opportunities* (Buckingham: Open University Press, 1996), pp. 108–123.

[3]Eugenia Hola and Rosalba Todaro, *Los mecanismos del poder: Hombres y mujeres en la empresa moderna* (Santiago: Centro de Estudios de la Mujer, 1992).

[4]Amartya K. Sen, "Gender and Cooperative Conflicts," in Irene Tinker (ed.), *Persistent Inequalities: Women and World Development* (New York: Oxford University Press, 1990), pp. 123–149.

REFERENCES

Aguirre, Rosario and Virginia Guzmán. *El género en el quehacer institucional de las ONGs afiliadas al CEAAL.* Santiago: CEAAL, 1996.

Anderson, Jeanine (with the collaboration of Rosa Mendoza). *Género en la docencia universitaria.* Lima: Programa de Estudios de Género, Pontificia Universidad Católica del Perú, 1998.

Hola, Eugenia and Rosalba Todaro. *Los mecanismos del poder: Hombres y mujeres en la empresa moderna.* Santiago: Centro de Estudios de la Mujer, 1992.

Largo, Eliana (ed.). *Género en el estado. Estado del género.* Santiago: ISIS Internacional, 1999.

Melgar, Walter. Informe de Encuentro sobre "Cambios Organizacionales y Demandas de Capacitación." Lima: Escuela para el Desarrollo, 1996, mimeo.

Melgar, Walter. Base de Datos del Area de Formación. Lima: Escuela para el Desarrollo, 1998, mimeo.

Pemberton, Carole. "Organizational Culture and Equalities Work." In Jenny Shaw and Diane Persons (eds.), *Making Gender Work. Making Equal Opportunities.* Buckingham: Open University Press, 1996, pp. 108–123.

Sen, Amartya K. "Gender and Cooperative Conflicts." In Irene Tinker (ed.), *Persistent Inequalities: Women and World Development.* New York: Oxford University Press, 1990, pp. 123–149.

Tinker, Irene. "A Context for the Field and for the Book." In Irene Tinker (ed.), *Persistent Inequalities: Women and World Development.* New York: Oxford University Press, 1990, pp. 3–13.

Leadership Training
Transformations and Transgressions

ALEJANDRA VALDÉS

Women's leadership is one of the most important political expressions of recent decades and a contribution to the political culture of our times. It is a notable event because it has emerged over time as a notorious social and political phenomenon that makes sense, that must be considered, thought upon, and that opens the door to new possibilities in the different public arenas where women appear. Reactions to this new player in the public sphere also merit observation.

In this sense, educational action and research about this "event" support not only an understanding of the women who are moving into the public sphere and their difficulties and achievements, but also how the women are changing, reordering, and transforming the public sphere. This chapter is based on educational work carried out by a team from the Women's Institute in Chile and adds to the collective effort of women who work to break down the spheres of domination and inequality between the sexes. This effort appears globally at this end of century and is manifested in the development of concrete proposals for change.[1]

The social transformation currently in process reflects the strong changes that are being produced among women leaders, who on the one hand adapt the masculine leadership model and on the other hand strengthen a new model for women as successful workers and initiators. Women in leadership positions today are a minority who experience the contradictions of both social demands to maintain the maternal, sacrificial, and "decent" model,[2] together with the rupture they find when they learn multiple skills and detect the weaknesses of a social structure that, in the case of the Chilean political process, demonstrates reticence about accepting the phenomenon of women leaders.

The historical context of the educational labor that led to this analysis is the major political transition initiated in Chile at the beginning of the 1990s, a product of the transformation of political institutions and the transition from the dictatorship to the period of democratic transition. This transition has been characterized by a willingness to participate in democratic reconstruction, but the reconstruction did not provide enough positions of authority for women that would have acknowledged women's decisive participation in the political process that brought an end to the dictatorship.

This paradoxical stage is marked by the disenchantment produced by the emergence of a public space that responds only to the logic of political representation within the party system and by a growing relocation of politics within the market framework and communications media. This loses the richness of the social framework constructed in the antidictatorial period. Many of the problems mentioned by women remain absent from the national public debate and face a new and fragile state institutionality of women, which has not succeeded in using the state structures to communicate women's demands and interests.

In this framework, women who lead diverse organizations within civil society express their need to learn new skills. They specify the need to construct discourses, to articulate their problems through a gender focus, to elaborate and bring to the public sphere proposals for change, to generate mechanisms to move into decision-making positions, and to participate in the new local power structures. And, what is even more important, they need to recognize the diverse positionings and the social and political insertions of women in this new context.

Women's greater visibility in the work force and more slowly in the formal political sphere, as well as the appearance of the governmental SERNAM (Women's National Service), helped women's discussion of problems and issues to have a greater impact. There has been growing legitimacy and presence in the communications media. This greater social and political presence coexists with the cultural weight of a daily reality that has undergone few changes in women's condition and with continued restrictions in the public institutional sphere that impedes the production of transformations.

Women have reclaimed clear positions with respect to power and their sphere of political action, and this has had a direct impact on the construction of democracy. The presence and strengthening of conservatism during the transition period, with its attempts to maintain women's exclusion from different political spheres and from decision-making places and to reverse the gains that women have won and continue to win, stimulated collective questioning about the best strategies to use for these times as well as questions of issues of representation and discourse construction.

POLITICAL LEADERSHIP:
THE INDIVIDUAL AND COLLECTIVE SUBJECT

Leadership as a form of exercising power "is a process through which the individual exercises more influence than others in the development of group functions, an influence that is exercised consistently and systematically and thus has predictable results."[3] An attempt to conceptually delimit leadership based on the study of several authors[4] shows that diversity is more common than a single and integrated image of leader. There are different images of leadership, some of them contradictory, which makes it difficult to synthesize all of them. One group of definitions defines leadership through the exceptions, the myths, the charisma, and the innate conditions of some subjects to exercise power, which assumes parameters of abnormality and looks at history as the terrain of great men who led with positive or negative historic legacy. Another group builds from a social and cultural vision that demonstrates collective creation, with people who share similar characteristics and who depend on each other and are obligated to confront together their needs, possible changes, and daily challenges. Leadership is always associated with collective references: It is a process that not only affects individuals in a determined moment, but which affects a relatively broad number of people and for a relatively long time period, depending on the historical situation in which they find themselves.

A perspective that contemplates psychological and structural aspects would allow an understanding of: (a) the political leadership related to the global social and cultural parameters of the context; (b the direct relation to the needs, expectations, and values of those legitimating the action; (c) reference to qualities, characteristics, and influences of individual development, which makes possible and potent the leadership of some and not of others; and (d) the phenomenon we face that is being transformed according to historical events and that does not allow for generalizations.

Leadership is in itself a concept that is made up of various concepts that are not possible to analyze separately, because they are linked together and it is in that relationship between the components that they become clear. A general leadership definition is that in which both leaders and followers interpret the context in which they should be acting and defining the goals and ways to implement the desired changes,[5] which immediately defines three central, interrelated components to permit the existence of the democratic leadership phenomenon: the leader, the followers or collaborators, and the historic context.

The conceptual framework of political leadership allows us to clarify the difference between leader and expert—an expert refers to the accumulation of technical knowledge that can permit leaders to move into specific professional fields, thus differentiating it from political leadership. The leader goes beyond the formal post, finds potential to articulate concerns with other issues beyond those defined by the organization, has the ability to convoke greater public impact, and plays an active role in planning change strategies, building on dissatisfaction and channeling it through collective action.

In democratic leadership, the leader as collaborator both interprets the context in which to act and defines the goals to be reached in order to make the desired changes. Summarizing the comments of Hannah Arendt,[6] a democratic leader can be associated with those who oppose forced collective action and the power of violence, understanding power as the potential to act together, and the unity between words and acts. Arendt emphasizes the plurality that should exist in the collective, which implies the existence of two elements: equality and distinction. Equality is sustained by communication and the ability to agree to collective action, while each individual's distinction appears in the collective and confirms itself through the discourse and actions.

Another central aspect in leadership is the communication process. The leader interprets, announces, and anticipates the needs, expectations, and desires of others, through diverse communication strategies. Leaders use particular communication codes that build the diversity of discourses, sustained in power relations, woven by negotiations throughout the diverse public spaces that produce distinct models of discourse. The uniformity of the masculine leadership model creates tensions, leading to transformations in the field of political and cultural disputes.

LEADERSHIP TRAINING:
METHODOLOGICAL TRANSGRESSIONS

In the experience of leadership formation, our work team had to choose methodological options that transgress common methodologies. The first transgression occurred by choosing to have leadership formation experiences be different from participation formation. Within the framework of popular education, participation training has traditionally been implemented in educational settings linked to class, age, productive sectors, party affiliations, or territorial location. All of this responds to a pedagogical relation that is not exempt from a power and class differentiation between educator and students and that is a form of traditional response, whether in the formal educational system, or in youth and adult education in work training, professionalization, and regular studies. This traditional educational situation does not allow the interchange of experiences between individuals who come from different sectors.

The intentional transgression of choosing leadership formation produces spaces where different women meet, which becomes a crucial element in program development and which creates a space for reflection with women from different social spheres, diverse socioeconomic strata, educational levels, and political positions.[7] From those spaces, it is possible to inquire into the meeting places and the differences, the concerns, and the needs of different women, and the experiences of each one becomes a support and a lesson for all, in addition to recognizing differences between women. In order to stimulate and privilege diversity of women's leadership, the goal is set of questioning uniformity of discourse, questioning the legitimized social and cultural models, and promoting the construction of unique styles, with the challenge of presenting this uniqueness in public.

A second transgression is the definition of methodological lines articulated around the political will to promote changes in Chilean social, cultural, and political institutions that produce and maintain gender inequities—which signifies incorporating into the thematic network of courses, workshops, and meetings a perspective of cultural deconstruction and reconstruction. This option translates into:

- Broadening the notion of what is political, to translate into rights those issues which are currently linked exclusively to women and relegated to the "private" sphere, and incorporate them into the articulations of different public spheres.
- Promoting the construction of political support networks between women, in order to relate learned issues with their organizational practices, with their coordinations and with eventual alliances between women.
- Building the potential of leaders in order to broaden the available models in our culture, which implies breaking out of identicality,[8]

differentiating and singling out women leaders with unique discourses, styles, and projects.

- Stimulating the integration of multiple definitions of their leadership, in the sense of understanding the diversity and complexity of identities that make them up: that of being women, residents, workers, citizens, natives, mothers, militants, daughters, wives, lovers, consumers, patients, and so on.

The methodological strategies privilege the workshop dynamics, that is, collective reflection to examine and look for responses through one's own history, by finding, recognizing, and separating oneself from others, on the path to seek and find new knowledge. The general criteria in the definition of these methodological strategies begin from looking at issues that should be analyzed in the complexity of their relations and referred to the thematic body that gives them particular meaning. Broad issues of gender, power, rights, conflict, and visibility cut across all proposals.

The working team should be part of a common search with the participants. They foster free associations in issues as a way to construct new meanings. They rescue knowledge that emerges from women's unconscious social practices, building from the assumption that the knots they express are an epistemological thread that can be developed in common.

The educational and research project is sustained by the educators,[9] as an attempt to critically and creatively synthesize issues like sexual identity, power relations in the family and the labor market, the biases in social policies, and the obstacles to the exercise of citizens' rights— issues that include the exercise of power, the notion of rights, the social construction of gender—with the final objective of allowing women leaders to exercise their leadership, to move forward incorporating concrete tools profoundly linked with content, like planning, oral presentations, conflict confrontation and resolution, and so on.

THE DESIRED TRANSFORMATIONS

The processes and skills we are trying to promote are related to the type of experience that we have wanted to create in the program, involving participants' cognitive and affective aspects.[10]

The development of individuation[11] and differentiation skills is a sort of vector of the process that seeks to link the educational program that contains continuous segments that we can translate into the development of the following skills:

Individuation skills: understood as the ability to have a singularized self-perception, with an individual project, with the ability to distinguish from the collective needs or social instances that contribute to identity formation.

- *Propositive ability:* understood as the ability to announce needs and to provoke collective identities; interpret others; evaluate and diagnose situations creatively; name conflicts, demands, and solutions; intercede appropriately; and incorporating in all analysis a critical gender vision.

- *Visibility:* the ability to develop in every leader the breaking with identicality[12] to distinguish oneself and set oneself apart from a position of equality in public spaces. This is translated into the ability to historify positions, to self-administrate in different areas, to place oneself satisfactorily with different public representations in such a way that the leadership has potential, breadth, and negotiating force.

- *Recognition of power in others and in oneself:* understood as the leader's understanding and management of her own ambition and that of others. It assumes the exercise of social and public recognition of other leaders, relating to them, naming them as equal, especially other women, to build parity among women. It assumes the ethical confrontation of different exercises of power and ambition of others as a necessary element of democracy.

- *The ability to address conflicts:* understood as the ability to recognize diverse interests based on the acceptance of otherness, overcoming the difficulty of recognizing one's own desires and confronting the diversity of positions at play in the origin of conflicts. And, therefore, it implies the development of negotiating abilities as well as the ability to resolve conflicts.

In our intention to strengthen women's leadership and to legitimize their desires and practices of power, the distinction between leadership and management is essential, because leadership is what defines the trajectory that we want women to move through in this formative process. We want to move beyond the limits of formal posts, develop abilities to articulate issues beyond their own—beyond local concerns and to articulate global concerns—to take on the challenge of greater summons, in terms of impact and the building of collective identities. We also want to question the organic frameworks in order to broaden them as contexts change, like the possibility of transgressing to transform and create new orders.

TRANSFORMATIONS, TRANSITS, OR POSSIBLE CHANGES

A study was done to evaluate this educational process,[13] which defined the points to be evaluated that, in our view, make possible the development of individuation by women, both assuming it and facilitating it. These points, which should be understood as a continuum in the process of deconstruction and reconstruction of women's perceptions with respect to their vital experiences, are those that go from uniformity to diversity, from "pre-civicism"[14] to citizenship, from invisibility to a propositive presence, and finally, from self-censure to the confrontation of conflicts.

From Uniformity to Diversity

From *power is a scab that I scratch* to *I didn't want to be left behind.*

To the degree to which women perceive power in a monolithic and uniform way, they have a greater sensation of their impotence to act and less of a possibility to develop their leadership. With respect to these monolithic visions of power, it could be affirmed that, to the extent to which the participants ponder and visualize the diverse powers, their sense of impotence is replaced by the analysis of different mechanisms that obstruct the exercise of their leadership. This analysis, however, is circumscribed within their most immediate spheres of participation, without looking at the macro-powers present in society, which leads to an incidence of their specific and isolated participation.

On the other hand, the essentialist perception and dichotomy of the relations between men and women with respect to power increases the impotence to establish strategies in relation to the distinct areas of power and to develop their leadership. This process of change is not linear, but is subject to tensions, to the mixture of discourses with articulations of gender and essentialist perceptions. One of the great challenges in the development of women's leadership is the development of the ability to establish personal power strategies based on articulations of gender that grow out of practice.

From Being Pre-Civic to Being Citizens[15]

From *I was outside of the community* to *to not to participate politically is not to express your opinion.*

If women value themselves as the subjects of rights, then they legitimize their political action and take on public spaces. If, however, they perceive of public places as far away from their personal and collective action, this reinforces their sensation of omission and exclusion. We conclude that even when public spaces are no longer perceived as radically distant, there is a prevalence of the sensation of a distance associated with a model of hierarchical institutionality that excludes social participation. Faced with this vertical logic, participants may participate, but only partially and without projecting ways of negotiating their integration.

It is worth noting the fact that women still continue to criticize and question, in their great majority, without a connection with national issues that would allow them to alter the path taken for public discussion, opening it up to incorporate problems and difficulties unique to women and marginalized groups. The construction of a discourse that competes with and places itself against the institutional discourses continues to be a pending challenge. Even more, the confusion of what corresponds to institutionality and to the role that civil society should play in the face of this is symptomatic of a lack of autonomy and citizen awareness. This is manifested even when women leaders continue or increase their participation in networks, which would be illustrating a political ability to work together and a way of reinforcing the collective intentions to exert pressure and citizen control.

The expression of women's desires (of recognition, of participation, of representation, etc.) is an advance to the degree that it implies greater self-valuation that points to the legitimacy of their interests and their space, which they defend, and thus a decrease in the obstacles to full citizen participation.

The Step from Invisibility
to a Presence with Proposals

From *we don't have any images with power* to *I don't like being behind anymore.*

The rupture with identity[16] increases the possibility of distinction and of setting oneself up from the position of equality in public spaces. It is in the public sphere where substantive changes can be noted in participants, and they succeed in positively visualizing other women in public spaces. Those who find themselves organized introduce a positive perception of other women in positions of power. They also evaluate the real influence of these women and recognize and name them.

The practice of identity makes it difficult to stand out as an individual, it provokes rivalries between women, and it only allows the validation of public visibility in massive form. Breaking with "protected" visibility and exposing oneself not only to the public view but also to the concrete tensions and contradictions means distinguishing oneself, separating oneself from identicity. This process also generates a change in negative judgments with respect to other women toward criticisms that emphasize the need for mutual support. It can be said that participants find themselves far from "the masses" with which they were confused, but they are still far from having the ability to establish networks of alliances with other women in conditions of individuation similar to their own. Linked to this point, and despite the advances that can be achieved (as noted earlier), subsist the expressions of rivalry between women, indicating that this problem continues to constitute one of the most persistent resistances to the development of power strategies among women.

It can be affirmed that to the degree to which women participate in relations that dispute power, rivalries will grow. The learning of competence, which allows one to imagine others as possible subjects of power, as peers with whom one can enter into disputes and negotiate, is only possible if the individuation process has advanced; to the degree to which it is incipient, women continue acting from rivalries.

Many leaders, when speaking of the explicit obstacles they face when accepting new positions or challenges when representing their organizations, manifest that it is women who express the strong opposition to naming women or delegating them to new positions of power. In the majority of cases, the rejection is manifested as: disqualification, lack of solidarity or loyalty, and many times a blind defense of men in the resolution of conflicts, without valuing the successes and skills of "the other person [woman] in question."

Women who have been part of this educational process move forward in the conscious expression of rivalry among women,[17] recognize their practices of disqualifying other women, especially those with whom they are disputing power, over things that they themselves have done or because of situations that they have been part of and in which they have felt impotent when they do not achieve their objectives. Loyalty and alliances between women is seen as a power strategy and as a possibility of overcoming conditions of inequality. However, it is also seen as an ideal to be reached in the degree to which women identify with each other, even if contradictorily, alienated and in a position of inferiority and inequality. Many recognize the need for the alliance, but they manifest that in their experience, "it has been through alliances with *powerful* men that women have gotten to new positions, candidacies and/or public recognition." There is still only a weak recognition that "women obtain social recognition in relation to men: fathers, partners, sons,"[18] and even less individual and collective reflection about the strength and political recognition of power among women.

From Self-Censure to Facing Conflicts

From *we don't want to create animosity* to *you can never please everyone.*

The difficulty in recognizing diverse interests, perhaps beginning with the difficulties in recognizing their own desires and interests, distances many leaders from the possibility of placing themselves within conflicts and constructing discourses and proposals from that position. Women, when they engage in conflict with others, inherently recognize their own desires and interests, develop strategies for confrontation, and resolve issues, in this way strengthening their leadership.

Leaders are very aware of women's difficulty in being labeled as "conflictive," attributing it to gender socialization, which in itself constitutes an advance in the recognition and questioning of gender attributes. Women recognize their own interests and defend them when necessary. This distances them from the role of conciliator in groups or mediators of conflicts, with the exception of members of women's organizations who link leadership to the notion of sacrifice. Thus, the demand for an altruistic feminine essence, fed by the maternal ideal, loses its strength, and issues of guilt feelings, which often predominate at the beginning of the process, are no longer present. This process is generally accompanied by a greater comprehension of the difficulties that women experience when facing conflicts. In conflicts with men there is an awareness that this is a transgression by women with respect to the place made for them in gender attributes.

This practice allows us to affirm that the act of putting oneself in power, of taking on the risks of public display, and of recognizing the conflictive field of leadership has positive effects on women leaders and on their social and political participation. Our curricular proposal and its evaluation we believe goes beyond educational processes and gender. Its applicability goes beyond the sense in which it was initially conceived, and despite its weaknesses, it can be a contribution to the education of young people and adults. In terms of developed educational models, it articulates dimensions that operate simultaneously, and shows what was defined as a process of individuation. Every training program that contributes to change in gender relations and to the strengthening of women's public participation should incorporate these methodological criteria and parameters in a transversal way to develop and elaborate the content of training programs and to evaluate their results.

NOTES

[1]The leadership formation team, which worked in the Women's Institute, included, from 1992 to 1997, Victoria Hurtado, psychologist; Guadalupe Santa Cruz, writer and adult educator; Alejandra Valdés, social planner and educator; and Lorena Nuñez, an anthropologist who participated between 1995 and 1996. The effort to build a collective work allowed the development of the methodological proposal and the experience that sustains the reflection developed in this chapter. The regular cycle of this methodological proposal is initiated with a Promotion Seminar, which sensitizes participants to issues of power, gender, and leadership and questions their assumptions, to deepen their understanding of leadership issues. These seminars consist of twelve hours over a two-day period, with an approximate participation of sixty women leaders of diverse organizations. After the Promotion Seminar, there is an intense workshop of twenty to twenty-four sessions one afternoon a week and every other Saturday. This workshop takes about two months, and has a maximum of thirty participating women. The experience accumulated by this team is inserted in an even larger program, which, in addition to a regular training cycle, includes other training activities for specific sectors of women who seek support to build leadership skills: nurses, fishing folk, workers from the National Association of Daycare Centers, temporary agricultural workers, social workers, and party leaders. About sixteen hundred women participated in this process during the team's work on this project.

[2]Elsa Chaney proposes decency as an ideal model of feminine conduct in Latin America. Decency should be linked to discretion, to a certain moral superiority and to service to others, attributes derived from maternity, a model that limits its public insertion. The author proposes that Latin American women would look to the "super-mothers" as a leadership model, the counterpart of masculinization. See Elsa Chaney, *Supermadre. La mujer dentro de la política en América Latina* (México: Fondo de Cultura Económica, 1992), p. 61.

[3]Jorge Sobral, "Conducta política individual," in Julio Seoane, Angel Rodríguez, et al. (eds.), *Psicología política* (Madrid: Ediciones Pirámide, 1988), p. 79.

[4]G. Hunt and L. Larson (eds.), *Crosscurrents in Leadership* (Carbondale: Southern Illinois University Press); Richard H. Hall, *Organizaciones: estructura y proceso* (México: Prentice Hall Hispanoamericana, 1983), pp. 155–158.

[5]B. Kellerman, *Leadership: Multidisciplinary Perspectives* (Englewood Cliffs, N.J.: Prentice-Hall, 1984).

[6]Hannah Arendt, *La condición humana* (Barcelona: Editorial Paidós, 1993), pp. 223–240.

[7]The participants have been leaders of social, party, union, cultural, feminist, ecological, territorial organizations, and so on.

Leadership Training

[8]We are referring to identicality as the indiscernability that women live in the private world, or world of identical. A place where they do not have to have their own seal, do not have to have a differential mark, susceptible to being judged. The difficulty of distinguishing women's competencies has its opposite in the public spaces, where competencies are measured and there is differentiation. See Celia Amorós, *Mujer, participación, cultura política y estado* (Buenos Aires: Editorial La Flor, 1990), pp. 9–10.

[9]Victoria Hurtado, Guadalupe Santa Cruz, and Alejandra Valdés, *Un indecente deseo/Escuela de formación de líderes. Metodología* (Santiago: Instituto de la Mujer, 1995).

[10]The thematic modules are: sexual identity, family and power relations, sexual division of work and jobs, civil society, and the state. See Hurtado et al., *op. cit.*, 1995, pp. 16–17.

[11]This notion of individuation has nothing to do with the mercantile concept of individualization; on the contrary, it signifies differentiation from others, mobilizations of one's own resources, construction of one's own profile at the margin of a single reason for social being, one's "ubi" as Amorós says.

[12]See Hurtado et al., *op. cit.*, 1995.

[13]Victoria Hurtado, Lorena Núñez, Guadalupe Santa Cruz, and Alejandra Valdés, *A contramano. Estudio evaluativo del impacto de la Escuela de líderes* (Santiago: Instituto de la Mujer, 1997).

[14]When speaking of pre-civic, it is an allusion to the lack of a notion of women's rights and the perception of social relations with guidelines previous to or independent of society's political organization. See Claudia Iriarte, *Mujer y legalidad en Chile. Una propuesta de cambio* (Santiago: Instituto de la Mujer, 1994).

[15]See Hurtado et al., *op. cit.*, 1995, p. 148; Hurtado et al, *op. cit.*, 1997, pp. 20–24.

[16]See Hurtado et al., *op. cit.*, 1997, p. 27

[17]See Hurtado et al., *op. cit.*, 1997, pp. 27–32.

[18]Marcela Lagarde, "Enemistad y sororidad: hacia una nueva cultura feminista," *Revista Memoria del CEMOS* (Septiembre–Octubre), vol. IV, 28, México (1989): 410–412.

REFERENCES

Arendt, Hannah. *La condición humana.* Barcelona: Ed. Paidós, 1993.

Amorós, Celia. *Mujer, participación, cultura política y estado.* Buenos Aires: Editorial La Flor, 1990.

Castells, M., R. Flecha, P. Freire, H. Giroux, D. Macedo, and P. Willis. *Nuevas perspectivas críticas en educación.* Barcelona: Paidós, 1994.

Coria, Clara. "Un paradigma de poder llamado femenino." *Revista Feminaria* año 2, no. 3 (Abril) Buenos Aires (1998).

Coria, Clara. *Los laberintos del éxito: Ilusiones, pasiones y fantasmas femeninos.* Buenos Aires: Editorial Paidós, 1992.

Chaney, Elsa. *Supermadre. La mujer dentro de la política en América Latina.* México: Fondo de Cultura Económica, 1992.

Derrida, Jacques. *Espectros de Marx.* Madrid: Ed. Trotta, 1995.

Foucault, Michel. *El discurso del poder.* México: Editorial Folios, 1983.

Fraisse, Genevieve. "La rupture revolutionnaire des femmes." In Dannielle Haase-Dubosc and Eliane Viennot (eds.), *Femmes e Pouvoirs sous l'Ancien Régime.* Paris: Rivages, 1991.

Freire, Paulo. *La educación como práctica de la libertad.* Montevideo: Tierra Nueva, 1967.

García Canclini, Nestor. *Consumidores y ciudadanos. Conflictos multiculturales de la globalización.* Madrid: Grijalbo, 1995.

Giroux, Henry. *Los profesores como intelectuales.* Ministerio de Educación y Ciencia. Barcelona: Paidós, 1990.

Hall, Richard H. *Organizaciones: Estructura y proceso.* México: Prentice-Hall Hispanoamericana, 1983.

Hunt, J.G., and L. Larson (eds.). *Crosscurrents in Leadership.* Carbondale: Southern Illinois University Press.

Hurtado, Victoria, Guadalupe Santa Cruz, and Alejandra Valdés. *Un indecente deseo. Escuela de formación de líderes mujeres. Metodología.* Santiago: Instituto de la Mujer, 1995.

Hurtado, Victoria, Lorena Núñez, Guadalupe Santa Cruz, and Alejandra Valdés. *A Contramano. Estudio evaluativo del impacto de la Escuela de líderes.* Santiago: Instituto de la Mujer, 1997.

Kellerman, B. *Leadership: Multidisciplinary Perspectives.* Englewood Cliffs: Prentice-Hall, 1984.

Kirkwood, Julieta. *Ser política en Chile: Las feministas y los partidos políticos.* Santiago: FLACSO, 1986.

Iriarte, Claudia. *Mujer y legalidad en Chile. Una propuesta de cambio.* Santiago: Instituto de la Mujer, 1994.

Lagarde, Marcela. "Enemistad y sororidad: Hacia una nueva cultura feminista." *Revista Memoria del CEMOS* (Septiembre–Octubre) vol. 4, no. 28, México (1989): 410–412.

Marshall, T.H. *Enciclopedia de las Ciencias Sociales.* Madrid: Alianza Diccionarios, 1991.

Molina Petit, Cristina. *Dialéctica feminista de la ilustración.* Barcelona: Anthropos, 1994.

Nun, José. *La rebelión del coro.* Buenos Aires: Nueva Visión, 1989.

Sobral, Jorge. "Conducta política individual." In Julio Seoane and Angel Rodríguez y otros (eds.), *Psicología política.* Madrid: Ediciones Pirámide, 1988.

From the Local to the Global and the Global to the Local
Lessons for a Strategy of Gender and Education

MARÍA BONINO AND CELIA ECCHER

INTRODUCTION

As the largest network linking nongovernment organizations (NGOs) that work with poor women in Latin America, REPEM (*Red de Educación Popular entre Mujeres de América Latina y el Caribe*) has been a fundamental participant in the development of educational projects within these organizations. NGOs have generated new levels of knowledge and attitudes about these processes and changes that can be better understood by looking at the evaluation and classification processes currently engaging those organizations.

The gender equity focus has been introduced in many educational processes. In some cases, it is the major focus of the group educational process. Participants, by reviewing their daily life and history, confronting the lives of other women, and analyzing them through the framework of understanding personal experience through cultural and social processes, resignify and reconstruct their place in the world. In other cases, these self-understanding processes accompany other learning processes that can include production, health, and community issues. Frequently, the process encourages women to reconstruct an identity that increases self-esteem and personal security, and this is reflected in changes in attitudes that have consequences both in the private and public sphere in terms of quality of life. These changes, however, are not linear and are not without their tensions.

As Jeanine Anderson has noted in a recent work, inner conflict and negotiation, as well as conflicts between women and men, appear to be an essential characteristic of these processes.

> The negotiation model, together with the social theories developed by actors with their diverse interests and flexible and strategic practices that are not predetermined by a system of roles, obliges us to accept that definitive solutions to conflicts cannot be the objective of a development project. Rather, objectives must include building procedures that are fair for all participants, eliminating coercion, reinforcing personal resources of some of the weakest actors, learning negotiation skills, and increasing self-esteem that allows the weaker actors to negotiate better terms of exchange.[1]

Breaking down the educational process that generates these changes reveals the importance of access to an explicit and explanatory framework. This framework both contextualizes personal situations and experiences in cultural and historical terms, and also explains those situations, which were initially experienced as individual issues and "bad times," as collective and social problems. That is, it is necessary to access (and this is the role of educators) a framework that legitimizes the process through which personal problems are transformed into social necessities. Many times legitimacy grows out of the role assigned to the educator and her place in group reflection.

The process takes on yet a different perspective if, instead of thinking of situations of inequity as "needs" to be covered, they are looked at in terms of "rights" to be acquired. If the concept of "need" places people in a passive and in some cases dependent role, the concept of "rights" places them in a place of equality in society, where they take their place as citizens. Nancy Fraser discusses the difference between a discourse based on "needs" and one based on "rights" in this way:

> I align myself with those who prefer to translate justified demands of needs into social rights. Like many radical critics of existing social welfare programs, I am committed to opposing forms of paternalism that emerge when demands for needs are separated from demands for rights. Treating the demands for justified needs as the basis for new social rights begins to overcome obstacles to the effective exercise of some existing rights.[2]

The process of broadening the notion of "rights" has been a key to contributing to equity and democracy. It allows people to make demands based on their needs, on equal rather than inferior terms. For women, and especially for women from popular sectors because of the double discrimination they face, this process also implies substantial changes. The notion of having a "right" to equity, a "right" to a life free of violence, a life with "sexual and reproductive rights," if they are truly taken on as such, implies the incorporation of half the population into a fuller citizenship.

SOME IMPACTS OF THE GLOBALIZATION PROCESS IN EDUCATIONAL PRACTICES AND GENDER EQUITY

The framework of women's rights and the need for justice in social gender relations has been greatly reinforced by the conferences and social summits promoted by the United Nations during the past decade: Vienna, Cairo, Copenhagen, Beijing, and Hamburg. In the degree to which these conferences offer world recognition of a situation of inequality, they have served to "legitimize" the demands and needs put forward by women's movements. At the same time, this cycle of conferences has served to verify what is known as the globalization phenomenon. The world is now interconnected, countries join together to make decisions for everyone, and certain decisions seem to be concentrated in ever fewer hands. This chapter, however, does not attempt to analyze the multiple economic, political, social, and cultural consequences of globalization for people around the planet.

As Gita Sen proposes:

> The globalization process requires global responses. . . . Now feminist organizations, by participating in the organization of the world conferences . . . know that these negotiation tables are new and highly visible spaces to challenge states and private patriarchal forces. Globalization, for its part, opens spaces for more global commitments, generating new demands, without eliminating earlier, territorialized, forms of mobilization.[3]

The cycle of conferences appears then to be associated both with this phenomenon of globalization and with the broadening of concepts of rights and citizenship. In effect, through the United Nations convocation of civil society to participate in these conferences, a new social entity has been generated: interaction among states, civil society, and international organizations. For the first time, civil society, through nongovernment organizations, thematic networks, and global networks, participates not only by raising new voices and demands but also by calling governments to account for or exercise control over government actions to implement agreements.

This new social practice of global participation contributes to and reinforces the notion of "citizens' rights." In effect it appears that, in this case, a world-level women's movement, though incipient, is exercising the right to a voice, to demand accountability, and to evaluate or monitor what these summits conclude. On the other hand, this "exercise of rights" forces civil society organizations, until recently moving in ways isolated from governments or international organizations, to rethink their action strategy. The fundamental change appears to be in the possibility, which can now be glimpsed and before could not be conceived of, of influencing governmental and super-governmental decisions and of using a logic of pressure, negotiation, and clarification, rather than of confrontation.

But this new practice demands of nongovernmental organizations new knowledge and skills: greater information about the way international organizations work, greater proactive ability, and new negotiation and lobbying skills. In synthesis, the globalization process and the United Nations cycle of conferences have had numerous effects on nongovernmental organizations, which until now worked only with women's groups, and especially on those networks that bring them together. There has been significant influence in the following areas:

- An explicit and justified framework that establishes gender equity as a citizen right that directly affects the possibilities and abilities of women from popular sectors to act.
- A new social practice that places NGOs and networks as actors with the ability to propose, pressure, and negotiate with national and international organizations associated with the exercise of citizen rights.
- The need for these NGOs and networks to better define this new role in the global world they are entering.

In this process, there have been various types of learning: greater awareness of their rights, greater knowledge in terms of developing processes with other organizations of procedures for decision making and the implementation of actions, and greater negotiating capacity. This has been a process where REPEM has accumulated local practices and transferred them to the global arena and is now beginning the reverse process: devolve what has been learned, carrying the global achievements to the local sphere, to women's groups and organizations, and to civil society.

These processes are not without their tensions and difficulties; much had to be learned to transcend from the local and regional to the global, and much is now being learned to make the reverse journey. Because, as Anderson and Sen describe the great tension for nongovernmental organizations—and which REPEM is not immune to—there is a need for professionalization in order to act in the global scene, while there is also a need to maintain work with the women's movement and with women from the popular sectors who are the origin and the reason for existence of the NGOs.

Significant experiences that demonstrate this give-and-take process from the local to the global and the learning generated by that process are considered below.

TWO EXAMPLES OF THE DYNAMIC BETWEEN LEARNING AND PRACTICE AT LOCAL AND GLOBAL LEVELS

The Lobby Manual in Popular Economy and Gender

As noted at the beginning of this chapter, REPEM has been working with women from the popular sector for a long time. Within this work, since 1994 it has been carrying out a systematic reflection process in the Gender, Education and Popular Economy Program about issues of women's economic enterprises from a gender equity focus.

The experience accumulated over decades by more than eighty NGOs that work with women in income-generating projects in micro-enterprises—and developed through many meetings and internal memos—demonstrates that women recognize that they have, in many cases, won autonomy in decision making, in the reevaluation of their personal identity, and in their role in the family.

Women's experiences in these NGOs also helps them break out of their isolation and to value the skills they have learned that allow them to improve their quality of life and that of their children, one of their greatest concerns. Evidence would indicate that belonging to a group of peers as well as taking on new responsibilities in the public sphere are key actions that help to break the cycle of poverty, illiteracy, and dependence.

Within the multiple lessons learned about methodology, one that emerges as key is that these processes require, as one of their components for success, that women accompany their technical training with reflections that help them overcome obstacles associated with gender. Thus, NGOs emphasize the importance of this educational component to their financial supporters.

This proposal to reach greater understanding about practices, successes, and advances of women's organizations has been presented to the Interamerican Development Bank in diverse meetings and at the Beijing and Hamburg conferences with the resolutions that declare the need for specific women's projects with a gender equity and economic leadership focus.

Another important lesson is that a fundamental factor for success lies in the ability of groups to associate together, to articulate their ideas, and to negotiate with other groups and organizations, whether private or public. The lessons learned by REPEM are key in the process of participation in the global sphere: greater awareness of and exercise of citizen rights, and greater ability to articulate ideas and negotiate with different government and super-government actors.

After learning how to navigate participation in conferences and in negotiation with different organizations, REPEM's great challenge has been to translate those lessons to women from the popular sectors—that is, how to help women from the popular sectors appropriate the notion of "rights" and to negotiate from a position of strength as they exercise those rights by making demands and proposals for the accountability of public organizations. In synthesis, the consideration is how they move from invisibility to being protagonists in the economic and political spheres.

The response to this challenge was the development of a Lobby Manual for Popular Economy and Gender titled *Así se hace: Emprendimientos exitosos liderados por mujeres y manual de lobby propositivo.*[4] The *Así se Hace* manual brings together a series of simple instruments for women's groups and economic organizations to extract knowledge to help them reach higher levels both in economic progress and in personal development and leadership skills.

An important instrument was to look at three experiences from successful economic experiences: economic skills, members' personal development, and interaction with local or national actors. The Latin American Competition of Women-Led Productive Enterprises was promoted to this end. The Competition took place in Bolivia, Brazil, Colombia, Ecuador, Mexico, Peru, the Dominican Republic, and Uruguay.

REPEM members in these countries mobilized and coordinated efforts in different sectors: with other NGOs, local and national networks, local governments, business leaders, the academic establishment, and government institutions that support micro-enterprises. One hundred and fifty-seven production projects were presented, representing 6,995 rural and urban women.

Eight winners were chosen: five of them produce and market food products, two make and sell artisan products, and one had developed a trash collection project. In all of them, women experienced a relatively stable economic income, greater personal development in terms of self-esteem and self-perception, and a greater ability to generate equitable relationships at home and with others, and successful strategies to relate to diverse social actors.

These types of projects, which involve the most vulnerable sectors of society, do not tend to be visible in the political agenda of their respective countries, nor are they generally the object of analysis, reflection, or concern in theoretical circles or among policy organizations. Thus, the first positive result of this competition is that the projects have become more visible in their countries. The competition demanded that local and national actors become visible, and for the first time in many cases the press treated these women as actors, and both government and cooperating agencies began to recognize the women's development projects and their demands that their experiences continue. It meant, finally, the recognition of the need to join together to better accomplish goals. This is a lesson learned at all levels: by the women's groups, by the NGOs that support them, and by government actors.

By systematizing these experiences, the *Así se Hace* manual allows other women to learn about the achievements and difficulties faced by women's groups and, fundamentally, to identify the factors that promote achievement in implementation. The manual distributes the accords from the Beijing Conference that deal with poverty and the economy, allowing women from the popular sectors to see themselves represented in government resolutions. The information and reflection about these accords are a key factor in the rebuilding of an identity based on a new concept of women's personal and collective rights.

The *Así se Hace* manual also integrates information about multinational organizations like banks and cooperation agencies, the way they work, as well as examples of negotiation experiences that allow women to appropriate the tools and use them in their own contexts.

These processes of appropriation are not easy; for women from popular sectors, the development of their social skills and practices can end up becoming a third workday. These processes are also slow; they demand support from NGOs, and they are arduous and often tedious. But they also signify the possibility of transcending the personal and collective, conceiving of much more ambitious projects and a better quality of life in economic, cultural, and social terms. REPEM will try to stimulate these processes at the local level by appropriating the Beijing commitments so that women from the popular sectors can make them their own.

Participation in and Follow-up of the Fifth World Conference on Adult Education

REPEM's participation in the Hamburg conference demonstrates the civil society's possibilities of influencing government decisions at the global level. While some global networks from northern countries already had experience in this area, REPEM's experience in Hamburg was a new one for Latin American NGOs. REPEM's first participation in international conferences had been in the Copenhagen Summit and the Beijing conference. Hamburg, however, was a great challenge because its specific focus on adult education offered an ideal space for presenting the gender equity focus.

REPEM developed a key strategy of presenting current knowledge about women's rights in both formal and nonformal education, almost all of which had already been identified in the education section of the Beijing World Action Platform. As a regional network, the proposal to be taken to Hamburg was debated by the national networks, concluding with a final document titled "Gender and Education for Young People and Adults." Many countries were able to publicize and debate the contents of the document at the national level.

Two actions followed this first stage: lobby training workshops with the support of women experts from the Development Alternatives with Women for a New Era (DAWN) network, and the development of material that publicized the accords about gender and education from previous conferences as a way to prepare and legitimize the pre-Hamburg process. Active participation in the different regional pre-conferences and conferences later became crucial, both because of the learning that took place as documents were developed and because of the links made with other women's NGOs and networks. Within these, the pre-conference meeting organized by UNESCO in Chiang Mai, Thailand, was especially important because the women's NGO participants agreed on their slogan to take to Hamburg: "Learning with Gender Justice."

REPEM took charge of the "women's caucus" at the Hamburg conference. The women's caucus is a tradition at the conferences, a place to share information as well as to plan and evaluate the lobbying work. The DAWN and Women's Environment and Development Organization (WEDO) global networks also offered solidarity support. The proposals were reviewed in this caucus, and amendments that included women's demands and rights were proposed. The caucus also planned the meeting with government representatives so that the amendments would be addressed. Finally, the caucus won the right to have a women's representative on the commission to draw up the final document. The gender equity focus was incorporated throughout, and the document addresses women's issues in every chapter and every recommendation.

All of this process was carried out with limited economic resources and with limited previous knowledge about the necessary procedures to achieve the goals. However, the lessons learned covered many areas: the ability to work, solidarity among women and the strength of the movement, and the recognition of skills achieved in terms of procedures, negotiations, and the ability to define issues. The work was broadly recognized by governments, by UNESCO (the conference organizer), by international cooperation agencies, and by many male ally participants. It is worth noting that the government delegations were only 25 percent women, while the nongovernmental delegations were 50 percent women.

REPEM, in addition to the lessons already mentioned, saw the possibility of linking itself with a world women's movement and saw that it is possible for local or national civil society organizations to influence at the global level, when the local organizations can articulate a common strategy. All of this effort, however, should be reflected in the implementation of agreements by national governments. And here begins the conference follow-up process that, as has been noted, is less "glamorous," drier, and longer than the preparations for the conference and the conference itself. REPEM has proposed a series of regional-level actions in response to this.

In the first place, it has proposed the publication of the conference accords as a didactic tool and its distribution among women's groups so that they can know about and appropriate them as their own. In the second place, it has proposed generating discussions and training in the countries about what it means to do follow-up, lobbying, and proposal-writing in relation to women's rights in education. In the third place, it has proposed a concrete monitoring tool that has already been implemented in five countries on the continent.

This tool identifies priorities for women within the accords, and transforms these into follow-up indicators in order to be able to observe and follow up on government actions in each country, and then compare the countries. This monitoring allows organizations in each country to question their governments about what they have and have not done, and to demand accountability, controlling what has happened, to propose, and to articulate, with the state, issues from the civil society position.

There are multiple challenges to the follow-up. Sónia Corrêa (1998) recently identified some of them in a REPEM organized seminar:

- Follow-up involves different state sectors, making it crucial to carry out sector analyses and an analysis of the specific dynamics for proposals to be integrated by sector.
- Since it is not possible to monitor all the accords, priorities must be identified.
- The characteristics of different actors must be identified, as well as the possibility of building alliances and identifying "openings" for lobbying efforts.

Monitoring the follow-up indicators for the accords also presents challenges:

- The construction of reasonably objective indicators for issues and variables that are not easily translatable into indicators, for example the "political will" indicators (a term taken from *Citizen Control*) that evaluate actions taken by different actors to fulfill the accords.
- Having sufficient and reliable information to evaluate the accord's fulfillment, and even more, gathering information that is often disperse.
- The indicator follow-up process should have a political evaluation of all the involved groups in terms of achieving the Index of Completed Commitments in gender and education from the Hamburg conference.

Despite these difficulties, this initial monitoring experience has already begun to give fruit; in many countries the mere seeking out of information has ended up being a lobbying tool. Many government organizations are being asked for information disaggregated by sex for the first time, and are being asked about their activities. Many government officials are learning, through these processes, about the Beijing and Hamburg conferences. Having a concrete instrument that indicates what has and has not been done in certain areas in contrast to what was promised opens the door to the exercising of their rights by groups and organizations that until now had not considered that possibility. The monitoring process also forces NGOs into a dialogue and involvement in government actions that allows them to both influence and to articulate their concerns and responses.

Through this experience, REPEM has also been dealing with the demands and rights of women in their local groups, national governments, and international organizations in order to contribute to channeling the demands, as well as supporting the women, and the tools that strengthen them and that give them power, voice, and efficacy.

CONCLUSIONS

REPEM has been learning lessons gradually because of the minimal efforts to systematize these experiences. Political activism is very time-consuming and rarely ends up producing historical reports that prioritize the most crucial points of daily lobbying and work. Within this context, the world conferences—which demand the development of documents for public presentation, the configuration of common objectives, and the identification of collective and efficient strategies—produce intense lessons that enable NGOs to create the inescapable links between the global and the local in the daily struggle.

NOTES

[1]Jeanine Anderson, Virtual REPEM Seminar, Internet, September 1998.

[2]Nancy Fraser, "La lucha por las necesidades: esbozo de una teoría crítica socialista-feminista de la cultura política del capitalismo tardío," *Debate Feminista, Del Cuerpo a las Necesidades* 2, 3 (1991): 3.

[3]Gita Sen, *Los Desafíos de la Globalización* (Montevideo: REPEM, 1998). (Originally presented as the lecture: *Globalization in the 21st Century: Challenges for Civil Society.* The UvA Development Lecture. Universiteit van Amsterdam, Amsterdam, June 20, 1997).

[4]REPEM, *Así se Hace: Emprendimientos exitosos liderados por mujeres y manual de lobby propositivo* (Montevideo: REPEM, 1999).

REFERENCES

Anderson, Jeanine. Virtual REPEM Seminar. Internet, September 1998.
Control ciudadano no. 1. Montevideo: Centro del Tercer Mundo, 1997.

Corrĕa, Sónia. *"Estrategias de seguimiento."* Talk presented at the Hamburg Follow-up Seminar, organized by REPEM, Santa Cruz de la Sierra, July 1998.

Fraser, Nancy. "La lucha por las necesidades: Esbozo de uan teoría crítica socialista-feminista de la cultura política del capitalismo tardío." *Debate Feminista. Del Cuerpo a las Necesidades* 2, 3 (1991): 3–40.

REPEM. *Así se Hace: Emprendimientos exitosos liderados por mujeres y manual de lobby propositivo.* Montevideo: REPEM, 1999.

Sen, Gita. *Los desafíos de la globalización.* Montevideo: REPEM, 1998. (Originally presented as the lecture: *Globalization in the 21st Century: Challenges for Civil Society.* (The UvA Development Lecture. Universiteit van Amsterdam, Amsterdam, June 20, 1997.)

PART III

International Development Agencies and Gender Equity in Education for Women and Girls in Latin America

Global Priorities and Local Predicaments in Education

REGINA CORTINA

This chapter explores contrasting perspectives that have emerged as education has moved to the top of the national agenda in developing countries and in the international dialogue and policy initiatives sponsored by donor countries and multilateral agencies providing financial assistance for development. Using the case of Latin American women and girls, I will examine the global imperative of education reform in light of local predicaments generated by national education and development policy.

From a global perspective, as donor countries and multilateral agencies focus on development in Latin America, education is seen primarily as a way of reducing poverty.[1] From a local or national perspective, education is also a way to use the cultural wealth of Latin America to strengthen the region's political and economic institutions. To build continuity, to incorporate the heterogeneous cultures of the continent into robust political and economic systems, education for all Latin Americans must become the most pressing goal for the new millennium.[2]

Whatever framework is used to analyze the problems, educating women and girls in the Third World has become an issue of growing visibility and importance. To gain historical perspective on the current situation, it is useful to contrast the present wave of international technical assistance with the first wave of reform during the 1950s and 1960s. During those years, aid for education and social development went from north to south in an effort to stimulate economic growth, the aim being to reduce the inequities between industrialized and underdeveloped countries. Both then and now, education has been at the center of foreign assistance initiatives. During the mid-century, however, most of the funding was directed

179

to higher education in Latin America, and this was mostly aid coming from the United States to a selected group of universities. The stated aims during those years were based on the assumption that investment in human capital would boost economic growth and national development. More specifically, the expansion of higher education was defined as building competence among the managers of development through the growth of the social sciences, thus cultivating the human resources needed for analyzing, planning, and managing the development process at the national level. Disparities in university training between the north and the south were seen as an explanation for unequal development.[3]

By the beginning of the 1970s, many of the educational programs embodying these aims were phased out because of strong criticism leveled at the imposition of Western values on the third world.[4] It had also become clear that such programs were not having the desired impact on the equity issue worldwide as the cleavage between the rich and the poor continued to grow. Nonetheless, programs of foreign assistance in the quarter century after World War II were successful at initiating a basic infrastructure of health and social services worldwide, which resulted, among other things, in rapid growth of the world population.[5]

The dramatic growth of the world population in the past twenty-five years, the decline in mortality rates, and increased life expectancy around the world have magnified the issues of poverty, sustainable development, degradation of the environment, and mounting evidence that social and economic inequalities continue to increase. In fact, 80 percent of the world population lives today in the third world.[6]

Since the 1970s, in response to these conditions, there has been a growing preoccupation among development and education specialists with issues of redistribution and the alleviation of poverty. The present wave of international assistance is occurring within a different economic context than that of the past. Today's context is one not of north-south relations but of economic globalization. The present wave has also attempted to take into account the fact that the expansion of education over the past few decades has not benefited the lowest income groups around the world. It is among the poor of the world that we see the largest expansion of the world population, as well as the most rapidly escalating demands for access to basic services along with a decreasing capacity to find productive employment in the local economies.

For the donor countries that constitute the main force in defining the economic global priorities, the renewed interest in educating the poor and in cultivating sustainable development can be explained by an overriding concern with political stability in the developing world. For without political stability, the present economic system and its increasing interdependence between all regions of the world would be jeopardized. Yet political stability is difficult to achieve when the fruits of globalization are not evenly distributed. Not only is a large proportion of the world's population living in poverty, but the wealthy are becoming wealthier at the local, national, and international levels.[7] Poverty in Latin America continues to afflict almost one-third of households. Although during the 1990s there was a small reduction in the number of people living in poverty—measured at the household level, poverty diminished from 41 percent to 36 percent between 1990 and 1997—inequality still increased overall during the same period. Since the median size of poor households was larger than for other income groups, the percentage of people living below the poverty line was 44 percent. Sixty-three percent of the population lived below the poverty line in rural areas and 37 percent in the urban areas. Five countries in Latin America consistently show high levels of poverty: Bolivia, Guatemala, Ecuador, Nicaragua, and Honduras.[8]

Since population growth is intimately tied to poverty, a key global priority for alleviating poverty has become the reduction of fertility rates among women belonging to the lowest income groups around the world. During the 1990s, all countries in Latin America continued to show a high percentage of teenage pregnancies. Thirty percent of women in rural areas had their first child before they were twenty years old.[9] A well-supported finding of research across cultures and nations is that additional years of schooling tend to decrease the fertility rate for women. Thus, the current focus is on the education of girls, as seen in the priorities set by international agencies such as UNESCO, the World Bank, USAID, and UNICEF, among others, and by programs of bilateral assistance sponsored by the United States.[10] Targeting the educational needs of girls, UNICEF argues that it is addressing one of the most disadvantaged groups in the third world, and that providing education for girls will help to create an advocacy group in the community to support the goals of educational improvement generally.[11] In contrast, however, when we look at the priorities set by many national ministries of education, the education of women and girls is just beginning to emerge in public discussions about how to reform education in the region.

The current global priority for education in national development took shape in a series of meetings sponsored by international organizations under the auspices of the United Nations during the 1990s, including UNICEF, UNESCO, and UNDP in cooperation with the World Bank and OECD. First was the World Conference on Education for All, in Jomtien, Thailand, followed by the World Summit for Children, in New York, both in 1990. At mid-decade, two other influential conferences took place, the World Summit for Social Development, in Copenhagen, and the Fourth Conference on Women, in Beijing. Based on agreements emerging from those meetings, we can summarize the global priority for education as follows: to provide basic education to all children and to eliminate gender disparities in basic and secondary education. Broad agreement on this priority was reached with the active participation of representatives from developing countries, including those from different sectors of those countries, such as the women's and feminist organizations from various Latin American countries that were present at the international women's conference in Beijing. For each particular country, national and local cultures, established social and political institutions, as well as the organizational and mobilization capacity of women's and feminist movements have tried to influence subsequent attempts to implement such global agreements.

All these discussions and consensus-building efforts come into clear focus when seen against the background of prevailing conditions of education in the region. In Latin America over the past few decades, the access of women to schooling has improved significantly, but during the years of rapid school expansion in the twentieth century little consideration was given to issues that concern us today: the extent to which school experiences are gendered, the differences in outcomes achieved in school by girls and boys, and the representation of gender roles for girls and boys in the curriculum and textbooks. Such issues are of concern today because we know that the early experiences, outcomes, and ways of representing girls and boys in school have a profound impact on the formation of femininity and masculinity notions.

Latin America has a low rate of primary school completion, showing rates of attrition that would be considered unacceptable not only in wealthier nations but in nearly all of the developing world. Only three countries in the region—Argentina, Chile, and Uruguay—are providing education beyond elementary school to more than 70 percent of the eligible population. That figure is particularly significant because middle-school completion is closely connected to the alleviation of poverty and to increasing levels of equity in social and economic development.[12]

For many years, the education research community has questioned the educational statistics for Latin America produced by UNESCO based on school surveys, which claim that there is universal access to schooling in Latin America. During the World Summit for Children in New York and in several follow-up meetings, the representatives of Latin American governments set regional standards and agreed on a common set of indicators to measure access to and completion of schooling. Rather than using the traditional school surveys, the new reported statistics are based on household surveys that provide a more accurate picture of schooling in the population. Based on these new tabulations published by CEPAL (Economic Commission for Latin America), we can confirm that there is a vast difference between the educational opportunities for students in urban schools as opposed to those in rural public schools across the region. For the majority of the population who participate in public education, a number of children do not enter school, a great many more never complete elementary education, and discrepancies in educational outcomes persist between boys and girls.[13]

In Latin America and the Caribbean, approximately 18 percent of the children of primary school age do not attend school, as compared to approximately 1 percent of primary school age children in the developed world.[14] The percentage of out-of-school children of primary school age in Latin America and the Caribbean is significantly higher for girls than for boys. In 1995, 91.9 percent of boys were enrolled in primary school, as compared to 85.7 percent of girls. Stated another way, only 8.1 percent of primary school age boys as opposed to 14.3 percent of primary school age girls were not enrolled in primary school, a gap of 6.2 percentage points.[15] Newly released statistics by CEPAL for selected Latin American countries on the completion rates for basic education—defined as six years of schooling—reveal the striking contrast in completion rates between urban and rural areas. Although the statistics show that during the 1990s, girls made significant improvements in their completion of basic education, in many cases achieving rates of completion significantly better than those of boys, they also make clear that for girls living in rural areas the rates of completion for basic education are well below the goal set by UNICEF for the year 2000. UNICEF stated that in both rural and urban areas, at least 70 percent of the children should be completing basic education by the year 2000.[16]

During the 1990s in Latin America, public dialogue about educational opportunities for women and girls received a substantial boost from the concerted efforts by international assistance programs, which helped to legitimize and clarify the goals for educating girls and boys in Latin America and the Caribbean. Despite such efforts to focus more intently on educational opportunities as a global and regional priority, it is important to bear in mind that income inequality and poverty influence education reform and magnify the local predicaments connected with economic and political development, since the poor have consistently lower rates of schooling. The larger the social and economic inequality within a country, the lower the rates of completion of the fourth grade for children, and girls are impacted most by these inequities.[17] Given the deep social and economic inequality that permeates countries in the region, discrepancies among boys and girls in the amount of schooling they receive can be explained by three main factors: family income, rural or urban residence, and racial or ethnic differences.[18]

In view of these factors, there are two lines of development along which education can have considerable impact on the alleviation of poverty. One is in the education of women and girls in indigenous or other rural communities, or who belong to an ethnic minority, since for them educational opportunities are most significantly lower than those of boys and men.[19] Even though we do not have a complete statistical pictures for these groups, it is among them that the greatest educational inequities related to gender remain. The other line along which education can have an impact on the alleviation of poverty is to increase the rates of middle school completion for girls.

LOCAL PREDICAMENTS: THE EDUCATION OF GIRLS

International organizations and programs of foreign assistance in leading industrialized nations have come to recognize that educating women has the potential to reduce poverty for both sexes, contributing to the overall productivity of society. Several of the assistance programs that have been sponsored in the past decade have focused on countries that have a high percentage of indigenous population, high fertility rates, and a young population, including Guatemala with a 60 percent indigenous population, Mexico with 30 percent, and Peru with 45 percent.[20] In all these countries, we see a significant difference between girls' and boys' rates of participation in school by ethnicity.

There is a link between the lack of education and family demand for domestic work. In half the countries of the region, the number of young men and females not in school and involved in domestic work is estimated by CEPAL at 15 percent to 25 percent in the urban areas and 25 percent to 50 percent in rural areas.[21] Furthermore, the involvement of children in domestic work is closely related to poverty. Research in nine countries in Latin America on the subsistence economy of impoverished families concluded that without the income of children aged thirteen to seventeen, the incidence of poverty in those countries would rise by 10 percent to 20 percent.[22] Child labor and education are directly linked, since poverty, which keeps children out of school, would rise without the supplementary income that children bring to the home, and under the duress of poverty, family survival takes precedence over children's education.[23] The challenge of increasing the educational opportunities of the poor is thus connected to economic development and its impact on the immediate choices available to families in poverty.

The inability to comprehend the choices and opportunities in poor families and communities stands in its own right as a major impediment to educational and economic progress. The assumptions of Oscar Lewis, the anthropologist writing in the 1950s about the poor in Latin America and focusing on the backwardness and cultural deficits of families in poverty, are very much present in the literature one encounters today. Lewis used the concept "the culture of poverty" when explaining the lack of social mobility, economic opportunities, and educational aspirations of the urban poor of Mexico City and Puerto Ricans in New York City. In his book about the urban poor in Mexico, *The Children of Sánchez*, Lewis described the main female character in the family story, Consuelo, as an illiterate woman.[24] Later scrutiny of the author's ethnographic notes found that this woman had provided him with a written autobiography of her life that he then used to describe her in the book. The most important fact, deleted from Lewis's account, was that his chief informant on the lives of the poor was educated and capable of writing. Jean Franco, in describing this finding, writes, "Of the four Sánchez children interviewed, Consuelo stands out as an anomaly, for although Lewis presented the material as if it all came from interviews (no doubt identifying orality with poverty), in fact Consuelo wrote down her own life history in a 170-page autobiography that forms part of the edited material of the finished book."[25]

The reason for poverty in this instance did not fit the conceptual framework developed by Lewis to explain the plight of the poor. In his conceptualization of poverty, education could not be present. Since Consuelo was still poor in spite of her education, it was necessary to erase the fact that she had been educated. It was necessary because he believed that schooling would transform all the constraining cultural beliefs that keep people poor. Yet, we know now that it is not only lack of schooling that keeps people poor. It must be acknowledged that poverty and its alleviation are complex issues that go well beyond the realm of education.

An assumption similar to that of Oscar Lewis's prevails today with regard to the perceived connection between educational opportunity and economic development. In current and recent projects of foreign assistance for education aimed at helping the poor in Latin America, essentially the same theoretical framework prevails, that of modernization theory, in which traditional culture and religious beliefs are used to explain economic isolation. Within this framework of analysis, lack of education is almost always relied upon as the explanation for the persistence of poverty.

What effect can education have on social and economic development within the present context of globalization? Today most indigenous and rural groups lack economic and social opportunity. In past decades, during the years of stable economic growth, learning Spanish in state-sponsored schools and forgetting the mother tongue had an economic rationale for people in local communities where Spanish was not the language of the home. Education and migration from rural to urban areas brought economic and social benefits, even though the dislocation brought a complete change of identity. As indigenous and rural people abandoned their villages, they accepted the new customs of town and cities and learned to speak Spanish. They stopped speaking their maternal tongue and also taught Spanish to their children. They were assimilated into the mestizo culture (or the *ladino* culture as it is called in the Central American and Chiapas region) that represents the majority in most countries in the region. Education during the 1960s and 1970s, in the decades of economic growth, provided social mobility and the creation of a small but expanding middle class.

Today, when migration to the cities only results in further poverty, the rural poor have two other choices: either migrate to the United States to do menial jobs, or recapture their ancestral culture and language, going back to their communities and reclaiming their Indian identity while working collectively to survive. Globalization of economies and the concomitant lack of economic opportunity for the poor are bringing back a resurgence of ethnic identity, rather than continued assimilation into the national cultures.[26] For girls whose lives are shaped by these trends, the imperative of family survival at the local level pushes the girls inexorably to do domestic work and denies them the opportunity to leave the household to attend schools. One additional compounding reason for the isolation of girls is that families are not willing to pay the private cost of schooling, including meals, uniforms, and textbooks. Since parents do not foresee productive employment for their daughters outside the home, there is no economic rationale for investing in their education. In Latin America, significant differences exist between urban and rural areas in the percentage of children between thirteen and fourteen years old who are working. In the rural areas during the 1990s, we see an increase in the percentage of children working. For example, in the case of Bolivia and Brazil, approximately 50 percent of this age group are working.[27] Work and especially participation in domestic work are undoubtedly affecting school completion, and the reasons are clearly related to family survival.

To further analyze the relationship between family survival and lack of participation in schooling, we turn now to the Mayan communities of Guatemala and southern Mexico. The choice of these communities is pertinent to the aim of this chapter, since international agencies, among them the World Bank, USAID, the *Agencia Española de Cooperación Internacional* (Spain's Agency for International Cooperation), Japan's Agency for International Cooperation, and NGOs funded by European countries are active in this area. These different agencies and countries have created programs during the 1990s for communities that have been described as among the most impoverished in the region, exploited by regional elites, and subsisting beyond the support provided by the Mexican and Guatemalan governments. The example of these communities will be used to illuminate the local predicament of education. Detailed studies of these groups tell a different tale than what is constructed by international organizations and development agencies. Undoubtedly, the Mayans have immense social and economic problems, but rather than assimilating as in years past, they are consciously rejecting incorporation into national political and economic structures as their strategy for survival. Not only is their number stable but the percentage of them speaking an Indian language has increased over in the past decade. The Mexican government attributes the conflict in Chiapas to the cultural backwardness of these indigenous communities, but it is through their strategy of not assimilating that these communities have been able to maintain their political autonomy. Moreover, there is considerable evidence showing the transformation of the culture in this area.[28]

The slogan developed by the USAID-funded program for educating Mayan girls in Guatemala is *Niña Educada: Madre del Desarrollo* (Educated Girl: Mother of Development). This slogan shows a lack of awareness on the part of planners and policy makers as to the conditions within the local community and an absence of understanding as to why, for indigenous groups today, it does not make sense to encourage their children to participate in state-sponsored schools.[29] Going to school is not connected with their strategy for survival. If investment in community economic development were taking place along with the effort to comprehend and constructively influence the sexual division of labor and gender roles in rural and indigenous communities, then perhaps the girls could indeed become the mothers of development. USAID represents one approach to educating girls in poor and rural communities, focusing on the schooling of girls without embedding the strategy in broader support for community development. The chapter in this section of the book by Stromquist and others presents an evaluation of the USAID project in Guatemala.[30]

Although multilateral agencies and bilateral cooperation have provided strategic assistance to Latin America to increase educational opportunity for the unschooled, during the 1990s there has been a departure from the earlier model of educational cooperation in the region. In previous decades, the aid came through the government from the multilateral agencies. Rosemberg in this volume describes the low-cost model of education expansion sponsored by multilateral agencies and its effect on the poor and blacks in Brazil.[31] Pursuing the low-cost model of educational expansion, a model in which cost-saving strategies do not stress the requirements for academic training of the teachers employed, many countries are following the recommendation of international organizations and expanding preschools in the region without the necessary investment in teacher training. This expansion is recommended as a solution for decreasing repetition rates at the first grade, since grade repetition is a wasteful educational practice that is affecting predominately poor children in the region. But the expansion of preschool education without necessary investments in teacher training can exacerbate the problem it is attempting to solve, as is evident in the case of Brazil, where the expansion of preschool education led to an increase in repetition rates among poor students mostly of African descent in the northeastern part of the country.[32]

The Colombia *Escuela Nueva* (New School) is another education model funded by international agencies to provide schooling to the poor and rural children in Latin America. In contrast to the low-cost approach model, the *Escuela Nueva* has emphasized, among other things, teacher training. The *Escuela Nueva* program, which originally started in Colombia in the 1960s, includes multigrade classrooms, automatic promotion from first grade, and the expansion of preschool programs. Evaluations have found that this program successfully helps to reduce the attrition rates and influence the achievement scores for both boys and girls in Latin American rural schools. One cautionary note, however, is that the model worked in its initial phase of implementation in Colombia because a significant investment was made in the training of teachers—many without formal training. The investment was calculated as three times more than in the regular schools.[33] Multigrade primary school models are being adopted in many other countries in Latin America under different names, from Venezuela and Chile to Nicaragua and Guatemala.

In the case of Guatemala, the *Nueva Escuela Unitaria* is a multigrade school in the rural areas. One of the central elements of success in the multigrade schools is the training of teachers, but in most countries in the region, teachers are being trained for conventional classroom work but not for multigrade teaching. The traditional role of teachers within the classroom emphasizes control through authority and transmission of knowledge. In the experience of the *Escuela Nueva* in Guatemala and Nicaragua, teachers from the community with no formal training have direct contact with the rural population and are more flexible in being able to teach in a multigrade classroom. The empowering of teachers as decision makers inside the schools and their level of training are central to the quality of multigrade classrooms. Within this context, gender-sensitive training for teachers has been initiated in pilot programs.[34] From the perspective of girls and how this more participatory program affects their chances for completing school, the evaluation of the pilot USAID project in Guatemala recommends further study of the gender of the teacher as an incentive for girls to stay in school but found that small scholarship programs were effective for reducing student attrition in the first three years of basic education.[35]

Indeed, among the programs that have been implemented to increase the rates of completion of basic education for girls in rural and poor communities, providing small scholarships for girls and their families has proven to be an effective approach in the case of Guatemala. This idea of scholarships directly to the family merits further study, since the school-family dynamic is crucial to keeping girls in school. The family shapes the social roles of girls, especially the participation of girls in domestic work, and the scholarship provides direct resources to the family and reduces the private cost of education. The free meals that have been furnished for many years in the schooling of the poor not only make resources available but also focus on the constraints faced by the poor within their local communities.

The uncertain impact of foreign assistance on educational change in the region is evident when one uses the lens of gender to interpret what has occurred. In some countries in Latin America, international cooperation has had a significant influence on the consolidation of the women's movement, but the overall impact that the women's movement has had on the strengthening of gender equity policies within formal systems of education is limited.[36] In some countries, the women's lobby has been effective, as shown by Colazo.[37] In other countries, such as Mexico, the debate about formal education is not a priority of NGOs connected to the women's movement. The work of NGOs offering services for women is concentrated on nonformal education such as reproductive health, family planning, violence against women, and human rights.[38]

Looking into the world of NGOs devoted to education, specifically for the schooling of girls and boys, we do not have systematic information on funding from foreign assistance for schooling, but we know that substantial funding is devoted to education of the poor. Much of that funding is coming from religious organizations and human rights and advocacy groups. The provision of schooling for children in poor communities by NGOs represents a change from the tradition of state-funded schools. It is funneling new resources and creating opportunities for completing basic education. Moreover, in these innovative forms of schooling, new curricula are being implemented, placing greater emphasis on the local community.

NGOs focusing on education bring to the local communities new resources beyond families and traditional community institutions, and they provide opportunities for education that complement the available state-sponsored schools. One successful example is a community center and school in San Andrés Cholula (Puebla, México), supported since the beginning of the 1990s by the government of Canada, among other private sources, and the income-generating activities of the community center. Today, this community center employs community women in the *maquila* (assembly plants) of towels and blue jeans for the international market. It also provides schooling for seven hundred children, has a day care center and a health center, and through its curriculum strives to create in the children a sense of community. Children and parents provide all the services that the school needs, from painting to daily cleaning, even participating in the construction of facilities. The success of this multipurpose institution owes much to international assistance, but its primary reason for success is the commitment of the rural community itself to providing educational opportunities for the girls and boys.[39]

The second international priority for poverty alleviation mentioned earlier in this chapter is the completion of middle school. The rate of completion of middle school is one of the most striking differences that exist today between Latin America and the developed countries. Research on the effects of education on economic opportunity in Latin America shows that for education to have an influence in the reduction of poverty and inequality, middle school needs to be completed. It is during the middle school years that students begin to realize the value of education for increasing their future opportunities based on the knowledge and skills they can acquire through further schooling. Unfortunately, middle school education is not a priority for agencies working on girls' education. They continue to place lower priority on this objective than on primary and higher education.

In terms of middle school, we have almost no research on how social and cultural dynamics influence the educational aspirations of girls, but the connection is clear: lower investment in middle schooling translates into greatly restricted opportunities, for all children but especially for girls. Investment in education is empty rhetoric unless there is a concerted effort to expand and strengthen middle schooling, which serves as the bridge to higher learning and the alleviation of intergenerational poverty.[40]

TOWARD GENDER EQUITY IN EDUCATION

Most countries in Latin America now have general policy statements about equal opportunities for women in education. Yet, to translate those policy pronouncements into concrete programs that might provide greater opportunities for girls is a task that remains to be done. At the public policy level, there is a need to frame goals and build national understanding of the importance of gender equity in education. To explore the link between policies and programs sponsored by international development agencies and government activities and their impact on equity issues in education, I will now present the most salient areas linking international priorities and government action.

Education Spending

Increasing education spending during the 1990s in most countries of Latin America has been directly related to the opportunities for the schooling of girls and boys. The increase in educational spending during the 1990s was devoted mostly to providing additional resources to Latin American educators, who suffered a devastating erosion in their salaries as a result of the wave of economic reform during the 1980s.[41] Alongside bolstering teacher salaries, attempts to provide equal educational opportunities for girls are intertwined with the need to improve the education that most children receive. In years past, the main concern was with children who had been excluded from basic education, especially in the more impoverished areas of the region. Today, we are concerned about equity issues, or differential access to learning opportunities and the quality of teaching that is offered.

The majority of students in Latin America now have access to low-quality schools. A recent report by the World Bank points out that educational quality, especially in the public schools of the region, is by all accounts extremely poor. The evidence available indicates that students in Latin America and the Caribbean perform significantly lower on standardized achievement tests than do students from other regions of the world.[42] In most countries of the region, the poor receive a starkly lower quality of education than people from more advantaged socioeconomic backgrounds within those countries. Studies conducted in selected countries in Latin America have found that results in achievement tests show a clear contrast between students in the lowest socioeconomic stratum who take standardized tests and those from the highest socioeconomic stratum that tend to score in the top quartile.[43]

Given the realities of education and economic inequality in Latin America, the challenge to provide a better learning situation for the poor is the framework within which we must situate the challenge to improve opportunities for girls and gender equity policies. Based on the experience of education projects funded through international cooperation, educational improvement is highly dependent on better training for teachers.[44] It is in this arena that educational spending can play a major role, since in most countries of the region, education professionals are paid less than other professionals with comparable years of training.[45] The economic incentives that teachers have to further their education and remain in the profession are extremely weak. Given these conditions, it is not surprising that in many countries and in predominantly poor and rural schools, there is increasingly a teaching force of women who in most cases have only a diploma equivalent to a high school education and who are teaching in preschool and elementary schools.

When recommending an action program for the education of girls, UNICEF stresses the complexities of change associated with the improvement of schools. One of the most difficult dilemmas to address is the tension between the need to build capacity, that is, to provide additional training for teachers, which is inherently a long-term process, and the need to improve the educational opportunities for the girls and women in a relatively short period of time.[46]

The most crucial area for implementing equity policies in education is teacher training. In Europe and the United States there are well-tested methodologies and procedures for training teachers in gender-sensitive issues. The research and training manual prepared by the *Instituto de la Mujer* based in Spain is being used in Latin America.[47] At the level of the national ministries of education in collaboration with local NGOs, readings and materials to sensitize teachers to gender dynamics within the classroom are starting to be distributed in some countries, such as Chile, Argentina, Paraguay, to teachers in the public schools. Evaluations of these manuals remain to be done, focusing especially on the teaching and learning taking place in Latin American schools. The collaboration of women's NGOs with national ministries of education in the preparation of manuals and courses for teachers is a contribution of international cooperation to furthering the understanding among teachers about gender and the school-and-family dynamics within the classroom.[48] Gender equity policies, like other compensatory policies in education, need additional resources, and national ministries of education are key players in channeling resources toward this goal. To strengthen gender training for teachers and gender equity policies, it is important to address them within the national goals for education in each country.

Public Policies

Projects sponsored by foreign governments and international organizations are short-term. They will not have a lasting effect on women's and girls' education unless national efforts complement the opportunities created by such projects. During the 1990s, countries in Latin America started organizing national policy initiatives to improve programs supporting the role of women in national development. All countries in the region have a national office created with the aim of coordinating public policies across sectors that might benefit women. In some cases, special programs were created to promote equity policies in education. Many other programs emphasize education as an important area of policy initiatives but do not discuss in detail what changes are needed in educational policy and how to implement gender equity policies.

For example, Mexico's document *Alianza la Igualdad* presents goals for the advancement of women as part of national policy in Mexico through the *Programa Nacional de la Mujer,* but only one section out-lines the need to focus on education. For the most part, this document reviews general issues such as the need to increase quality and access. Quality is described principally in terms of female representation within textbooks, literacy programs directed toward women, and improving health and child-care opportunities so that women can go to school. There is no mention of schooling or the fact that girls need to be educated from a young age, as the document directs its attention more to educating adult women.[49] Effective coordination of policies toward women and girls needs to be developed within the context of equal opportunity in education.

The education of the poor and the improvement of opportunities for women and girls have been identified as an international priority. The international agreements of the past decade are broader than the changes that have taken place in the region for the completion of basic education and middle-school education for girls. Programs of foreign assistance during the 1990s promoted different strategies and supported diverse projects with the hope of changing the realities of education in the region: from the low-cost preschool models of education promoted by multilateral agencies, to strengthening voices within civil society in order to lobby for gender equity policies in education promoted by Euro-pean NGOs, to the incorporation of the private sector and community initiatives promoted by the USAID in the Guatemala project, to creating new frameworks for action in women's and girls' education promoted by UNESCO in Latin America. These are all examples of the many ways through which the foreign assistance programs are providing technical assistance and resources to address the educational needs for women and girls in Latin American. As this chapter has argued, they must do so in the context of local predicaments rooted in social and economic inequal-ity, which shapes the educational opportunities throughout the region.

In this chapter, I have summarized the predicaments that countries in Latin America face within the global priorities for education reform. It is clear that the support for girls' schooling needs to be complemented with broader support for economic development, since the lack of economic opportunity the families face at the community level discourages girls and their families to further their education. Moreover, as long as inter-national agencies furnish mainly project-level support for NGOs, mak-ing only a short-tem investment without providing help for sustained capacity building, the local predicament is that without serious invest-ment by the state in teacher training, the learning that has been achieved through such projects will not ensure lasting influence in the educational systems of the region. Finally, the projects being funded are capable of improving the completion rate in primary schools without promoting the expansion and completion of middle school opportunities. The overriding local predicament is that given the social and economic inequality that exists today in Latin America, for most Latin Americans the alleviation of intergenerational poverty is not a reality in the foreseeable future.

NOTES

[1]Development Assistance Committee, *Shaping the 21st Century: The Contribution of Development Co-operation* (Paris: OECD, 1996).

[2]For an eloquent discussion of this priority, see Carlos Fuentes, "Prólogo," in *Educación la agenda del siglo XXI: Hacia un desarrollo humano* (Programa de Naciones Unidas para el Desarrollo, 1998), pp. xvii–xxi.

[3]Daniel C. Levy, *To Export Progress in the Americas: U.S. Golden Age Assistance to Latin American Universities,* book manuscript in progress.

[4]Robert Arnove, *Philanthropy and Cultural Imperialism* (Boston: G.K. Hall, 1998).

[5]Francis X. Sutton (ed.), *A World to Make: Development in Perspective* (New Brunswick, N.J.. Transaction Publishers, 1990).

[6]Development Assistance Committee, *Shaping the 21st Century: The Contribution of Development Co-operation* (Paris: OECD, 1996).

[7]The topic of globalization and political stability in world development appears in most policy initiatives of the European Union. In a roundtable on foreign policy in the European Union focusing on relations between the European Union and Latin America, Pierre Schori, Minister for International Cooperation of Sweden, stressed this point by quoting J. Wolfensohn, president of the World Bank: "If we do not have greater equity and social justice, there will be no political stability. And without political stability, no amount of money put together in financial packages will give us financial stability." Barcelona, November 26–27, 1998. <www.ud.se>; printed May 5, 1999.

[8]Comisión Económica para América Latina y el Caribe (CEPAL), *Panorama social de América Latina 1998* (Santiago de Chile: CEPAL, 1999), pp. 17, 35, and 40.

[9]CEPAL, *Panorama social 1998,* p. 30.

[10]UNESCO, The Education of Girls and Women: Towards a Global Framework for Action (Paris, UNESCO, 1995).

[11]UNICEF, Girls' Education: A Framework for Action, Program Division, New York, January 1997.

[12]CEPAL, "Rol estratégico de la educación media para el bienestar y la equidad," 23 de Abril de 1996.

[13]CEPAL, *Panorama social 1998,* Table V. 11, p. 184.

[14]UNICEF, The State of the World's Children 1997 (New York: UNICEF, 1997), p. 52.

[15]UNESCO, Mid-Decade Meeting of the International Consultative Forum on Education for ALL, June 1996, Amman, Jordan. Table entitled "A Statistical Picture: Improvements since Jomtien."

[16]With the purpose of implementing the recommendations of the World Summit for Children, in New York, 1990, UNICEF established the goal for the year 2000. For an evaluation of the achievement in Latin America, see Evaluación del cumplimineto de las metas en favor de la infancia fijadas para el año 2,000 en los compromisos de Nariño y Santiago, *Panorama social 1998,* pp. 152–169.

[17]CEPAL, *Panorama social 1998,* p. 29.

[18]*Educación la agenda del siglo XXI* (Programa de Naciones Unidas para el Desarrollo, 1998), pp. 63–66.

[19]Ibid.

[20]World Fact Book, <www.odci.gov/>, 1998, May 26, 1999.

[21]CEPAL, *Panorama social 1998,* p. 30.

[22]CEPAL, *Panorama social 1995,* <http://www.eclac.cl/espanol/Publicaciones/ps95/ps2b3.html>.

[23]UNICEF, *Education and Child Labour* (background paper), n.d.

[24]Oscar Lewis, *The Children of Sánchez: Autobiography of a Mexican Family* (New York: Vintage Books, 1963).

[25]Jean Franco, *Plotting Women: Gender and Representation in Mexico* (New York: Columbia University Press, 1989), p. 163.

[26]For ethnic and cultural revival in Guatemala, see Kay B. Warren, *Indigenous Movements and Their Critics: Pan-Mayan Activism in Guatemala* (Princeton: Princeton University Press, 1998); in the case of Mexico, Juan Pedro Viqueira, "Los peligros del Chiapas imaginario," *Letras Libres* 1 (Enero de 1999): 20–28.

[27]CEPAL, *Panorama social 1998,* Table V. 16, p. 197.

[28]Juan Pedro Viqueira, "Separate Identities or Collective Identities? The Relationship between Indigenous People and Ladinos in Chiapas," El Colegio de México, unpublished manuscript.

[29]Slogan of campaign of the USAID Girl's Education Project in Guatemala.

[30]Stromquist *et al.,* in this volume.

[31]Rosemberg, in this volume.

[32]Rosemberg, *op. cit;* and Fúlvia Rosemberg, Educaçâo, gênero e raça. Paper presented at the XX International Congress of the Latin American Studies Association, Guadalajara, México, April 17–19, 1997.

[33]George Psacharopoulos, Carlos Rojas, Eduardo Veléz, "Achievement Evaluation of Colombia's *Escuela Nueva*: Is Multigrade the Answer?" *Comparative Education Review* 37, 3 (1993): 263–276; Patrick J. McEwan, "The Effectiveness of Multigrade Schools in Colombia," *International Journal of Educational Development* 18, 6 (1998): 435–452.

[34]Oscar Mogallón, presentation in panel "New Knowledge: Studies in Girl's Education," at the conference, "Educating Girls: A Development Imperative," May 6, 7, and 8, 1998, International Trade Center, Washington, D.C.

[35]Ray Chesterfield and Fernado E. Rubio, "Incentives for the Participation of Guatemalan Indigenous Girls in Primary Education: Final Evaluation of the *Eduque a la Niña* Pilot Project, Guatemala, February 1997.

[36]María Luisa Tarrés, "Las Organizaciones del movimiento de mujeres en la reforma politica," in Alberto Olvera (ed.), *La sociedad civil: De la teoria a la realidad* (El Colegio de México, 1999); in the case of Peru, describing the connection of NGOs to the women's movement, Virginia Vargas, "Las actuales vertientes del movimiento de mujeres," in Patricia Ruiz Bravo (ed.), *Detras de la Puerta: Hombres y mujeres en el Peru de hoy* (Lima: Pontificia Universidad Católica del Perú, 1996).

[37]Carmen Colazo, in this volume.

[38]María Luisa Tarrés, *op. cit.*

[39]Interviews at educational center by the author, March 1999.

[40]Naciones Unidas. Comisión Económica Latina América y el Caribe. Rol estratégico de la educación media para el bienestar y la equidad. LC/G.1919. Santiago de Chile: CEPAL, 1996.

[41]International Labour Organization, *Impact of Structural Adjustment on the Employment and Training of Teachers* (Geneva. ILO, 1996).

[42]Shadid Javed Burki and Guillermo E. Perry, *The Long March: A Reform Agenda for Latin America and the Caribbean in the Next Decade* (Washington, D.C.: World Bank, 1997), p. 98.

[43]United Nations, *The Equity Gap: Latin America and the Caribbean and the Social Summit* (Santiago: ECLAC-CEPAL, 1997), pp. V-112–V-113.

[44]Rosemberg, *op. cit.*; Laura Randall and Joan B. Anderson, *Schooling for Success: Preventing Repetition and Dropout in Latin American Primary Schools* (Armonk, N.Y.: M.E. Sharpe, 1999).

[45]CEPAL, *Panorama social 1998,* p. 29.

[46]UNICEF, Girl's Education: A Framework for Action, New York, January 1997.

[47]Marina Subirats and Cristina Brullet, *Rosa y Azul: La transmisión de los géneros en la escuela mixta* (Madrid: Instituto de la Mujer, 1992); Marina Subirats and Amparo Tomé, *Pautas de observación del sexismo en el ámbito educativo* (Barcelona: Instituto de Ciencias de la Educación, 1992); and Eulalia Lledó, *El sexismo y el androcentrismo en la lengua. Análisis y propuestas de cambio* (Barcelona: Instituto de Ciencias de la Educación, 1992).

[48]*Mujeres y hombres en la escuela y la familia: Estereotipos y perspectivas de género* (México: Secretaría de Educación Pública, Comisión del libro de texto gratuito, 1999). A collection of short readings for teachers on gender issues resulted from a collaboration between a Spanish NGO and a Mexican NGO.

[49]*Alianza para la Igualdad,* Programa Nacional de la Mujer, 1995–2000 (México: Diario Oficial, Agosto 21 de 1996).

REFERENCES

Alianza para la Igualdad. *Programa Nacional de la Mujer, 1995–2000.* México: Diario Oficial, Agosto 21 de 1996.

Arnove, Robert. *Philanthropy and Cultural Imperialism.* Boston: G.K. Hall, 1998.

Burki, Shadid Javed and Guillermo E. Perry. *The Long March: A Reform Agenda for Latin America and the Caribbean in the Next Decade.* Washington, D.C.: World Bank, 1997.

CEPAL. "Rol estratégico de la educación media para el bienestar y la equidad." 23 de Abril de 1996.

Chesterfield, Ray and Fernado E. Rubio. "Incentives for the Participation of Guatemalan Indigenous Girls in Primary Education: Final Evaluation of the *Eduque a la Niña* Pilot Project. Guatemala, February 1997.

Comisión Económica para América Latina y el Caribe (CEPAL). *Panorama social de América Latina 1998.* Santiago de Chile: CEPAL, 1999.

Comisión Económica para América Latina y el Caribe (CEPAL). Rol estratégico de la educación media para el bienestar y la equidad. LC/G.1919. Santiago de Chile: CEPAL, 1995. <http://www.eclac.cl/espanol/Publicaciones/ps95/>.

Development Assistance Committee. *Shaping the 21st Century: The Contribution of Development Co-operation.* Paris: OECD, 1996.

Franco, Jean. *Plotting Women: Gender and Representation in Mexico.* New York: Columbia University Press, 1989.

Fuentes, Carlos. "Prólogo." In *Educación la agenda del siglo XXI: Hacia un desarrollo humano.* Programa de Naciones Unidas para el Desarrollo, 1998.

International Labour Organization. *Impact of Structural Adjustment on the Employment and Training of Teachers.* Geneva: ILO, 1996.

Levy, Daniel C. *To Export Progress in the Americas: U.S. Golden Age Assistance to Latin American Universities* (book manuscript in progress).

Lewis, Oscar. *The Children of Sánchez: Autobiography of a Mexican Family.* New York: Vintage Books, 1963.

Lledó, Eulalia. *El sexismo y el androcentrismo en la lengua. Análisis y propuestas de cambio.* Barcelona: Instituto de Ciencias de la Educación, 1992.

McEwan, Patrcik J. "The Effectiveness of Multigrade Schools in Colombia." *International Journal of Educational Development* vol. 18, no. 6 (1998): 435–452.

Mujeres y hombres en la escuela y la familia: Estereotipos y perspectivas de género. México: Secretaría de Educación Pública, Comisión del libro de texto gratuito, 1999.

Psacharopoulos, George, Carlos Rojas, and Eduardo Veléz. "Achievement Evaluation of Colombia's *Escuela Nueva*: Is Multigrade the Answer?" *Comparative Education Review* vol. 37, no. 3 (1993): 263–276.

Randall, Laura and Joan B. Anderson. *Schooling for Success: Preventing Repetition and Dropout in Latin American Primary Schools.* Armonk, N.Y.: M.E. Sharpe, 1999.

Rosemberg, Fúlvia. "Educação, gênero e raça." Paper presented at the XX International Congress of the Latin American Studies Association, Guadalajara, México, April 17–19, 1997.

Subirats, Marina and Cristina Brullet. *Rosa y Azul: La transmisión de los géneros en la escuela mixta.* Madrid: Instituto de la Mujer, 1992.

Subirats, Marina and Amparo Tomé. *Pautas de observación del sexismo en el ámbito educativo.* Barcelona: Instituto de Ciencias de la Educación, 1992.

Sutton, Francis X. (ed.). *A World to Make: Development in Perspective.* New Brunswick, N.J.: Transaction Publishers, 1990.

Tarrés, María Luisa Tarrés. "Las organizaciones del movimiento de mujeres en la reforma política." In Alberto Olvera (ed.), *La sociedad civil: De la teoría a la realidad.* El Colegio de México, 1999 (forthcoming).

UNESCO. *The Education of Girls and Women: Towards a Global Framework for Action.* Paris: UNESCO, 1995.

UNICEF. *Education and Child Labour* (Background paper), n.d.

UNICEF. *Girls' Education: A Framework for Action.* New York. January 1997.

UNICEF. *The State of the World's Children 1997.* New York: UNICEF, 1997.

United Nations. *The Equity Gap: Latin America and the Caribbean and the Social Summit.* Santiago: ECLAC-CEPAL, 1997.

Vargas, Virginia. "Las actuales vertientes del movimiento de mujeres." In Patricia Ruiz Bravo (ed.), *Detrás de la puerta. Hombres y mujeres en el Perú de hoy.* Lima: Pontificia Universidad Católica del Perú, 1996.

Viqueira, Juan Pedro. "Los peligros del Chiapas imaginario." *Letras Libres* 1 (Enero de 1999): 20–28.

Viquiera, Juan Pedro. "Separate Identities or Collective Identities? The Relationship between Indigenous People and Ladinos in Chiapas." El Colegio de México, unpublished manuscript.

Warren, Kay B. *Indigenous Movements and Their Critics: Pan-Mayan Activism in Guatemala.* Princeton: Princeton University Press, 1998.

UNESCO and the Education of Girls and Women in Latin America and the Caribbean

MARÍA LUISA JÁUREGUI

NORMATIVE FRAMEWORK FOR EQUALITY OF OPPORTUNITY

UNESCO has been working on issues of equality of opportunity for many years, and several conventions and recommendations go back to the 1960s. The conventions are legal frameworks that oblige states, to a certain extent, to promote equality of opportunities and to fight against the discrimination that has historically affected girls and women alike.

The first of these conventions is the 1960 "Convention Against Discrimination in Education," which favors women's participation in education. This was followed by the 1966 "Recommendation Concerning the Status of Teachers," which demands women's access to the teaching profession; the 1974 "Convention on Technical and Vocational Education," which favors young women's access to vocational education; and, finally, the 1976 "Recommendation for the Development of Adult Education," which calls for women's access to adult education programs.

UNESCO has played an important role in numerous regional and world meetings. For example, at the Sixth Regional Conference for Women's Integration in Economic and Social Development in Latin America and the Caribbean, a preparatory meeting for the World Conference on Women held in Mar del Plata (Argentina) in September 1994, UNESCO participated in designing a regional strategy to promote equal opportunities in girls' and women's education.[1]

Of the world conferences that have been held in the 1990s, special note should be taken of the "Education for All" Conference, which gave a new push to girl's and women's education. At all the world conferences that took place in these years, governments committed themselves to improving the education of girls and women. Nevertheless, we consider that movement toward this goal has been very slow. This is due mainly to cultural reasons, as we will see later.

After the Beijing World Conference for Women (1995),[2] UNESCO redefined its goals and decided to consider women as a "Priority Group" and to consider girls and women's programs as a transversal subject in all of UNESCO's fields (education, science, culture, communications) and to give emphasis to the following areas of the Beijing Platform for Action:

- equal access of girls and women to education;
- women's contribution to a culture of peace;
- women's contribution to the management of natural resources and the protection of the environment; and
- eradication of illiteracy among women.

In order to achieve these objectives, UNESCO launched a global strategy that is based on three orientations: (1) an analysis in terms of gender of the ensemble of the process for formulation of policies and planning, program execution, and evaluation of activities; (2) promote women participation at all levels and areas of activity, giving particular attention to the priorities and perspectives of women themselves in the redefinition of the objectives and means of development; and (3) develop specific programs and objectives for girls and women that promote equality, the creation of endogenous capacities, and full citizenship.

The new UNESCO's Program for Gender Equality and the Improvement of Life Conditions of Girls and Women at the world level has the following objectives:

1. To foster education to confer greater autonomy to women.
2. To promote equal access to knowledge in all disciplines, particularly scientific and technological, and increase women participation in teacher training at the highest levels.
3. To support human rights of women, promoting initiatives that facilitate a wider ratification and a more effective application of normative instruments related to women, in particular the Convention on the Eradication of All Forms of Discrimination Against Women.

4. To promote gender equality, full citizenship, and women participation—on equal terms—at decision making, as a prerequisite to a real democracy in the local, national, and international levels.
5. To promote co-participation and dialogue and to reach a new contract between the genders.
6. To introduce the gender perspective, the conceptualization, application, and evaluation of policies in relation to development, peace, and security.
7. To trigger creativity and freedom of expression of women, among others, by giving support to women's activities and research in the UNESCO fields of competence (mentioned earlier).
8. To support pluralistic and independent communication means, favoring an ample and active participation of women in decision making and giving impulse to a more diversified, realistic, and nondiscriminatory image of women.
9. To contribute to building a culture of peace in the minds of women and men, recognizing the leadership capacity of women and their contribution of solving conflict through nonviolent means.[5]

UNESCO'S REGIONAL ACTIVITIES

UNESCO's regional action in favor of girls' and women's education can be seen in the light of the three following moments: (1) the launching of the Major Project for Education (1983); (2) the Education for All World Conference held in Jomtien (1990); and (3) the Regional Platform for Action for Gender Equality in Latin America and the Caribbean Region adopted in 1994 at the Sixth Conference for the Regional Integration of Women to the Economic and Social Development in Latin America and the Caribbean.

The Major Project for Education, which is ending in the year 2000, and started in 1983, had the following objectives: the universalization of primary education, the improvement of educational quality, and the eradication of illiteracy. The project was a framework for governmental action, supported by agreements and recommendations made by ministers of education, which met every two years to look at progress achieved and new challenges.

The first objective, the universalization of primary education, has been achieved, with very few exceptions (children of indigenous areas, children living in remote rural areas, etc.). There has been an increase in the quality of education, as there is now more consciousness of the importance of the contents and relevance of education and there have been a series of educational reforms that have been launched in recent years to deal with this subject. Finally, the third objective, the eradication of illiteracy, is still pending, as it affects particularly indigenous populations living in rural areas. This is in spite of numerous campaigns and programs launched by the governments with more or less success.

Also in Latin America and the Caribbean, particularly since the Education for All World Conference (1990) and the Beijing World Women's Conference (1995), efforts have concentrated on the following: (1) identify structural programs that are affecting girls' access to education; (2) increase public expenditure for education; (3) guarantee disaggregated data by sex in all statistical information; (4) develop research methodologies and obtain the necessary information to design educational policies that include the gender perspective; and (5) identify and get more information on the "feminine" qualifications mentioned in the job descriptions in the labor market.

UNESCO's role has been to give strong support to the items listed earlier, to alert public opinion, and to convince governments to offer the best quality education to girls and women as a fundamental step toward the implementation of efficient educational programs.

In 1990 and 1992, UNESCO conducted case studies on the situation of girls' education in Chile, Colombia, and Mexico, which was found to be satisfactory. As a whole, UNESCO's efforts of giving visibility to the situation of girls' and women's education has been regularly disseminated through a biannual publication, *The State of Education in Latin America and the Caribbean,* which is based on official statistical data provided by the ministries of education from the region in the framework of the Major Project for Education.[4]

Another publication in 1994 examined the relation between education, income, and employment of women and youth. It was produced by UNESCO and UNDP under the title *The Educational Perspective of Human Development in Latin America.* The study was based on household surveys conducted in ten countries.[5] In addition, in 1997, a manual and a video for use in teacher training at the secondary level was produced by UNESCO, the Spanish Institute for Women, and the Chilean NGO La Morada. The film was made in close cooperation with secondary-level students of both sexes who expressed their knowledge and appreciation of "gender relations" in their own language.[6]

There have also been numerous efforts to consider the gender perspective in sexual education programs conducted by UNESCO and the United Nations Population Fund (UNFPA) in the formal education systems in Argentina, Brazil, Colombia, Chile, Costa Rica, El Salvador, Haiti, Honduras, Panama, Mexico, and Peru, as well as in all the English Caribbean countries. In spite of these activities, we still have much to do in order to include the gender perspective in all the official curriculums throughout the region.

In statistical terms the situation of girls' education has greatly improved. The census carried out in the 1980s indicated that differences in educational levels by sex essentially disappeared (except when the analysis is done by ethnicity). Furthermore, in half of the countries the situation is being reversed and women actually have greater access to primary and secondary education.

Boys drop out more often than girls because they see no relevance in the subjects they study at school to their own life and needs. Often, when they come from poor families, boys tend to look for work very early, rather than "waste their time" at school. As for girls, the greater numbers of dropouts come from girls who are pregnant and are either obliged by their families or by their schools to remain home.

In the case of the Caribbean states, female schooling rates are surpassing those of males, both at the secondary level, as well as at the higher education level, thus presenting unforeseen problems.[7] The case of the Caribbean is troublesome. The governmental authorities have requested UNESCO to look upon the matter of the important dropout rates of boys and greater permanence of girls in school.

With respect to the situation of the introduction of the gender perspective in the official curriculum of the schools, we can only ask ourselves why there has been so little progress. There are no rational answers, so perhaps we must look to the psychological or cultural realms. We know that the gender perspective demands that we reflect upon our own work; it obliges us to question our own thoughts and actions, which sometimes makes us realize our own, often painful, contradictions, and resultant mixed reactions. Perhaps this makes it difficult to address gender in the current educational agenda. We need to develop concrete proposals incorporating the gender perspective and providing the appropriate tools for those involved, including the planners mentioned earlier, in order to help them implement the proposals in the official curricula of our countries.

The other objective, which has still not been reached, is total literacy of all girls and women in the region. This is not solely an educational issue, but has other social and political implications, and its success depends very much on the political will of the governments concerned.

The next sections examine some of UNESCO's activities in the field of literacy. We also look at other subjects related to equality of opportunities among men and women, both at various educational levels and in other areas of concern to UNESCO, in order to find alternative ways to achieve our objectives of social justice.

WOMEN'S ILLITERACY

It has been estimated that in the year 2000, only seven countries in Latin America will have illiteracy rates over 10 percent. In Central America and the Caribbean, Guatemala has 38 percent illiteracy, Haiti has 37 percent, El Salvador has 20 percent, and Honduras has 19 percent. In the rest of Latin America, Bolivia, Brazil, and the Dominican Republic have rates higher than 10 percent but less than 15 percent.[8]

Looking at women's illiteracy, it is estimated that their rates are higher than the regional averages in Bolivia, Ecuador, Guatemala, Mexico, and Peru. All of these countries have indigenous populations living in rural areas where many girls do not go to school.

UNESCO has done research and organized numerous workshops for women indigenous leaders to determine the reasons why girls do not attend school. In many cases, in the rural areas, schools are located away from the people's homes, and this implies dangers for the girls who must walk long distances to and from school. There are several other reasons, including economical reasons: When the family has to choose who to send to school, they prefer to send boys rather than girls; there are physical reasons, including bad roads, enormous distances, girls' undernourishment, and so on.

There are also cultural reasons: Women are less valued than men. There is the belief that women's productivity is less than that of men. There is no recognition of the cultural role of women. The schools provide education in Spanish rather than in the mother tongue, thus making learning achievement more difficult.[9]

The region also faces significant functional illiteracy rates. UNESCO has been conducting in-depth research since 1990 in various countries of the region to determine the degree of functional illiteracy. Seven countries participated in the most recent research: Argentina, some states in Brazil,

Colombia, Chile, Mexico, Paraguay, and Venezuela. This research did not specifically consider the gender perspective, but rather interviewed a comparative number of men and women. It discovered, among other things, that men surpassed women in mathematics and women surpassed men in writing skills. Future studies should consider the gender perspective to see how it influences the acquisition of functional literacy in both sexes. The lack of a gender perspective both in research projects such as the one mentioned earlier, and in programs targeting adult women, is another matter of concern.

UNESCO'S LITERACY ACTIVITIES

In 1992, UNESCO asked Peruvian sociologist Patricia Ruíz Bravo to prepare a systematization of nonformal innovative education experiences targeting poor women in the region, in order to publicize these programs and improve or duplicate them. Programs considered included literacy, income generation, health, ecology, and the protection of the environment.[10]

The study concluded that the most successful innovative experiences were those that included both a material and a subjective dimension. Programs that prioritized both improving the quality of life of women and their families by increasing economic resources and also increased women's self-esteem and self-affirmation were the most successful.

Many of these programs did not start out with a gender perspective, but adopted one along the way, in practice rather than institutionally. Thus, the achievements mentioned had more to do with changes of attitude among the women and an improved sense of their individual value and self-esteem, rather than with changes in the level of income, productivity, or efficiency. When women start working, they often face opposition from their husbands around their need and right to become literate and their need to work. Women have to overcome their shame and succeed in improving their sense of self-worth.

In the programs examined, there exists a growing concern about combining and responding simultaneously to two lines of action: one offering training and/or education and the other offering technical and/or economic services. This combination of the social and economic aspects signals a change in comparison to previous experiences that gave preference to one aspect, leaving the other unattended. There is currently acknowledgment of the importance of considering both components to respond to the survival needs of poor women. It is important to provide women not only with material resources (credits, land, food, etc.), but also with symbolic resources (education, information, and training), that give them access to decision making and to influencing the sustainability of projects.

The research mentions the importance of supporting activities that free women's time to allow them to participate successfully in these programs. This includes but is not limited to offering child care and introducing technologies and infrastructure to reduce women's time spent on household chores. Variables such as the age of women, stage in their life cycle, number of children, and literacy level are all characteristics that either encourage or discourage their participation in these programs.

The study by Ruíz Bravo also acknowledges that another factor affecting the success of these programs is the degree to which they recognize and value the abilities and capacities that women already possess. Successful programs begin by assuming women's real abilities to exercise control over the products of their work, and they improve their access to resources.

As women have more confidence in themselves, acquiring more security and reaching greater autonomy, the personal perspective is linked to the economic one and success is achieved in the educational program. When these women feel capable, with rights and with the ability to express their own opinions, they improve their relationships with their husbands and their children. This in turn gives them more self-value, energy, and security to improve their quality of life and that of their families.

UNESCO has carried out many other studies in recent years. Among them, we can mention the following: Between 1993 and 1994, the Andrés Bello Convention and UNESCO organized a Contest of Monographs on Women's and Children's Education in Poor Sectors. The results of the contest were published in 1995, under the same title.[11]

Another important research project, financed by UNESCO and UNICEF, was prepared by the Chilean sociologist María Eugenia Letelier, which concentrated on the examination of women's illiteracy in Chile, both in the rural and indigenous areas, as well as in marginal urban areas. The results of this research were published in 1996.[12]

Besides promoting research, UNESCO organizes literacy training workshops and launches projects at the national level. In recent years, important projects have been implemented in Bolivia, Ecuador, and Peru, supported by UNESCO and by other United Nations agencies.

The Bolivian project, which was financed by UNESCO, UNDP, and AGFUND (Arab States Fund), utilized audiovisual media to carry out the literacy program. The most innovative aspect of this project was the use of videos, which allowed women to view themselves while the learning process was taking place.

The Ecuadorian project was an excellent example of interagency cooperation. Besides UNESCO, FAO (World Food Programme), UNDP, and UNFPA collaborated in this effort. In this case, the peasants that participated in the literacy program received food. Literacy was a training component to facilitate productive work. The project also included sexual education and family planning. Today, the women who participated in this project are creating their own cooperatives and small businesses.

In the case of Peru, for example, at this moment we are preparing the second stage of a literacy and civic education project, targeting indigenous peasant women and displaced women, with the support of UNESCO and Denmark's International Cooperation (DANIDA). The first stage was conducted in Cajamarca and Cuzco, between 1992 and 1994, and literacy was offered in Spanish, Quechua, or both languages, as appropriate for the population concerned. Three hundred and forty-nine literacy promoters were trained, the majority from the same community. Almost five thousand women were taught to read and some one thousand received post-literacy courses linked to income-generating activities.[13]

The project's literacy activities were implemented by three Peruvian NGO's: *Asociación Perú-Mujer* in Cajamarca; the Ecology and Development Association (APED), and the Andean Center for Education and Promotion (CADEP) in Cuzco, under the coordination of the Ministry of Education of Peru. The project produced a voluminous amount of educational materials for literacy in Quechua, Spanish, and both languages. Complementary post-literacy material was also developed for training in cultural and civic education and in gender issues for peasant women, using charts, manuals, texts, and booklets with songs, stories, local legends, and guessing games.

Emphasis was placed on civic and gender education and was based on histories and testimonies of the women themselves. In Cuzco, two testimonial books were written in Quechua, one about the life of a peasant woman, Asunta, and the other about the history of an indigenous district. The book about Asunta offers a strong testimony of the marginalization, oppression, and discrimination that Quechuan indigenous women suffer. The second book is the story of an indigenous district as told by its own inhabitants. The books were utilized to help women reflect upon their own situation and to find alternatives to deal with their problems.

The post-literacy stage combined strengthening of acquired literacy skills with knowledge of women's civic rights, agricultural training, crafts production, and environmental conservation. This combination produced integration, communication, and interrelations with the rest of the community and contributed to the integral development of women as literate members of the community.

In a search for continuity, efforts were made to link post-literacy with existing productive projects. One of the greatest achievements of this first stage were the agreements and conventions subscribed to by the educational authorities in Cajamarca and Cuzco to continue with the literacy work started by the NGOs. The project's activities encouraged the existing civic and social organizations in these areas to continue working with new literacy programs, and the communities firmly advocated the use of Quechua in the literacy programs instead of the Spanish-only program.

The evaluation of the project documented the positive effects of the methodological proposal that links the literacy process and the issue of the indigenous and peasant woman's intercultural self-affirmation. The process of selection, training, and literacy offered by the community literacy workers was also considered to be successful. The bilingual literacy process also received a positive evaluation. Some difficulties included: problems of coordination among the implementing agencies, the lack of exchange of experiences, and the lack of available scholarships. Finally, there were difficulties in the post-literacy stage, which lacked clarity with respect to the content and the operational aspects of the educational activities.

HIGHER AND SCIENTIFIC EDUCATION OF GIRLS AND WOMEN IN THE REGION

Higher education is not addressed in the Major Education Project, implemented by the Santiago UNESCO Regional Office for Education. However, UNESCO supports the improvement of higher education and women's participation at the university level.

In 1994, together with Gloria Bonder (then at the Ministry of Culture and Education in Argentina) and UNESCO, and in the framework of the Mar del Plata Regional Conference, we organized a Sub-Regional Meeting on Women's Studies at the Universities, with participants from five countries of the Southern Cone. It was very interesting to note that gender and/or women's studies were still very marginal and were not officially recognized in the universities represented. Professors were not directly paid for those courses, since most of them were part of other faculties such as the social sciences, and their efforts to include a cross-curricular gender perspective at their universities did not always achieve the expected results. While the situation has improved since then, as was demonstrated at recent regional events in Santiago de Chile, it still remains a subject of concern.

The subject of women's studies at universities in the region does not emerge as an important theme in the Regional Preparatory Conference of the World Conference for Higher Education in the XXI Century. In the Conference Declaration, which took place in Havana in 1997, concern for women's access to universities is mentioned in general terms, but with insufficient strength and content.

If we examine the "World Declaration on Higher Education for the XXI Century: Vision and Action," we find that in the chapter dedicated to the "Strengthening and Promotion of Women's Access and Participation" there have been advances, at least at the level of discourse. Among the principal advances, we underline the following:

- the need for increased efforts to eradicate all stereotypes based on gender in higher education, taking into account the gender perspective in the different disciplines, consolidating the qualitative participation of women in all levels and disciplines in which they are not sufficiently represented and, above all, increasing their active participation in decision making;
- [the need] to promote gender studies (or studies related to women) as a specific field with a strategic role in the transformation of higher education and society;
- [the need] to make efforts to eliminate political and social obstacles that allow women to be under-represented and to favor, in particular, women's active participation at the policy and decision-making level, both in higher education as well as in society.[14]

This Declaration will help us to continue advancing in the establishment and official recognition of women's studies at our region's universities. It will also help us open UNESCO chairs of women's studies and to build links with other universities, from both the north and the south, in order to profit from the experiences and knowledge of one another in this field.

Finally, I would like to examine the preparations for the World Conference on Sciences, which was held in Budapest in July 1999. There have been numerous preparatory meetings on the specific subject of women's role in science and technology, in Paris (July 1998), Bariloche (October 1998), and Santo Domingo (February 1999).

Seventeen Latin American countries participated in the "UNESCO Regional Forum on Women, Science and Technology in Latin America: Diagnosis and Strategies," which took place in Bariloche in October 1997. The final document declares:

> Although the number of women dedicated to science and technology in Latin America has increased, they remain concentrated in certain branches, and their presence is minimal at decision-making levels. At the same time, they face specific obstacles and difficulties in their professional lives, a result of both intrinsic factors of the models and practices characteristic of scientific institutions, and of socio-cultural conditions that limit women's full development.[15]

The Regional Forum made certain recommendations for gender equity in professional development: the provision of scholarships and special subsidies, the establishment of spaces and quotas, the promotion of work sites that are "friendly to women," child-care services, and the creation of networks.

With respect to education, the forum recommends the promotion of qualitative scientific and technical education (formal and nonformal) that integrates the gender perspective, the promotion of flexible and innovative educational practices that are linked to everyday life and to community issues, the incorporation of leisure activities that favor the development of self-esteem and the altering of stereotypes, and the stimulation of an active and creative position vis-à-vis science and technology.

Furthermore, the forum proposes the use of new technologies to enhance women's position, an examination of the relation between science and technology and the private sector, the development of biotechnology, and the elaboration of policies and programs at regional and national levels that favor the participation of girls and women in the region.

WORLD REPORTS ON EDUCATION AND CULTURE

The International Reports on Education and Culture presented to UNESCO in recent years are the product of two independent commissions. Both are the result of worldwide processes of consultation and analysis over a period of years.

In the case of education, the International Commission on Education for the Twenty-First Century, was chaired by former European Commission president Jacques Delors.[16] In the case of culture, the commission was created by UNESCO and the United Nations in 1992, under the leadership of Javier Pérez de Cuéllar, former secretary general to the United Nations.[17] Both reports contain important guidelines to consider in the next century, which include the strengthening of personal identity as the ultimate goal of education for every human being, and as the first step to consider the importance of learning to live with others and with our environment. The earlier-mentioned reports on education and culture contain important ideas developed through consultations with specialists from diverse fields and cultures who agree on the importance of strengthening the self-identity of every human being. In summary, *Education for the XXI Century* is conceived, in this report, as a permanent and lifelong process, encompassing all spaces, and at the same time including all human beings, all institutions, and all structures.

The report on *Education for the XXI Century* emphasizes four pillars of education: to learn to be, to learn to know, to learn to do, and to learn to live together. In the context of this document:

- to learn to be a woman is a challenge that implies self-knowledge, self-development, and self-esteem, which forms the basis and expression of values and beliefs;
- to learn to know, to learn throughout life, not only in school, but also outside, in everyday life;
- to learn to do, to acquire the skills that will allow us to survive, to maintain ourselves and our families, through a profession or through employment or through an income-generating activity; and
- to learn to live together implies the improvement of relations with other people, to promote respect, tolerance, cooperation, solidarity, justice, peace, and love, without forgetting links to the environment.

According to María E. Irigoin, there have been advances in guaranteeing educational gender equity in the Latin American and Caribbean region:[18] (1) through actions that favor access, by guaranteeing broad publicity and preventing sexist selection and orientation (however, she insists that the most notorious discrimination continues to be feminine illiteracy among indigenous women and among women living in rural areas, as well as the consecration of "feminine careers"); (2) through strategies within and outside education, such as efforts to incorporate gender as a cross-curricular subject in the curriculum or child-care initiatives to support women's presence in training programs for women; and (3) through actions related to the results of the educational process.

The gender issue can also be considered from the cultural point of view. We are in a period of transition, where the roles of men and women are changing. It is for this reason that we must find places to nurture ourselves in the cultural area in order to be able to continue moving forward. The UNESCO report on cultural development has dedicated an important space to the subject of gender. According to this report,

> gender has become one of the most delicate questions in a changing world, even more so since any transformation in this field encompasses inevitable ruptures of the identity models for both sexes and it is related to matters of domination (thus of power).
>
> Development processes are changing the perceptions of the vital cycle of men and women, of their social participation, besides the relations among each other. According to a criteria of equity, one cannot discriminate against women in any area, and at the same time a criteria of efficiency calls for a better employment of the productive capacities of women in order to reach a better level of life and to improve the quality of life of all concerned.[19]

The subject of gender has distinct categories; it is simultaneously ethical, political, economic, and cultural. To refer to gender implies questioning the life projects of men and women, as well as their relationships among and with each other. The traditional role of man as the sole provider for the family is currently in crisis, as is the role of woman as housekeeper. Research in the region shows that the differences of life projects among girls and their mothers are greater than those between sons and fathers. Today, opinion surveys show that women aspire in the first place to study and travel, and marriage and childbearing come in sixth place.[20]

Significant differences among men and women continue to exist in the region, and the differences are consecrated by authority, tradition, and religion. These differences can be associated with socialization processes legitimated by "what is," and include the sexual division of the workplace and the distribution of roles, assigned behaviors, and dispositions.

The major task is to increase women's contribution to the construction of society and men's contribution to the family. Each person should follow his or her "own vocation," and each one should try to "negotiate" his or her own possibilities, which may not always mean observing the socially imposed vocations. In other words, women's work outside of her home should not be seen as an "abandonment of her family," but it does imply the creation or negotiation of a new order of relations with her partner, where men take up household duties as their own responsibility as well.

Gender encompasses both culture and justice. Gender inequality compromises peace, since peace is based on relationships of equality. Irigoin considers that the following primary strategies have been employed thus far in relation to gender and gender discrimination:

- Increasing visibility of existing differences (for example, showing how language sanctions masculine power: phrases such as "men's work," etc.).
- Facilitating policies that counter discrimination (such as the utilization of quota systems during the government elections). This is a transitory measure until women gain access to political positions or positions of responsibility. These measures must be temporary or else they incur new types of discrimination.
- Empowering women, which is a long-term process that cannot be postponed. As mentioned before, there is a need to count women's potentials and abilities on equal terms as men's, and for the betterment of all. When we mention that it is a long process, we do so because we have seen resistance to change in many areas and in particular in this one. Men are not ready to give away the power situation where they have remained for years, and that is why we need to find more clever ways to "renegotiate" women's gains and advances, so that they do not seem frightening to men.

The development of research on subjects related to the cultural dimensions of education becomes a central element of any strategy. There is a need for systematic work on the cultural models present in Latin America and the Caribbean and their consequences for the educational processes in the region.[21] Furthermore, academic institutions must be stimulated to participate in the conceptualization of a new history, capable of offering the space that corresponds to women as protagonists in the history of our countries.

CONCLUSION

As we mentioned earlier, the introduction of the gender perspective in education implies cultural change and thus it is resisted. We have seen how among traditional (often indigenous) populations, there is a strong resistance to change. This is so because they still have many other problems to consider and they prefer women's role to remain the same.

We must continue working to achieve a qualitative change in the distinct areas of education, including but not limited to: achieving the introduction of the gender perspective as a cross-curricular subject, promoting nonsexist images in textbooks, introducing women's contribution in the history of our countries, training teachers with a gender perspective, training public functionaries—from all ministries—on the gender perspective, and increasing the use of educational indicators with a gender perspective.

We, who work in so many distinct professional tasks, must use the opportunities we find in our respective professional areas to introduce and address the gender issue. This must be our objective and our commitment. Other activities distract us from this task, but we can also profit from the enrichment different disciplines provide to improve work in our own fields. I believe that we will be able to initiate cultural change through a permanent construction of knowledge and the exchange of experiences through formal and nonformal networks of women and men interested in these issues.

At this moment, as our countries are addressing the urgency of adapting education to the needs of modernization, women must take on new forms of leadership, of management, and of decision making. This entails a significant increase in women's participation in scientific and technological progress and in the production of knowledge in general, which will have implications for the definition of production, the sexual division of work, and the cultural values that are being integrated and developed in society.

NOTES

[1]Dainne Almerás and María Luisa Jáuregui, *Hacia una estrategia educativa para las mujeres de América Latina y el Caribe.* ECLAC, Document DDR/6 for the IV Regional Conference of Women and Economic and Social Development (Santiago: ECLAC, 1994).

[2]María José García Oramas, "Actividades de la UNESCO en pro del mejoramiento de las condiciones de vida de niñas y mujeres en América Latina y el Caribe: Avanzando hacia la igualdad entre los géneros. Plataforma de Acción de Beijing en seguimiento a la IV Conferencia Mundial de la Mujer" (Paris: UNESCO, 1999).

[3]García Oramas, *op. cit.*

[4]UNESCO/OREALC, *The State of Education in Latin America and the Caribbean, 1980–1994* (Santiago: UNESCO, 1996).

[5]NESCO/PNUD. *Perspectiva educativa del desarrollo humano en América Latina* (Santiago: UNESCO, 1996).

[6]Olga Grau and Gilda Loungo, *Cambio de piel* (Video) (Santiago: Corporación del desarrollo de la mujer, La Morada, 1997); Olga Grau and Gilda Loungo, *Cambio de piel. Textos escogidos y guías de trabajo sobre género para la enseñanza media.* Material complementario del video *Cambio de piel* (Santiago: Corporación del desarrollo de la mujer, La Morada, Area de Educación, 1997).

[7]UNESCO/OREALC, *op. cit.*

[8]UNESCO/OREALC, *op. cit.*

[9]UNESCO/UNICEF. *Mujer, educación, género e identidad. Informe del curso-taller para mujeres líderes indígenas (Cochabamba, Bolivia, 13–25 de septiembre de 1993)* (Santiago: UNESCO, 1994).

[10]Patricia Ruíz Bravo, *Género, educación y desarrollo* (Santiago: UNESCO/OREALC, 1992).

[11]Patricia Ruíz Bravo, *Mujer y educación de niños en sectores populares* (Santiago: UNESCO/Convenio Andrés Bello, 1995).

[12]María Eugenia Letelier, *Analfabetismo femenino en Chile de los 90* (Santiago: UNESCO/UNICEF, 1996).

[13]Gonzalo Portocarrero, *Vamos creciendo Juntas. Alfabetización de la mujer campesina en Perú* (Santiago: UNESCO/OREALC, 1995).

[14]*La declaración mundial sobre la dducación superior en el siglo XXI: Visión y acción,* approved at the World Conference for Higher Education, which took place at UNESCO, Paris, from 5 to 9 October 1998.

[15]UNESCO, Foro Regional UNESCO, *Mujeres, ciencia y tecnología en América Latina: Diagnósticos y estrategias,* final document (draft version) (Bariloche, Argentina, October 1998).

[16]UNESCO, *Learning: The Treasure Within.* Report to UNESCO of the International Commission on Education for the Twenty-First Century (Paris: UNESCO, 1996).

[17]UNESCO, *Our Creative Diversity.* Report of the World Commission of Culture and Development (Paris, September 1996).

[18]María E. Irigoin (UNESCO consultant on gender issues) at the Round Table on Education and Gender at the follow-up meeting of the V World Conference on Adult Education for the Andean Countries. Cochabamba, Bolivia, January 1999.

[19]Pages 28 and 29 of the Spanish version of the summary version of the report.

[20]Irigoin, *op. cit.*

[21]María Luisa Jáuregui, "Equal Educational Opportunities: Myths and Realities," in the *Major Education Project Bulletin for Latin America and the Caribbean,* No. 35 (Santiago: UNESCO/OREALC, 1994).

REFERENCES

Almerás, Dainne and María Luisa Jáuregui. *Hacia una estrategia educativa para las mujeres de América Latina y el Caribe.* ECLAC, Document DDR/6 for the IV Regional Conference of Women and Economic and Social Development. Santiago: ECLAC, 1994.

García Oramas, María José. "Actividades de la UNESCO en pro del mejoramiento de las condiciones de vida de niñas y mujeres en América Latina y el Caribe: Avanzando hacia la igualdad entre los géneros. Plataforma de Acción de Beijing en Seguimiento a la IV Conferencia Mundial de la Mujer." Paris: UNESCO, 1999.

Grau, Olga and Gilda Loungo. *Cambio de piel* (video). Santiago: Corporación del Desarrollo de la Mujer La Morada, 1997.

Grau, Olga and Gilda Loungo. *Cambio de piel. Textos escogidos y guías de trabajo sobre género para la enseñanza media.* (Material complementario del video *Cambio de Piel*). Santiago: Corporación del desarrollo de la mujer, La Morada, Area de Educación, 1997.

Jaúregui, María Luisa. "Equal Educational Opportunities: Myths and Realities." In *Major Education Project Bulletin for Latin America and the Caribbean,* no. 35. Santiago: UNESCO/OREALC, 1994.

Letelier, María Eugenia. *Analfabetismo femenino en Chile de los 90.* Santiago: UNESCO-UNICEF, 1996.

Portocarrero, Gonzalo. *Vamos creciendo juntas. Alfabetización de la mujer campesina en Perú.* Santiago: UNESCO/OREALC, 1995.

Ruíz Bravo, Patricia. *Género, educación y desarrollo.* Santiago: UNESCO/OREALC, 1992.

Ruíz Bravo, Patricia. *Mujer y educación de niños en sectores populares.* Santiago: UNESCO-Convenio Andrés Bello, 1995.

UNESCO. *Learning: The Treasure Within.* Report to UNESCO of the International Commission on Education for the Twenty-first Century. Paris: UNESCO, 1996.

UNESCO. *Our Creative Diversity.* Report of the World Commission of Culture and Development. Paris: UNESCO, September 1996.

UNESCO. Foro Regional UNESCO *Mujeres, ciencia y tecnología en América Latina: Diagnósticos y estratégias.* Final document (draft version). Bariloche, Argentina, October 1998.

UNESCO/OREALC. *The State of Education in Latin America and the Caribbean, 1980–1994.* Santiago: UNESCO, 1996.

UNESCO/UNICEF. *Mujer, educación, género e identidad. Informe del curso-taller para mujeres líderes indígenas.* (Cochabamba, Bolivia, 13–25 de septiembre de 1993) Santiago: UNESCO, 1994.

UNESCO/PNUD. *Perspectiva educativa del desarrollo humano en América Latina.* Santiago: UNESCO, 1996.

Restructuring Bilateral Aid for the Twenty-First Century

REGINA CORTINA WITH HELEN PORTER

Achieving the civic, economic, and social goals of any society is intimately connected with providing adequate basic education for all. Human and social development cannot be measured solely by economic development and national income, but must be viewed within a broader context of well-being and the capacity for personal and social betterment. This approach to development, when voiced by nations and international agencies in the context of restructuring bilateral aid, offers the promise of a symbiotic relationship between the reduction of poverty, the strengthening of basic education, and human capacity-building. But it is empty rhetoric without educational equity for all groups in society.

The idea that poverty reduction must be tied to an increase in basic education for all the world's poor became a central conclusion of the May 1996 meeting of the Development Assistance Committee (DAC), a group of member nations who belong to the Organization for Economic Cooperation and Development (OECD).[1] This meeting threw a spotlight on the scope and direction of development aid worldwide as DAC set forth a strategic plan to help the more than one billion people still living in poverty throughout the world. Outlined at this meeting were key objectives that global development partnerships should pursue into the twenty-first century.

The first objective was that economic well-being should yield "a reduction by one-half in the proportion of people living in extreme poverty by 2015." Other objectives were "universal primary education in all countries by 2015; demonstrated progress toward gender equality and the empowerment of women by eliminating gender disparity in primary and secondary education by 2005; a reduction by two-thirds in the mortality rates for infants and children under age five and a reduction by three-fourths in maternal mortality, all by 2015; access through the primary health-care system to reproductive health services for all individuals of appropriate ages as soon as possible and no later than the year 2015."[2]

In order to attain these objectives, DAC stressed the importance of active engagement and contributions by the people and governments of the developing countries, so that implementation reflects both local conditions and the development strategies adopted to improve them. The industrialized countries were urged to commit to mutual cooperation with development partners, to provide improved coordination of assistance as well as coherence between aid and other policies and adequate resources. DAC called for adherence to the "widely accepted volume target of 0.7 percent of GNP established by the United Nations in 1970 as an appropriate level for official development assistance."[3]

Unfortunately, despite the written agreements, the actual contributions of donor countries to development assistance has been in decline during the 1990s. Far from reaching the stated goals, average development aid as a percentage of the GNP for DAC countries was 0.22 percent in 1997.[4] Since the 1960s, when all OECD countries established bilateral development assistance programs, the level of bilateral educational aid among these countries remained relatively constant at an average $4.2 billion in constant 1994 U.S. dollars until the recent decline.[5]

DAC cited humanitarian issues as a principal motivation for these strategic development goals. Nearly one-fifth of the world's population lives in extreme poverty, lacking access to clean water, adequate health care, sufficient nourishment, and basic literacy. Thus, a "moral imperative" exists to participate in development assistance. Another motive supporting strategic development goals is the idea of "enlightened self-interest." Development benefits all participants, both donors and receivers. In addition to the obvious humanitarian gains to developing countries, development expands economic markets of industrialized countries and increases human security by reducing social and environmental stresses and encouraging political stability. A third motive for international development support is the building of a world community. Sustainable development enables people from several nations to work together toward common global goals in environmental protection, decreased population growth rates, nuclear nonproliferation, and eradication of epidemic diseases.[6]

Despite the stated goals for human development worldwide since 1990 and international targets for equity in primary education completion and gender equality, the global picture for education remains highly uneven, and the evidence of success in educational advancement is skewed toward more highly developed countries and toward males. In 1997, 404 million of the world's children under the age of eighteen were out of school. This figure represents 38 percent of the children of the world. At the basic education level, 140 million children or 23 percent of children in developing countries are not attending school. Girls represent two-thirds of out-of school children.[7] In 1990, women represented two-thirds of the world's 948 million illiterate adults. In the lowest-income countries, the disparity in primary school enrollment between boys and girls varies by as much as 20 percent.[8]

To identify new directions in developmental education aid since 1990, especially for girls and women, this chapter examines bilateral aid programs in Latin America. A look at these new directions is especially relevant since countries such as the United States and the Netherlands are continuing to revise their bilateral goals to reflect the strategies and target outcomes outlined at the DAC conference. New players in bilateral aid such as Spain are now present in Latin America and are also embracing aspects of the DAC strategies. Through explanation and comparison, it is possible to illuminate the policies and projects sponsored in Latin America today. It is especially useful to compare how different countries implement bilateral cooperation. Each donor country presents a different aid philosophy, and a unique perspective on the education of women and girls emerges in each case from national legislation and education traditions. European countries such as the Netherlands, Spain, and Sweden tend to channel their funding through their own nongovermental organizations (NGOs), whereas USAID (United States Agency for International Development) relies on direct implementation with United States subcontractors who work with the government, private sector, and NGOs of each county. Our analysis will focus on the assistance provided by three countries: Spain, the United States, and the Netherlands.

SPANISH SUPPORT FOR GENDER EQUITY PROGRAMS

Among the priorities of the *Agencia Española de Cooperación Internacional* (Spanish Agency for International Cooperation, AECI) in its development assistance toward Latin America is gender equality and the strengthening of the women's movement in the countries where the agency is working. Spain, which only a few years ago was receiving aid from advanced industrial countries, today is in the position to provide development assistance to Latin America. AECI, started in 1988, has offices (*Oficinas Técnicas de Cooperación*) in twenty Latin American and Caribbean countries, and Latin America is the agency's priority region. In the years to come, AECI is planning to finance and provide technical assistance to design and implement gender equity policies in Latin America. Guatemala was chosen as the first country in which to develop this strategy.[9]

Following the strategy used in Latin American countries by the international cooperation programs of other members of the European Union, primarily Sweden and the Netherlands, the Spanish strategy is to strengthen the women's lobby in the country. To accomplish this goal, AECI undertook the responsibility of supporting the *Oficina Nacional de la Mujer en Guatemala* (National Office for Women in Guatemala), support that included the creation of offices to represent the national office in each one of the departments of the country, and subsidizing administrative expenses of these regional offices, such as the salary for the directors and certain program expenses.[10]

The goal is to establish the Spanish agency as the first international agency that finances and helps to shape the design and implementation of a national gender policy in a Latin American country.[11] By simultaneously providing funding on gender training projects for women within different education levels, the agency aims to influence public policies to improve the situation of women in Guatemala at the national, municipal, and community levels. To achieve its goals, the AECI supports gender training programs within higher education and at the secondary schools level as well as funding the inclusion of gender training in all the development projects supported by AECI. The priority of the gender training in the development projects is achieved by providing a special budget for the gender component.[12] Within higher education, the agency funds gender awareness programs as a graduate diploma for women in leadership positions. At the secondary level, the agency provides specialized training for women who are working as educators and facilitators in short courses designed for women within NGOs in order to improve their technical and planning skills. The agency also funds basic literacy programs for rural and indigenous women.

Gender training for women leaders, such as businesswomen, professionals, politicians, and university faculty, is funded as a postgraduate degree for women leaders in Central America. Such training is offered collaboratively with the Jesuit University, Rafael Landivar University, and with FLACSO (*Facultad Latinoamericana de Ciencias Sociales*). The objective is gender awareness for female leaders in Central America in topics such as human rights, politics, culture, economy, and work "within a Spanish program with prestige and academic quality." The course had been organized through the Guatemalan Institute for Hispanic Culture, a Spanish-funded cultural institution, and with the help of the Spanish Embassy.[13]

Gender training and literacy are the basic education components of the rural development programs that the Spanish government is sponsoring in Guatemala. For rural women, the objective of the gender training programs is to promote women's participation and to improve women's self-esteem and the well-being of women with regard to education, health, family, and political integration.[14] The gender projects sponsored by the Spanish Agency are implemented in the larger context of rural development projects following the experience developed in Spain by the *Instituto de la Mujer* (Women's Institute). By 1998, AECI had supported the creation of fourteen regional offices of the National Office for Women. Within each region, this office in collaboration with local NGOs organizes formal and informal courses for women with a gender training component. All projects are managed in a decentralized way within each region.

By the end of 1998, there were gender training specialists working in six of the regions of Guatemala and ongoing development projects with a gender component in eight other regions. In Huehuetenango, one of the regions in Guatemala, the projects for rural development and the twelve local offices of the national office for women in operation have different projects with a gender component. These projects promote the organization of women, provide literacy training, train women in the use of medicinal plants, prepare rural promoters to communicate about issues of gender and health, and train rural promoters as midwives.[15] Projects similar to these are receiving funding from Spain in rural communities all over Guatemala through a combination of Spanish NGOs, local NGOs, and government organizations.

In the case of Mexico, the projects supported by AECI are geared toward different education levels. But in contrast to the Guatemalan programs just described, there is no mention of women or gender training courses. The argument is that because of Mexico's level of economic development, no basic assistance programs are needed. Within higher education, in cooperation with ANUIES (*Asociación Nacional de Universidades e Institutos de Enseñanza Superior*), doctoral graduates from

Spanish universities come to teach in Mexican universities. Within basic education in cooperation with Mexico's National Ministry for Education (SEP, *Secretaría de Educación Pública*), the program funds short courses on school management for school supervisors, principals, and teachers in different states of the country, and a new project is being developed for special education teachers. At the middle school level, short courses are funded for faculty in technical education and school to work programs. Another important element of the education program is scholarships to increase exchanges between Mexican and Spanish universities.[16] The funding priorities of the Spanish agency in Mexico show that for Spain the gender programs are part of their effort to alleviate poverty and are not seen exclusively as a way of empowering women in society or creating a women's lobby.

USAID: HOW DOES IT SUPPORT GIRLS' EDUCATION?

Since World War II, the United States has taken an active role in foreign aid development. USAID is responsible for designing and administering "sustainable development assistance," including programs involved in improving girls' and women's education. In 1998, the agency was placed under the State Department, reporting to the Secretary of State. Building upon USAID's pioneering development of Women in Development (WID) programs, the Gender Plan of Action began in March 1996, developed with the DAC Conference goals in mind and as a follow-up to the Fourth World Conference on Women. This plan focuses on women's pivotal participation in economic and social development.[17]

For fiscal year 1999, USAID budgeted $98.2 million from the Child Survival and Disease Program account to fund basic education programs. This dollar amount is about the same as was allocated in 1998.[18] Funds are targeted toward quality, universal access, and effective primary education, especially for women and girls.[19] Countries and other partners must be equally committed to these goals for USAID to assist them.[20] USAID maintains that over the years the agency has learned that local commitment is critical to program success. Sustainable development must involve and utilize local resources and draw upon a wide cross-section of the country's people, targeting women and other disadvantaged groups.[21]

USAID recognizes that progress in basic education is uneven throughout the world. In the case of Latin America, only 50 percent of students who begin school complete primary education. The results of these huge dropout rates are that students cannot compete with their counterparts in industrialized countries or integrate into their own country's modern sector of the economy. In the area of educational performance, most low-performing students are from low-income areas. Thus the poor receive the least education, and this situation perpetuates lack of opportunity, advancement, and social inequity.[22] Poor educational opportunity and quality have a pronounced impact on women and girls in Guatemala and Bolivia. In 1995 in Guatemala, illiteracy rates for females were 51 percent, while rates for males were 38 percent, a difference of 13 percent. In Bolivia, the difference in the illiteracy rates between females and males was even more extreme: Female illiteracy was 24 percent compared to male illiteracy of 9.5 percent, a difference of 14.5 percent.[23]

To help address these education concerns in Latin America, USAID has designed several programs that make use of education development software to collect and analyze data for use by ministries of education, provide guidelines for educational reform, and replicate lessons learned from successful education reforms in Latin America and the Caribbean.[24] The agency has also produced studies on the impact of gender socialization on young children to assist NGOs and ministries in promotion of early learning and parent education.[25]

Over the past few years using gender as a funding criterion, USAID has given priority to programs that directly benefit women and girls and has budgeted $10 million in fiscal year 1999 for WID programs in girls' education, women's reproductive health, women's participation in micro-enterprises, political participation, and legal rights.[26] Within girls' and women's education, program guidelines emphasize training for female teachers, scholarships for girls, and increasing girls' retention and completion of elementary school. The guidelines encourage involvement from the private sector by calling on businesses to support girls' education and to raise parents', educators', and religious leaders' awareness of the importance of girls' education at the community and national levels.[27] The evaluation of Stromquist and colleagues of USAID's project in Guatemala presents a detailed analysis of how these guidelines were implemented within a nationwide project. The evidence from Guatemala supports USAID funding scholarships for girls but does not show that the involvement of the business community was effective in raising nationwide awareness on behalf of girls' education.[28]

Women's literacy has a major impact on a nation's population, health, and nutrition. Research indicates that high rates of national female illiteracy are linked directly to higher fertility and infant mortality rates. Furthermore, it has been estimated that for every year a girl stays in school beyond fourth grade, child deaths drop by 10 percent, family size decreases by 20 percent, and female wages rise by 20 percent.[29] USAID supports programs in population and family planning and women's reproductive health to help save lives worldwide. USAID maintains that women who are repeatedly pregnant cannot participate in their own social and economic progress.[30] Child health and nutrition are targeted areas of intervention. In developing nations, women are most frequently responsible for providing safe drinking water and nourishing, vitamin-enriched food for their families. Education and literacy give women the required knowledge for safer choices about nutrition and overall health.

In the case of Mexico, research indicates that formal education helps girls to acquire the dispositions that result in positive health choices and smaller families when the girls become mothers.[31] Smaller families, in turn, enable the mother and father to have more time and money to devote to their children's health needs. During the period of 1990–1995, Mexico was one of the Latin American and Caribbean countries with the lowest birth and mortality rates. By contrast, Bolivia and Haiti had among the highest birth and mortality rates in the region.[32]

In the case of Honduras, the Basic Education for All project, funded by USAID and implemented by the Division of Adult Education in 1992, provides basic education and training to adults using interactive radio instruction and textbooks. Areas of training include reading, writing, math, social studies, science, business, vocational training, and civics. USAID's Basic Education and Skills Training (BEST) Project and EDUCATODOS, implemented by the Secretariat of Public Education in 1995, are ongoing projects also utilizing interactive radio and textbooks. Women in Honduras are targeted for participation in these programs to increase their overall basic education and literacy, technical training, and business and entrepreneurial skills.[33]

USAID uses many different temporary subcontractors to implement its programs. To improve in the design and development of educational research and programs, USAID created a project entitled Advancing Basic Educational Literacy (ABEL). The ABEL projects work with a consortium of international consulting firms and universities that includes the Academy for Educational Development, Creative Associates International, Inc., Education Development Center, Inc., Florida State University, Harvard Institute for International Development, and the Research Triangle Institute. In the area of girls' and women's education, ABEL has had projects in Bolivia, the Dominican Republic, El Salvador, Guatemala, Haiti, Honduras, Jamaica, and Nicaragua. Expenditures in fiscal year 1995 from USAID to support these projects totaled approximately $25 million.[34] Yet, despite this level of expenditure, evaluations are not available in published form to guide future research and implementation of other programs. As of February 1999, countries in which ABEL remained active were Bolivia, Ecuador, El Salvador, Haiti, and Honduras.[35]

USAID's WID office has programs in Bolivia, Honduras, and Peru and works with a consortium led by the Institute for International Research. This group includes Abt Associates, CARE, Management Systems International, PLAN International, and World Education.[36] Most recent research and evaluation of girls' and women's education programs have been subcontracted to Juárez and Associates, Inc., and the Academy for Educational Development. Research projects on girls' education focuses on the concept of sustainability, which in the 1990s revolves around the central theme of human capacity-building to enhance the quality of life. Global comparisons of national economic and social indicators over time, such as per capita incomes, life expectancy, and educational attainment levels, are inadequate measures of quality of life issues because of the great disparities between the rich and poor people in most countries. Over the past ten years, the number of people living in poverty has increased. Therefore, a broader working definition of sustainability of girls' education programs today includes quality of life across generations. Factors such as educational access, enrollment, and completion rates for the poor and underserved populations are included in current sustainability analysis, as is a nation's ability to provide funding, technical capacity, and civic and political support. Sustainability also requires that start-up donor funding from outside the country be replaced over time by the country's own resources, whether it be from government funds or private sector support. A strategic form of new research is analyzing trends cross-nationally to ascertain whether some of the factors helping to sustain quality of life are more important than other factors such as access and completion rates.[37]

Juárez and Associates, Inc., is currently conducting a research study for USAID's WID office to create indicators for monitoring sustainable girls' education programs around the world. The project includes data collection, development and measurement of sustainability indicators, in-depth case studies, and revision of indicators based on research.[38] Preliminary conclusions indicate that foreign-sponsored programs for girls' education might influence the internal allocation of funds but have no influence on the amount of national education spending.[39]

Among the initiatives from the WID office to promote girls' and women's education, World Education is involved in a project called Girls' and Women's Education Activity, Component III (GWE III).[40] The research project focuses on sustainability in Honduras, Bolivia, and Peru, and is examining the outcomes of pilot and existing projects in girls' and women's education to help governments to create and implement cost-effective girls' and women's education programs.[41]

In Honduras, illiteracy has been linked to the high population growth rate, low-earning power, and the precarious lives of the poor. To reduce the problems caused by illiteracy, a five-year longitudinal study began in 1996 with a completion date expected in 2001 to measure the impact of the integrated women's literacy program, EDUCATODOS, which started in 1995 in three regions. Using interactive radio instruction and community volunteers as program leaders, the program is offered to women who have not had access to basic education, training in reading, writing, math, social studies, science, business, and vocational areas. The research is measuring change in seven areas including participation in economic activities, involvement in children's education, and use of health care.[42] A key question in the research is the degree to which women's participation in interactive radio instruction changes their attitudes and behavior when compared to a control group of women who have not participated in the program. The goal is to assess the long-term impact on women's socio-economic development after participation in adult literacy programs. Prior research does correlate formal primary education of girls and indicators of social and economic development.[43] However, literacy instruction for women without prior formal primary schooling has not yet been linked to indicators of social and economic development. USAID hopes that the results of the study will help to assess the effectiveness of non-formal versus formal training and fill a serious gap in the knowledge concerning cost-effective women's literacy programs.[44]

The research by World Education's five-year longitudinal study in Bolivia (1998–2002) is measuring the impact on the social and economic development of individual women participating in integrated basic education programs provided by well-established NGOs in Bolivia such as Pro-Mujer and Gregoria Apaza. The study attempts to design indicators of women's social and economic development, monitor changes in women's behavior and attitudes, and identify positive relationships between the basic education programs and women's behavioral and attitudinal changes. Specifically, the study will attempt to measure how women are affected in the areas of economics, children's education, health, agriculture, participation in community activities, legal rights, and political awareness.

Women participants in the integrated basic education programs will be compared to women who do not participate in the programs.[45]

World Education's longitudinal study in Peru is concerned with the reasons for the large disparity between adult male and female illiteracy. In 1995, 17 percent of females were illiterate, while only 5.5 percent of males were illiterate. Peru was selected for the study because anecdotal evidence suggests that local beliefs about puberty influence girls' schooling. The Peruvian study seeks to determine the average age and reasons for girls' dropping out of school before finishing primary education, investigate why girls begin school late, understand the role of puberty in dropout rates, and explore strategies to encourage girls to start school earlier and finish primary education.[46]

In sum, USAID is hoping to generate empirical knowledge, following the DAC commitment, on the relationship between nonformal and formal education of girls and women on the one hand, and economic and social development on the other. For girls, USAID is looking to confirm effects of school completion on reducing poverty and economic and social development. For nonformal programs and adult women, USAID is seeking confirmation for the social and economic benefits of investing in those programs. The strategy is to use the knowledge generated to inform and mobilize national leaders in government, business, and religious communities to create a national commitment to promoting gender equity. The overall strategy of USAID is a top-down model of change that is to hoping to promote gender equity by persuading national leaders of the value of providing additional knowledge and skills to women and girls so that they can participate more fully in national development. To gain more perspective on USAID's strategy, we will turn our attention to the funding priorities that are, in contrast, offered by the Netherlands.

GENDER AND DEVELOPMENT AND DUTCH NGOS

The Netherlands has a co-financing agreement with four major NGOs. This formal funding relationship between the government and the NGOs is set up to give the latter considerable autonomy in the implementation of gender and education programs. The model used by the Netherlands to provide funding to developing countries through their national NGOs stands in sharp contrast to the approach followed by the United States. The Netherlands follows a bottom-up model of change strengthening organizations in society that can lobby for the education of women and girls.

The four co-financing organizations sponsored by the Netherlands include ICCO (Protestant-Inter-church Organization for Development); BILANCE (Catholic Organization for Development Cooperation); NOVIB (Netherlands Organization for International Development), and HIVOS (Humanist Institute for Cooperation with Developing Countries). These organizations together receive approximately 10 percent of the budget for international cooperation of the Netherlands Ministry of Foreign Affairs. Of the four national NGOs, two of them are renowned for their contribution to strengthening women's organizations and development programs with a gender component. We turn our attention now to their programs.

NOVIB is the largest of the Dutch NGOs, and since 1981, it has been concerned with the needs of women. Today the priorities for NOVIB's funding include gender and development, the environment, and human rights. The goal of this NGO is to contribute to the empowerment of women in development programs. The funding priorities distinguish between Women in Development or WID programs and Gender and Development or GAD programs. The latter category includes programs that promote women's organizations, women's participation in decision making, and women's access to economic and natural resources and basic social services. The overriding goal of GAD programs is to change the "unequal relations between women and men."[47]

The programs being funded by NOVIB in Latin America are devoted to alleviating poverty by providing credit for income-generating activities, strengthening civil society by increasing cooperation between NGOs and local governments, and advocacy. To provide just a few examples of the many programs funded in Latin America, in 1996 three thousand women from rural NGOs coming from all countries in Latin America met in Brazil to discuss how to implement gender awareness programs in their respective organizations. Another concern of NOVIB is reducing the dependence of Latin American NGOs on international funding by organizing workshops to build local capacity and financing strategies.[48] In 1998, NOVIB had partnerships with 269 local NGOs in Latin America and was funding more than three hundred projects focusing on these three concerns.[49]

A 1996 evaluation found only 30 percent of the NGOs financed by NOVIB followed its priority on gender and development. To reduce the gap between funding priorities and implementation, NOVIB developed programs and strategies to integrate a gender perspective more deeply into the organizations with which is has established a partnership.[50] To create a stronger gender perspective among its Latin America partners in Chile and Peru, NOVIB is funding a project to develop indicators "to make visible the improvement of the position of women." Working with one women's organization in Guatemala, *Fundación Manuel Colom Argueta,* NOVIB is involved in a project introducing an ethnic dimension to public debate about women in Guatemala.[51]

A new priority for NOVIB, as a result of international commitment to the eradication of poverty and to the goal that all children should receive at least primary education, is to increase access for girls to formal schooling. Even though NOVIB in the past was not directly involved in funding education projects within formal education, special priority is being given now to the training of teachers for primary schools as well as tutors for nonformal programs.[52]

Another major Dutch NGO is HIVOS. Embracing a view similar to the priorities just described, HIVOS focuses on strengthening civil society through national NGOs. The aim is "to support organizations that enable people to assert their rights and improve access to decision making."[53] HIVOS gives priority to strengthening organizations, not just to funding their activities. Internal evaluations of its gender programs offer several conclusions regarding the impact of NGOs on women's well-being. Support of women's NGOs is their most important achievement. Long-lasting support of women's NGOs has contributed to "the relevance of issues such as violence against women's and women's reproductive rights." The evaluations also point out, however, the limited impact of women's NGOs on women's economic empowerment. Another conclusion is that without gender training courses for staff, the impact of the gender component on development projects is limited.[54]

These organizations are committed to advocacy for the advancement of women and the poor. The Dutch NGOs contribute part of their funding to global networks, supporting international networks such as the Women's Global Network on Reproductive Rights and DAWN (Development Alternatives with Women for a New Era). To promote awareness in the north of the situation in the south, NOVIB is funding an international campaign to raise awareness of the international commitment to eradicate poverty and child labor.[55]

The evaluation of programs sponsored by Dutch co-financing organizations is coordinated by the Policy and Evaluation Department of the Ministry of Foreign Affairs. Each of the NGOs favors different types of evaluations. NOVIB, for example, encourages self-evaluation for the receiving organizations to view and adopt the programs as their own, while HIVOS prefers thematic evaluations in a specific region, for example, on gender programs in Central America.[56] The evaluations are crucial for monitoring the type of learning that is happening to assess the effectiveness of the aid provided.

CONCLUSIONS

Looking to the twenty-first century, the donor countries and their agencies are seeking ways of strengthening basic education for the reduction of poverty worldwide. For each of the donor countries reviewed in this chapter, agencies and programs for international cooperation are rooted in national legislation and cultural traditions and institutions. International assistance is a two-way process for donor countries. The building of international cooperation provides a channel for promoting the donor country's cultural institutions, universities, and consultants. The kinds of projects funded can often be explained by internal priorities within the donor country and do not necessarily reflect the priorities of the receiving countries.

In all cases reviewed in this chapter, funding for the education of women and girls is part of an international effort to alleviate poverty. The chapter describes three main strategies of donor countries in the establishment of their international cooperation. USAID draws upon consultants and academic institutions in the United States to generate knowledge that might be used by the private sector and government in Latin American countries to create awareness of the national need to educate women and girls. The strategic concern of Dutch NGOs is the empowering of women to generate social and economic development and the eradication of poverty. Within this overall concern, they support women's NGOs to strengthen advocacy organizations and the women's movement within a country in order to create a national lobby to promote educational opportunities for women and girls. The Spanish model is based on close collaboration with the government of Latin American countries to implement gender equity policies. Spain's funding priorities are to increase the delivery of programs devoted to women as well as providing educational opportunities to women within different levels of the education system using Spanish consultants, NGOs, and higher education institutions.

Research on the dynamics of gender in schools in Latin America is just starting. The research presented in this chapter shows that education research concerning Latin American perceptions is not a priority of the programs being funded. Moreover, when agencies of donor countries include a gender component in their projects, it is based on their own experience and research, both in the United States and Europe. For each of the three donor countries reviewed, the inclusion of gender or a gender component in the development process has different meanings. USAID is focusing on increasing literacy training for adult women and schooling completion for girls in the hope of influencing economic and social development. The Netherlands aims to strengthen women's power and decision making within income-generating projects or to support women's advocacy through different means. Spain is promoting national policies on gender equity by incorporating gender awareness and gender training into courses for women at different education levels.

As the number of funded projects multiplies, the need to build a gender perspective into education with greater attention to the reality and cultural perspective of receiving countries becomes crucial. National universities and researchers in the developing countries need to play a more central role in international cooperation in order to create research capacity in those countries that might help the education initiatives promoted to have a long-lasting effect. Research provided through short-term contracts to highly paid international consultants, as is the case with USAID, might not capture the many cultural dynamics that must be engaged to promote long-lasting change, since the research instruments are designed in English and then translated to Spanish and in many cases the researchers might not be sensitive to local and regional differences. When it comes to building capacity, the interests of the donor countries and receiving countries can be at odds, since foreign assistance is a way for donor countries to promote their own research capacities, develop and employ their own professionals, and market their own cultural products.

International cooperation is a crucial element of reform in Latin America. In light of the obstacles that a gender perspective faces when implemented at the national level, the participation of international donor agencies is significant because it helps to legitimize this type of education reform. But such a contribution is inevitably short-lived unless at the national level there is an active lobby to promote these reforms and incorporate them into the national education laws. In the case of the program funded in Guatemala by the Spanish agency, there is a clear statement of this issue and the need to make women leaders aware of these reforms.

The cases reviewed in this chapter reflect a trend in bilateral aid—increasing access to basic education in order to alleviate poverty—that will undoubtedly continue into this century. Countries are following their DAC commitments and reshaping bilateral assistance in an effort to reduce poverty and overpopulation in the developing world. The cases highlight the multiple projects and NGOs being funded and the many levels of intervention through which donor countries have chosen to participate in Latin America.

NOTES

[1]OECD, "Shaping the 21st Century: The Contribution of Development Cooperation"(Paris: OECD, 1996).

[2]OECD, "Shaping the 21st Century," p. 2.

[3]OECD, "Shaping the 21st Century," p. 16.

[4]OECD/DAC, Table V-1, Official Development Assistance Flows in 1997, in OECD/DAC Statistical Reporting System, <www.oecd.org>.

[5]The authors' calculations are based on information provided in Table 2: UNESCO and the Expansion of Educational Multilateralism, 1965–1995, in Karen Mundy, "Educational Multilateralism in a Changing World Order: UNESCO and the Limits of the Possible," *International Journal of Educational Development* 19 (1999): 27–52, see table p. 35.

[6]OECD, "Shaping the 21st Century."

[7]UNICEF, *The State of the World's Children 1997* (New York: UNICEF, 1997), pp. 48 and 52.

[8]United Nations, "UNICEF Strategies in Basic Education" (New York: UNICEF, 1995), p. 7.

[9]Agencia Española de Cooperación Internacional, *Ley de cooperación internacional para el desarrollo* (Madrid: Ministerio de Asuntos Exteriores, Septiembre 1998).

[10]Agencia Española de Cooperación Internacional, "La Agencia Española de Cooperación Internacional y la igualdad de género en la ayuda oficial al desarrollo, Informe 1998," n.d., p. 14.

[11]Ibid.

[12]*op. cit.,* p. 21

[13]*op. cit.,* p. 15.

[14]Ibid.

[15]*op. cit.,* Tabla: Proyectos de Desarrollo con Componentes de Género, 1. Proyectos en Ejecución, p. 7.

[16]La Cooperación Española en México, Nota Informativa, Marzo de 1999.

[17]USAID, "Congressional Presentation Central Program" (1999, www.info. usaid.gov/), 18.

[18]USAID, "Congressional Presentation Special Interests" (1999, www.info. usaid.gov/), 6.

[19]USAID, "Congressional Presentation Program Performance" (1999, www. info.usaid.gov/), 7.

[20]USAID, "Congressional Presentation Special Interests" (1999, www.info. usaid.gov/), 6.

[21]USAID, "Congressional Presentation Program Performance" (1999, www.info.usaid.gov/), 1.

[22]United Nations, *The Equity Gap: Latin America, the Caribbean and the Social Summit* (New York: United Nations, 1997), p. 112.

[23]IIR Consortium, "Key Issues in Development Guatemala, Key Issues in Development Bolivia, Key Issues in Development Honduras" (Arlington, Virginia: n.d.). For detailed information about Guatemala, see Stromquist et al. in this volume; for Bolivia, see Lazarte and Lanza in this volume.

[24]USAID, "Congressional Presentation Central Programs" (1999, www.info.usaid.gov/), 17.

[25]USAID, "Congressional Presentation Central Programs" (1999, www.info.usaid.gov/), 17.

[26]USAID, "Congressional Presentation Central Programs" (1999, www.info.usaid.gov/), 18–20.

[27]USAID, "Congressional Presentation Central Programs" (1999, www.info.usaid.gov/), 19.

[28]Stromquist et al., in this volume.

[29]USAID, *Genderaction* vol.1, no. 2 (winter 1996/97): 8.

[30]USAID, "Congressional Presentation Program Performance" (1999, www.info.usaid.gov/), 8, 9.

[31]Florinda Riquer Fernández, *Aspectos sociodemográficos de la población rural y urbana* (México: Consejo Nacional de Población, 1995).

[32]United Nations, *The Equity Gap: Latin America, the Caribbean and the Social Summit* (New York: 1997), p. 131.

[33]IIR Consortium, "Key Issues in Development Guatemala, Key Issues in Development Bolivia, Key Issues in Development Honduras" (Arlington, Virginia: n.d.). The published reports do not provide information on how many women are served in Honduras.

[34]Christina Rawley for Creative Associates International, Inc., "Including Girls in Basic Education: Chronology and Evolution of USAID Approaches" (Washington, D.C.: 1997). Annex 4. Note: FY 1995 does not include expenditure in Guatemala.

[35]USAID, "Education & Training Building Knowledge, Skills, Participation, Empowerment and Hope" (1999, www.info.usaid.gov/).

[36]IIR Consortium, "New Frontiers for Girls' Education" (Arlington, Virginia: 1998).

[37]Juárez and Associates, Inc., USAID, "Sustainability of Girls' Education Initiatives: A System to Monitor the Sustainability of Girls' Education Initiatives" (Washington, D. C.: n.d.), pp. 1–3.

[38]Juárez and Associates, Inc., "Educating Girls; A Development Imperative New Knowledge: Study on Sustainability of Girls' Education Initiatives (Washington, D.C.: 1998).

[39]Juárez, "Sustainability of Girls' Education Initiatives," p. 9.

[40]World Education, "Girls' and Women's Education Activity, Component III," Boston, January 1998.

[41] IIR Consortium, "New Frontiers for Girls' Education" (Arlington, Virginia: 1998).

[42]World Education, "Research Design for Honduras Girls' and Women's Education Activity, Component III, Boston, January 1998.

[43]Paul Schultz, "Return to Women's Education," in King and Hill (eds.), *Women's Education in Developing Countries* (Baltimore: Johns Hopkins University Press, 1993), pp. 51–99.

[44]World Education, "Research Design for Honduras Girls' and Women's Education Activity, Component III, Boston, January 1998.

[45]World Education, "Research Design for Bolivia Girls' and Women's Education Activity, Component III, Boston, September 1998.

[46]World Education, "Attachment 1 Girls' and Women's Education Activity, Component III (GWE III) Program Description," Boston, September 1998.

[47]NOVIB, *More Power, Less Poverty: Novib's Gender and Development Policy until 2000* (Novib, 1997), Box 2: Gender and Development, p. 9.

[48]NOVIB, *Summary of Annual Report 1996*, p. 16

[49]NOVIB, *Summary of Annual Report 1998*, p. 18.

[50]NOVIB, *More Power, Less Poverty*, p. 5.

[51]NOVIB, *Summary of Annual Report 1998*, p. 18.

[52]*op. cit.*, pp. 10 and 21.

[53]Stein-Erik Kruse, "The Netherlands Case Study: NGO Evaluations Policies and Practices," Diakonhjemmets Internasjonale Senter (DIS), Oslo, May 1997. Appendix 5 of a report prepared for the OECD/DAC expert group on evaluation, "Searching for Impact and Methods: NGO Evaluation Synthesis Study, the University of Helsinki, Finland, <www.valt.helsinki.fi/ids/ngo/app542>, printed May 6, 1999.

[54]Stein-Erik Kruse, Box A5–3: Gender Evaluations, summary of evaluations conducted in 1991, 1992, 1993, 1994, and 1995.

[55]NOVIB, *Summary of Annual Report 1998*, p. 21.

[56]Stein-Erik Kruse, "The Netherlands Case Study," Chapter 4, Evaluation Methodologies, 4.1 NOVIB; 4.2 HIVOS; see appendix one for a complete listing on program evaluations.

REFERENCES

Agencia Española de Cooperación Internacional. "La Agencia Española de Cooperación Internacional y la igualdad de género en la ayuda oficial al desarollo, Informe 1998." n.d., p. 14.

Agencia Española de Cooperación Internacional. *Ley de cooperación internacional para el desarrollo.* Madrid: Ministerio de Asuntos Exteriores, Septiembre 1998.

IIR Consortium. "Key Issues in Development Guatemala, Key Issues in Development Bolivia, Key Issues in Development Honduras." Arlington, Va., n.d.

IIR Consortium. "New Frontiers for Girls' Education." Arlington, Va., 1998.

Juárez and Associates, Inc. "Educating Girls; A Development Imperative New Knowledge: Study on Sustainability of Girls' Education Initiatives. Washington, D.C., 1998.

Juárez and Associates, Inc., USAID. "Sustainability of Girls' Education Initiatives: A System to Monitor the Sustainability of Girls' Education Initiatives." Washington, D.C., n.d.

La Cooperación Española en México. Nota Informativa, Marzo de 1999.

Mundy, Karen. "Educational Multilateralism in a Changing World Order: UNESCO and the Limits of the Possible." *International Journal of Educational Development* 19 (1999): 27–52.

NOVIB. *More Power, Less Poverty: Novib's Gender and Development Policy until 2000* (Novib, 1997), Box 2: Gender and Development.

NOVIB. *Summary of Annual Report 1996.*

OECD. "Shaping the 21st Century: The Contribution of Development Cooperation." Paris: OECD, 1996.

OECD/DAC. Table V-1. Official Development Assistance Flows in 1997, in OECD/DAC Statistical Reporting System, <www.oecd.org>.

Rawley, Christina. Creative Associates International, Inc. "Including Girls in Basic Education: Chronology and Evolution of USAID Approaches." Washington, D.C., 1997, annex 4.

Riquer Fernández, Florinda. *Aspectos sociodemográficos de la población rural y urbana.* México: Consejo Nacional de Población, 1995.

Schultz, Paul. "Return to Women's Education." In Elizabeth M. King and M. Anne Hill (eds.). *Women's Education in Developing Countries: Barriers, Benefits and Policies,* pp. 51–99. Baltimore: Johns Hopkins University Press, 1993.

Stein-Erik Kruse. "The Netherlands Case Study: NGO Evaluations Policies and Practices." Diakonhjemmets Internasjonale Senter (DIS): Oslo, May 1997.

UNICEF. "The State of the World's Children 1997." New York: UNICEF, 1997.

United Nations. *The Equity Gap: Latin America, the Caribbean and the Social Summit.* New York, 1997.

United Nations. "UNICEF Strategies in Basic Education." New York, 1995.

USAID. "Congressional Presentation Central Programs" (1999, www.info.usaid.gov/).

USAID. "Congressional Presentation Program Performance" (1999, www.info.usaid.gov/).

USAID. "Congressional Presentation Special Interests" (1999, www.info.usaid.gov/).

USAID. "Education & Training Building Knowledge, Skills, Participation, Empowerment and Hope" (1999, www.info.usaid.gov/).

USAID. *Genderaction* vol.1, no. 2 (winter 1996/97).

World Education. "Attachment 1 Girls' and Women's Education Activity, Component III (GWE III) Program Description." Boston, September 1998.

World Education. "Girls' and Women's Education Activity, Component III." Boston, January 1998.

World Education. "Research Design for Bolivia Girls' & Women's Education Activity, Component III. Boston, September 1998.

World Education. "Research Design for Honduras Girls' & Women's Education Activity, Component III." Boston, January 1998.

USAID Efforts to Expand and Improve Girls' Primary Education in Guatemala

NELLY P. STROMQUIST,
STEVEN J. KLEES, AND SHIRLEY J. MISKE

INTRODUCTION

Guatemala is characterized by strong ethnic differences, marked economic disparities, and widespread poverty. After thirty-five years of civil war, Peace Accords were signed in December 1996 by the major parties in the conflict, the Guatemalan National Revolutionary Army (UNRG), the government, and the army. The civil war was extremely costly, with between 150,000 and 200,000 civilians killed or disappeared and a large segment of the population left in destitute status, including some 45,000 widows and an estimated 100,000 to 240,000 orphans. At present, one in six households is headed by a woman, and most live in extreme poverty.[1]

Educational statistics in Guatemala are imprecise; nonetheless, this country has one of the least educated populations in Latin America. Conservative estimates indicate that 43 percent of all women over fifteen years of age are illiterate, compared to 28 percent of all men.[2] While 78 percent of girls in urban areas enroll in primary school, in rural areas this percentage falls to 59 percent.[3] Girls have lower initial enrollments and lower retention than boys in rural areas because domestic work, agricultural work, and poverty greatly reduce the demand for their education. The compound effect of gender and ethnicity contributes to an even greater disadvantage for Mayan women compared to *ladino* (mestizo) women, with the former's illiteracy rate at 72 percent or almost three times greater than that of the latter (25 percent). Indigenous women average 0.9 years of schooling compared to 4 years among non-indigenous women. The current Peace Accords call for special attention to be given to the Mayan people, who speak twenty-one of the country's twenty-three indigenous languages and constitute between 50 percent and 60 percent of the population.

Educational supply lags substantially behind demand, further diminishing enrollments. Guatemala has a large number of one-classroom schools (*escuelas unitarias*), 95 percent of which are in rural areas. These schools, which usually cover three to four grades and provide low-quality teaching, do not enable students to attain stable literacy levels. Some 800,000 children—two-thirds of them girls—do not have access to primary schooling.[4] A 1992 study estimated a deficit of approximately twenty thousand classrooms.[5] Current rates of repetition and dropout absorb 20 percent of the Ministry of Education's (MOE) budget.

AN INITIATIVE TO ADDRESS GIRLS' EDUCATION

This chapter, which focuses on USAID initiatives in Guatemala since the mid-1980s, is based on an evaluation conducted in 1997.[6] The authors conducted fieldwork during a three-week period; data gathering methods included semi-structured interviews with a wide array of MOE personnel, private foundations, NGOs, and organizations interested in gender and bilingual issues. Numerous reports, evaluations, and plans concerning education in Guatemala were reviewed. In seven rural schools, the team observed classrooms and interviewed parents and teachers.

USAID began work on girls' education in Guatemala in 1987, when it funded a nongovernmental organization called the Guatemalan Association for Sexual Education (*Asociación Guatemalteca de Educación Sexual*, AGES) for four years. The project provided scholarships for about six hundred girls a year in thirty-three communities as a way to further girls' education, delay childbearing, and reduce fertility. An evaluation of AGES found that girls receiving scholarships completed their elementary education in 6.9 years of schooling—more efficiently than the national average, which over the years has oscillated between 7.5 and 11.6 years of schooling. The same evaluation found that in addition to the scholarship funds, the role of community promoters was crucial in disseminating the importance of girls' education and motivating parents to be supportive and aware of their daughters' education.[7]

Major support for primary education by USAID was initiated in 1989, when it created the Basic Education Strengthening Project (BEST). Its basic strategy called for a mix of activities that sought to "balance broad systemic improvements with specific classroom support, and institutionalization of project activities into existing organizational units."[8] BEST also planned for the investment of $30 million in development assistance grant funds over a period of six years. A component on "girls and women's education," later renamed the Girls' Education Program (GEP), was added in 1991. A midterm evaluation of BEST in 1992 led to a substantial reassessment and redesign of the project. The changes included a reduction of USAID project allocation from $30 million to $25.7 million, an extension of the project until the end of 1996, and an expanded role for GEP in two of the major BEST activities: bilingual education and the *Nueva Escuela Unitaria* (NEU).

To achieve its goals, BEST counted on coordinating its activities with the World Bank's Secondary Education Project in Guatemala in 1989. However, the government of Guatemala fell into arrears in its payments to the International Monetary Fund and the Bank project was delayed for three years. Moreover, the original BEST Project design was predicated on the expectation of a ten- to fifteen-year USAID commitment to education in Guatemala, which would support expansion of BEST activities. By 1992, as regional political tensions eased, USAID resource allocations fell sharply for Central America. The resources for the USAID mission in Guatemala (for all sectors) went from a high of almost $175 million in 1987 to less than $50 million in 1992, with an accompanying reduction in mission objectives. In 1992, USAID decided to withdraw support from the education sector in Guatemala by 1997. The December 1996 Peace Accords brought increased importance to education in the context of national reconstruction and thus to continued support by USAID, but BEST and GEP activities operated under a context of funding uncertainty and reduction.

Under the revised BEST project, the MOE was required progressively to assume recurrent costs and to hire staff necessary to expand BEST programs. Institutionalization was to be further ensured by linking the redesigned BEST to a new World Bank loan and to a large education loan from the Inter-American Development Bank. Both loans were expected by 1995, but were not signed until 1997.

A major design feature of GEP was its emphasis on private sector participation as a means to accomplish policy changes aimed at transforming how the Guatemala educational system dealt with gender issues. The private sector was seen to have two main roles: to form a group of private sector leaders to spearhead nationwide attention to girls' education, and to help the Ministry of Education and USAID to implement some specific components of GEP. It is also noteworthy that in designing and implementing GEP, an explicit decision was made to avoid treating gender issues as issues of equity. In the words of the USAID officer who played a key role in

the design and implementation of the gender efforts, "because of the polarization that exists on gender issues related to the discrimination of indigenous populations in Guatemala, girls' educational issues must be framed as
a social and economic question, not as an equity issue."[9]

It is of particular interest to examine the experience and trajectory of
GEP in Guatemala because it: (a) was accompanied by efforts to evaluate
some of the impact of the gender initiatives across a three-year period;
(b) was predicated upon the principle of cooperation among donor agencies; and (c) enabled an examination of the role of the private sector.

BASIC GEP COMPONENTS

The initiative to work on gender was amorphous, comprising several elements but having no major cohesive mechanism. Its major objective was
to increase girls' retention in schooling and, if possible, ensure that they
would complete the sixth grade. According to the initial design, two key
activities were to be *Eduque a la Niña* (Educate the Girl) and *Franja
Curricular* (Integrated Curriculum). *Eduque a la Niña* was a three-year
pilot project designed to test the impact of three different "packages"
implemented to improve the retention and achievement of girls in primary school. *Franja Curricular* was to involve the development of materials and programs for "integrating concepts, attitudes, and methods of
improving girls' attendance and retention" in all primary schools throughout the country.[10]

The *Franja Curricular* also called for training of MOE personnel at
all levels and in all regions in gender issues.[11] To carry out GEP activities, USAID hired a three-person local team, promoted the creation of an
Association for Girls' Education (a group comprising private sector
notables and education authorities), and contracted with private sector
foundations to implement specific GEP components. In this section, we
review some of these basic components of GEP. The activities of private
sector foundations in GEP will be examined in the section that follows.

Eduque a la Niña. This component of GEP was designed as an experiment to test three treatments designed to increase the retention of girls in
primary school, each implemented in twelve rural schools. The thirty-six
intervention schools and twelve matched control schools were spread over
six provinces with large Mayan populations. The three interventions were:

1. the provision of scholarships accompanied by the presence of
    social promoters to sensitize parents to the importance of girls'
    education;

2. the creation of parents' committees supported by promoters; and
3. the provision of gender-sensitive educational materials to teachers (without the support of promoters or parents' committees). This component was carried out by a foundation representing the large sugar growers of Guatemala, FUNDAZUCAR.

As with most such field experiments, there are serious deficiencies in the USAID-sponsored evaluation of GEP, especially in terms of the comparability of control and experimental schools.[12] Nonetheless, some results were visible.

While neither the creation of parents' committees nor the provision of gender-sensitive materials by themselves showed the expected positive effects, the awarding of scholarships (combined with parental participation) did show beneficial results. The approximately 420 girls receiving scholarships each year showed rates of attendance, promotion, and completion better than the control group and better than overall national statistics.[13] The greatest impact was on girls in grades 1 and 2. Longitudinal follow-up data, available only for 1996, corroborated these findings: Only 2 percent of girls with scholarships did not return to second grade in 1996, contrasted with 11 percent of girls without scholarships.[14]

Principals and teachers in scholarship schools reported more girls attending higher grades. As one teacher stated, "We are seeing more girls in fourth grade. A few years ago, I would have seen four in my class, now I have eight. Our school has now two girls *in ciclo básico* [the first three years of secondary schooling]." Some teachers also reported less timidity in girls. Evaluation results indicate that the yearly attendance of both girls and boys was higher in schools in which girls received scholarships than in the control schools, a phenomenon that suggested that boys are not hurt by efforts to help girls.

The scholarships the girls received amounted to $4.30 per month. Why such a small amount should make a significant impact must be examined in the light of the extremely poor rural economy. When remunerated jobs are available in the countryside, a typical wage is between $1.70 and $3.40 per day. It is not uncommon for rural parents to spend between $5 and $7 on notebooks and school materials at the beginning of the school year.[15] Girls and parents reported that, in addition to purchasing school materials, they used scholarship monies to buy clothing, food, and medicines. In other words, the scholarship amount, although minute by most standards, in the context of a rural subsistence economy, allowed Mayan campesinos to offset some of the direct costs of girls' schooling and provided a little cash for other necessities.

Educational Materials. The GEP team produced teachers' guides and sample activities to motivate girls' participation in the classroom. These materials were used in the *Eduque a la Niña* (for the third "treatment") and as part of the technical support given to the NEU and the *Dirección General de Educación Bilingüe* (DIGEBI). The *Eduque* materials packet included a flip chart showing the differential life chances of women with and without education; worksheets for students to review a day in the life of a girl and a woman; four short stories; a map of "famous" women in the world; and a motivational poster for girls bearing the slogan, "We will reach sixth grade." A teacher's guide, *A favor de las niñas,*[16] provided a lengthy introduction to social and economic reasons for educating girls along with a set of lessons intended to promote girls' and boys' self-esteem and to communicate the importance of diversity and cooperation. While the information and suggested activities seemed appropriate, the teacher's guide offered no direction on how to include girls' interests, needs, and life stories in daily lessons; how to correct for gender inequities in textbooks; or how to integrate the self-esteem building and other activities with regular subject matter. Moreover, the GEP team was not able to produce grade-specific materials to introduce gender throughout the primary school cycle.

The GEP technical assistance team developed a second manual, *Un mundo en común,*[17] during the final year of the project. This manual, addressed to the MOE's inservice teacher trainers, seeks to promote equal participation of girls and boys in the classroom. It offers a detailed discussion of attitudes that can be enhanced through classroom exercises and presents several exercises to foster the development of such attitudes. Unfortunately, the proposed innovative activities are "supplementary" and thus not integrated to the curriculum; they are "add-ons" that teachers can use or set aside.

Bilingual Education. The role of USAID in the promotion of bilingual education in Guatemala is widely recognized. In 1979 the agency began a pilot program which led to the establishment of the *Programa Nacional de Educación Bilingüe* (PRONEBI) within the MOE in 1984. In 1989, USAID's ongoing bilingual education activities were incorporated as a BEST activity. In 1995, under the leadership of the first minister of education of Mayan origin, PRONEBI was transformed into DIGEBI (*Dirección General de Educación Bilingüe*).

DIGEBI is still far from being institutionalized within the operations of the MOE. Bilingual education coverage is minimal compared to the prevailing Mayan composition of the student population. It operates in only 5 percent of existing schools (800 out of 16,000 schools), with 1,200 teachers classified as bilingual (out of 50,000 teachers nation-wide). Moreover, 60 percent of the bilingual schools provide bilingual education in grades one and two only. It is estimated that bilingual education covers only 8 percent of the Mayan children in their first year of primary school and only 2 percent of those in fourth grade.[18]

Although girls' education concerns were to be integrated into the provision of bilingual education with the expansion of GEP in 1993, gender-motivational materials and teacher training began reaching small numbers of DIGEBI teachers only in 1995. Within DIGEBI there arose conflicts regarding the acceptance of gender issues, many staff members generally preferring to give less attention to these matters. DIGEBI made some of its textbooks and flip charts more gender-sensitive; there was widespread agreement that much more needed to be done.

The Peace Accords empower the National Council on Mayan Education (CENEM), an NGO comprising twenty-two Mayan organizations, to monitor and contribute to the ongoing educational reform to ensure that it is appropriate to the linguistic and sociocultural reality of the country. The educational themes being treated by CENEM include inter-cultural sensitivity, inter-ethnic tolerance, education for peace, and education and the environment. When asked about gender issues, a CENEM leader indicated that they would be covered under the inter-ethnic tolerance theme, which is to include the elimination of sexual stereotypes. Thus, gender issues, though present, were limited among the Mayan reforms in education.

Nueva Escuela Unitaria. GEP also intended to influence the NEU. This program, based on the *"escuela nueva"* model that has been success-ful in Colombia, was adopted in Guatemala as a pilot project through BEST. It uses flexible individual and group study and active participation of learners. A focus on gender sensitization was not part of the original NEU design, yet as the NEU moved teachers away from traditional peda-gogical methods and introduced the use of small groups in the classroom, the innovation permitted girls to participate more actively and to have their experiences and knowledge recognized. The NEUs also benefited from some GEP motivational materials and training related to girls' education.

NEU evaluations confirmed that the use of participatory learning methods in the classroom, accompanied by motivational materials in favor of girls' education, increased girls' classroom participation and their per-sistence in higher primary grades. Nevertheless, girls continued to lag behind boys in primary school completion by about 6 percent during the final year of the project,[19] an outcome that argues for the need to give more special attention to girls.

In an attempt to integrate NEU innovations with bilingual programs and gender-sensitive materials of *Eduque a la Niña*, in 1995 DIGEBI initiated a program it called NEU-DIGEBI-Niña (NDN). This program was implemented by USAID on a pilot basis in thirty-six schools (different from those of *Eduque a la Niña*). Another adaptation of NEU, the *Educación Bilingüe Activa* (Active Bilingual Education, EBA) was instituted by the MOE in sixty schools in one Guatemalan department in 1996. These two programs—NDN and EBA—can be interpreted at one level as positive responses by the MOE to institute gender-related changes in the schools, but at the time of our study both were still small-scale pilot projects with no evidence on their effects.

GEP's Implementation Resources. To implement GEP on a day-to-day basis, BEST subcontracted with a U.S. firm to provide three locally hired experts, supplemented by short-term assistance. This GEP core team offered technical assistance on girls' education to the two other BEST programs—NEU and bilingual education—for planning and integrating gender concepts in the classroom. The GEP team also trained some MOE personnel (mostly supervisors and teacher trainers) on strategies to foster girl's attendance and retention and on instructional techniques to motivate girls' participation in class.

While the technical assistance provided by the GEP team was generally seen to be of high caliber, it had limited coverage. The small *Eduque* experiment was best served, with 95 percent of the teachers in the thirty-six "treatment" schools reporting having received training in girls' education in 1996. Teachers in NEU received less attention, with 62 percent reporting having had such training, and almost no DIGEBI teachers reported training in *Eduque* materials.[20] According to GEP staff members, the targeted NEU teachers benefited from the equivalent of eight days of gender training per year, while the few bilingual teachers reached were give only four hours of training per year on gender. Training was limited, therefore, to personnel in the USAID experimental and pilot projects, and in the case of one important group, the bilingual teachers, it seems to have been very brief and limited to a single occasion.

PRIVATE SECTOR ROLE

A major—and widely publicized—component of GEP involved the private sector in girls' education. The strategy was based on a belief in the comparative advantages of leading business firms to influence decision makers in government, to raise funds, to offer efficiency and transparency in management, to assist with strategic planning for external efficiency, and to mobilize resources. To accomplish these ideas, GEP worked with the Association for Girls' Education (AEN) and with three private sector foundations, as we discuss later.

One of the most successful outcomes of the early girls and women activity was a national seminar on girls' education in 1991, attended by numerous persons from various sectors of society. While some have argued that this seminar resulted in a national plan for girls,[21] it is more accurate to say that a commission on girls' education was formed at that conference and that, with strong input of the USAID mission, an "Action Plan for Girl's Education" was developed the subsequent year. Rather than constituting a coherent plan, this document listed a set of thirty-seven separate projects seeking potential adopters/implementors. A few of these projects were adopted by business firms, the most important being the *Eduque a la Niña* experiment, discussed earlier, and a social marketing campaign to promote education for girls.

AEN. An outcome of the 1991 national conference on girls' education, the AEN was incorporated as a nonprofit institution in 1994. It comprised at that time twenty-five persons from the private sector, from MOE, and from GEP, and sought to coordinate efforts in the private sector and to engage in fund-raising to help girls' education. AEN was organized as a collection of individual members rather than institutions. Some of the individuals who joined AEN did so because of their friendship with AEN's first board chair, the wife of Guatemala City's mayor. When she left AEN, several others followed. By 1997, only ten of the twenty-five members were active and only four paid their monthly fees of $85. During its first four years, AEN had two presidents and three executive directors. Substantial internal disagreements had arisen over objectives, administrative procedures, bilingual education, action on literacy, and the provision of technical assistance. The association had never had a regular budget for its own staff; as a consequence, many of the executive director's efforts were focused on AEN's own survival. In part through their participation in AEN, three private sector foundations did become involved in GEP activities.

FUNDAZUCAR. This sugar growers' foundation implemented and administered the experimental projects of *Eduque a la Niña*. The foundation was given a one-year USAID-funded contract, renewable if it was able to raise a promised $100,000 in private funds. This target was never met; nevertheless, each year the contract was renewed. FUNDAZUCAR received payment from USAID for its role in *Eduque a la Niña* (estimated at $1.5 million). It also received contributions from other international donors (about $840,000 in total from the Spanish and Japanese aid agencies and UNESCO). By FUNDAZUCAR's accounting, it did contribute its promised $1.4 million of its own money to the *Eduque* project. There has been no independent audit, and many are skeptical of that figure, noting the small number of schools covered and the limited nature of the three experimental "treatments."

Following the three-year demonstration project, FUNDAZUCAR evinced little interest in continuing its efforts in girls' education. According to a FUNDAZUCAR spokesperson, it had given the MOE "scientifically validated findings about what works and what does not," and that it was now up to the government to broaden its coverage to many more girls. According to FUNDAZUCAR, it had served 5,000 girls and now it was up to the government to intervene to serve the 500,000 girls estimated to drop out or never enroll in school. The foundation perceived the government as not interested and found this regrettable.

Fundación Castillo Córdova. This foundation, representing a beer and food producers' foundation, conducted two projects. The largest was a nationwide social marketing campaign to promote girls' education mentioned earlier. Billboards were put up in various parts of the country carrying the message: "Educated Girl: Mother of Development." (This message, although in favor of girls' education, was ambiguous in that it also reiterated their roles as mothers.) Many radio stations and TV channels collaborated through the provision of free airtime for the campaign. The foundation reportedly contributed $1.4 million to the campaign. In addition, the foundation initially engaged in a very successful, albeit small, mobilization campaign in eight villages in 1993 that sought to increase the enrollment of girls in primary schooling. The campaign brought together community leaders, university students, and Ministry of Culture staff for several days of community meetings, talks, plays, and contests. They were successful in increasing families' interest in girls' education, only to discover that the schools were unable to satisfy the demand following such an intensive mobilization. The mobilization was not repeated as a part of the nationwide social marketing campaign. Costs may be a partial factor, although foundation staff said both projects did not take a substantial amount of their resources because many of those involved contributed time and other resources.

Fundación Castillo Córdova initiated a new program in 1997 entitled *"La Cocina en mi Escuela"* (The Kitchen in My School). This program targets girls and provides them with cooking classes and recipes using products sold by the firms supporting the foundation. Staff at AEN, FUNDAZUCAR, and others observed that the emphasis on cooking for girls conveys a very stereotypical message of girls as domestic workers and was designed to promote sale of the foundation's products. The foundation justifies this emphasis by saying that its programs cover much more than cooking, as they also offer knowledge of nutrition and health and that its nutritious products are sold at a very reduced rate.

Fundación para el Desarrollo Rural (Foundation for Rural Development; FUNRURAL). Representing the coffee growers, this group was hired in 1996 by the MOE to administer its ailing girls' scholarship program. FUNRURAL has shown better administrative ability than the government in delivering the scholarship funds to the schools: The distribution of funds to parents' committees via bank transfers appears to be faster and more transparent. Since the foundation represents coffee growers whose operations are located in the highlands, FUNRURAL has been able to use its network of member firms in implementing its system. FUNRURAL receives a 7 percent commission of the MOE scholarship money for administering the scholarships, but by its own financial accounting that does not cover the foundation's costs. Another 3 percent of the MOE scholarship money goes to AEN to do some community work to motivate parents for girls' education.

Other Private Sector Involvement. An internal retrospective account of GEP[22] states that GEP has been assisted by seven public and private donors. The involvement in girls' education of private firms other than those mentioned earlier was modest. Shell Oil Company funded the training of teachers and the printing and distribution of one thousand girls' education flip charts. A few U.S. individuals, one North American NGO, and several Guatemalan individuals have contributed to girls' scholarships. The Baha'i Community donated notebooks for some scholarship recipients. Rafael Landívar University was involved in the production of short stories for the girls' educational materials, but this was a contractual relationship, not a donation.

MISSING ACTORS FROM CIVIL SOCIETY

GEP worked almost exclusively with the government and major private commercial/foundation sector organizations. It is striking to see the absence of important social groups in this project to promote girls' basic education. Women's groups and teachers' unions play important roles in the education of girls, roles widely recognized in the educational and social science literature and in international forums since 1985. Even though a few women's groups and NGOs were invited to the 1991 First National Conference on Girls, there was no subsequent involvement. AEN included only individuals associated with large business or governments. At least in part, reluctance of USAID to include a broader group of actors in the promotion of girls' education was due to the polarization in Guatemala as the civil war was ending.[23] This seems to have contributed also to the separation of emphasis on "women" and "girls." The GEP was originally called "Girls and Women in Development," but operationally it was defined to mean only girls and subsequently renamed to reflect that definition.

GEP's avoidance of conflict in general, and of equity issues and women's rights in the efforts to promote girls' education, were justified on the grounds of building consensus and promoting constituency for girls' education. Unfortunately, a broad consensus could not be forged given the narrow definition of civil society involvement. A number of women's groups as well as relevant NGOs and the teacher unions were in existence at the time GEP was initiated. Even the National Women's Office (ONAM), an official organization in existence since the late 1980s, was never included in GEP, despite having created a joint commission with the MOE to work on the elimination of sexual stereotypes in school textbooks in 1992. At the time we evaluated this project (August 1997), many of the women's groups we spoke with were not aware of the MOE initiatives in girls' education.

THE LIMITS OF GEP

While success and failure are ends of a complex continuum and hindsight is always easier than foresight, GEP could have accomplished much more than it did. What accounts for GEP achieving so much less than the system-wide impact that was planned?

First, GEP soon abandoned its explicit intent to promote systemic change. When GEP began, it encountered resistance almost everywhere within BEST and within the MOE;[24] gender issues were perceived as extra work by most people and unnecessary by some. *Franja Curricular,* the key system-wide curriculum reform and teacher training strategy, was dropped very quickly. The result of abandoning the system-wide *Franja* left GEP serving a limited audience within the BEST project, through *Eduque,* NEU, and the bilingual program.

The inability or unwillingness to involve major stakeholders in girls' education was another strategic flaw in GEP. As GEP began, there was recognition of the need to involve other groups[25] and even some attempt to do so in the first national conference. Regrettably, other than this, there was no serious attempt to engage the participation of the broader civil society.

Aid agencies often avoid controversy, especially in times of political turmoil. This is understandable, but such avoidance is never total—it is a matter of degree. Girls' education cannot be apolitical; by its nature it is about unequal access, disparate opportunities, and system-wide imbalance, that is, discrimination, sexism, oppression. The controversies generated by groups who advocate for gender equity is inherent to broader civil society's participation in girls' education initiatives, but such participation is essential to system-wide change.

In Guatemala, GEP's focus on big business foundations in the private sector was innovative and relatively politically safe. A few business-sponsored foundations made a contribution to the education of girls, but it is clear that much of this contribution had financial returns. In the case of FUNDAZUCAR, USAID gave it $1.4 million for its involvement in the demonstration project. In the case of *Fundación Castillo Córdova,* the social mobilization campaign engagement allowed it entry to the schools to pursue later efforts such as "The Kitchen in My School," which promoted their products and contributed to the gender stereotyping that GEP was supposed to combat. From the perspective of long-term support, it should be asked whether big business, which has a vested interest in keeping down taxation and hence the revenues available for education, can really become partners with the MOE and USAID in efforts to expand and improve schooling nationwide.

It was through GEP efforts that girls' education attained public salience; also through GEP the pressing issue of girls attaining complete primary education received public attention. GEP also succeeded in promoting a strong interest for girls' education among some leading business firms and other private sector groups. GEP personnel succeeded in organizing two national seminars focusing on the issue of girls' education and provided technical assistance as well as materials on girls' education to NEU and DIGEBI.

In part due to the previous work by AGES, but also due to its contacts with GEP, the Ministry of Education, under a woman minister, initiated a broader pilot program of scholarships for indigenous rural girls in 1994, at the same time *Eduque* was starting. The goal of the initial MOE pilot project was to reach six thousand girls a year, but serious implementation problems, especially irregularities and inefficiencies in the distribution of the funds, led to smaller and sporadic coverage. Despite these problems, the MOE expanded the goal to a single cohort of 36,000 girls (grades 1 to 3) for three years, to raise "a generation of educated girls." As discussed earlier, MOE contracted with a private foundation, FUNRURAL, to administer and implement the program. While the original scholarship program targeted Mayan girls, the revised program includes all girls without specifying that Mayans will receive any sort of priority. There are over 600,000 girls in primary school and another 500,000 in this age cohort who are not enrolled, the vast majority of whom are poor and Mayan.[26] The scholarship program is modest, covering only 7 percent of the enrolled girls. On the other hand, it represents one of the few instances in which a government has funded a scholarship effort on its own.

As an integral part of the BEST Project agreement, the government of Guatemala agreed to a variety of conditions that were never complied with. Perhaps of most importance to the implementation and institutionalization of BEST activities throughout an expanded primary school system, the government of Guatemala agreed to almost double its support for education (to 3 percent of its GDP). The government also agreed to provide counterpart funds for BEST equivalent to $59.5 million, and progressively to assume the recurrent costs of BEST activities, reaching 100 percent support by 1996. The MOE also made various commitments to hire new personnel, including two girls' education specialists.

The MOE and the government of Guatemala did not meet any of these conditions or agreements. Specifically regarding GEP, it was only in 1997, the final year of the project, that GEP's technical assistance got a counterpart in the MOE to develop guidance for gender-sensitive textbooks and teacher training. Given the magnitude of the proposed changes along gender lines in basic education in Guatemala, with multiple fronts and activities, the staff available to work on the GEP project—three full-time members (only one of whom had postgraduate studies in education)—was simply much too small. Moreover, the staff did not work within MOE facilities, which further contributed to isolate the impact of GEP.

Policy reform concerning girls' education has been minimal. In the redesigned BEST, GEP was to have as its major objective the promotion of policy reform through the work of AEN and the *Franja Curricular* process.[27] However, no new policy analysis unit was formed, AEN barely functioned, and the *Franja Curricular* was not pursued. The minister most supportive of the girls' education (a woman) enacted a series of policy principles in favor of girls' education in 1993, written up in a brochure. These principles called for increasing the enrollment, retention, and achievement of girls; strengthening the national curriculum with content that promotes girls' education; sensitizing the school community, especially parents, about the need to promote girls' education; and linking with various social sectors to develop activities to promote girls' education. The principles in this brochure appear with no identified timelines, resources, or delegation of responsibility within the MOE to enact them. While persons associated with GEP identified this brochure as constituting a government policy,[28] when we conducted the study, the brochure was out of print, very few people knew of it, and there was no evidence of implementation.

Looking for other signs of policy change, we found that Guatemala's current Five-Year National Plan stated that the government of Guatemala will increase the coverage of preprimary and primary schooling, emphasizing bilingual/intercultural education and girls' education in both rural and marginal urban areas to attain universal primary education (six grades) by the year 2000.[29] The government of Guatemala activities previewed in the plan to expand coverage of schooling include decentralization, the expansion and strengthening of PRONADE (an initiative to have parents' committees at the school level), school construction, school feeding programs, adoption of schools by the private sector, and the provision of "innovative and alternative modalities to expand coverage." None of the specific activities consider girls or indigenous girls, nor is the provision of scholarships to facilitate girls' education mentioned. The activities for the specific objective of improving the quality of education do include the "elimination of any type of discrimination in teaching materials and methods,"[30] but this text makes no direct reference to gender or ethnic issues. On the positive side, although not linked directly to gender, the share of primary education as a proportion of the educational budget in 1997 was 61 percent, a notable increase from the 32 percent registered in 1992.[31]

In November 1996 the MOE attempted a policy reform to create in the teacher training schools a curriculum component addressing girls' education, increased parental involvement in the administration of their schools, and more bilingual education programs. According to ministry officials, this reform was rejected by the teachers' unions, fearing more work for the same pay and changes in hiring and firing procedures. As a result, the MOE dropped this initiative.

Donor coordination was supposed to be a key element in the plans to expand and sustain GEP and other BEST activities. Successful BEST programs (including GEP) were expected to be taken to scale by the government of Guatemala through loans from the World Bank and the Inter-American Development Bank (IDB). However, as discussed earlier, there were lengthy delays in lending that allowed for little coordination. When the loans finally did materialize, there was little evidence that girls' education was going to receive much attention. The World Bank loan ($33 million) emphasizes decentralization and incorporates little from BEST programs: Bilingual education and girls' education are allotted only 2 percent of project funds. The IDB loan ($15 million) seeks to "improve the quality of education at preprimary and primary levels" of all Guatemalans through the provision of textbooks, teacher training, and curriculum revisions. Content analysis of the proposed IDB activities indicate a desire to adapt the materials to the cultural and linguistic heritage of Guatemala. Only passing reference is made to the need for girls' education, which is mentioned as a concern when developing new curriculum guides that are to include "an appreciation . . . of girls' education in the learning process" and in inservice teacher training, which is to include "the importance of girls' enrollment and completion of studies."[32] We do not know, at this point, about the implementation of such concerns.

LESSONS LEARNED

In addition to the need to work with a broader sector of civil society and to espouse conflict as a natural element in the process of social change, some lessons emerge.

Target Girls Specifically. USAID targeted the most disadvantaged social group in Guatemala: indigenous girls. Wherever BEST resources were applied to girls' issues—in scholarship incentives, material development, social marketing, parental involvement—they helped change people's attitudes, awareness, and behavior. A focus on girls, in this particular case, Mayan girls, is particularly important to the strategic objective of reducing poverty.

Provide Scholarship Support. Positive results were seen in the *Eduque* pilot project's scholarship package. The direct and opportunity costs of schooling continue to be major barriers to the schooling of poor girls and boys in Guatemala and elsewhere. While there are political and financial obstacles to instituting large-scale scholarship programs, a nationwide program, even if short-term, directed toward the most disadvantaged girls could make a substantial contribution to closing the gender gap in primary education.

Involve Parents. Mothers and fathers (although not in large numbers) in rural areas took advantage of the opportunity to participate in parents' committees in two of the experimental "treatments." Mayan parents, especially mothers, saw education for their daughters as very important for giving the girls the possibility of "getting out of bad marriages," the ability to "plan their number of children," and the capacity to "make their own decisions." In economic terms, parents saw education as helping their daughters get "better jobs." When parents were asked if they thought a woman's place was in the home, a common reply was, "Times have changed. Now we need more income to survive." Parental participation, in terms of making an impact on girls' attendance and retention, appeared significant only in the case in which parents' committees were accompanied by scholarships. This suggests that under conditions of extreme poverty, as in rural Guatemala, changes in parental attitudes and knowledge is not sufficient to offset the cost to the family associated with girls' schooling.

Link Girls' and Women's Education. There should be an integral connection between the education for girls and women; their separation was not productive in Guatemala. It is not possible to isolate girls' education from the substance and politics of women's concerns. With democracy, women are an increasingly strong political force and, potentially, a voice for girls' needs and interests. There are many ways of linking education for girls and women in meaningful ways including, for example, encouraging mothers to participate more actively in their daughters' education and assisting NGOs working with adult women to address formal and nonformal education issues. All work done in girls' education should make possible the active engagement of groups concerned with women's education and development.

Mobilize All of Civil Society. The fabric of society comprises much more than large business firms. The focus on this segment of the private sector did little to change girls' education. The private sector can contribute to education, including to the support of girls' education. However, it is unlikely to be a major sustainable source of resources for field activities. Businesses can contribute to tasks integral to their activities, such as school-to-work programs, efficient administration, management, and strategic planning. For broad social issues, like the expansion and improvement of girls' education, the private sector can be a participant in a broad mobilization of civil society, but there are many other constituencies who must be included in fundamental ways in order to yield progressive social change.

Bring Successful Projects to Large Scale. Too many efforts unnecessarily take the form of pilot projects, absorbing substantial resources that could be used more effectively by trying to bring well-demonstrated activities and policies to nationwide scale. Beginning a system-wide innovation on a small scale is usually necessary, but donor-run pilot projects, especially experimental ones like *Eduque,* are usually very expensive and so isolated and insulated that they are seldom scaled up. Pilot projects generally should be run by governments with expansion plans built into the pilot, with support from donors where appropriate. In Guatemala, support for NEU and the MOE scholarship program would have made more sense than *Eduque.*

Choose Conditions and Agreements Carefully and Endorse Them. USAID is well known in development circles for its insistence on agreements and conditions established with "partner" countries and, in fact, has been characterized as "high interventionist."[33] Questions of sovereignty and practicality make conditionality a very complex issue. For example, conditions designed to support IMF-style economic reform are quite different from those that could be designed to further Peace Accord social reform. In our view, conditions should be chosen that would have popular support among those who are supposed to be the beneficiaries of aid.

Surprisingly, in USAID's dealings in Guatemala on education, and gender in particular, there was an obvious disregard by the government of Guatemala for agreed-upon actions, ranging from doubling its education sector support to hiring two girls' education specialists in the Ministry of Education. This disregard for commitment certainly contributed to make the effort for girls' education fragile and unstable.

Improving the education of girls in Guatemala, and elsewhere, is clearly a very difficult task. Too often, despite good intentions, the efforts of donors and countries serve more to legitimate that "something is being done" rather than to mobilize the resources and the people that could make progressive change possible. In Guatemala, unfortunately, this has been true of GEP. The lead role that was supposed to be played by the private sector did not materialize and the relatively few resources USAID put into GEP was spent on very small-scale efforts instead of system-wide change in the education of girls, as had been envisioned. Today, GEP has ended and USAID is funding a new project to promote girls' education in Guatemala, *Proyecto Global,* as one part of a global effort in this area. The project started in 1997 for a five-year period with a total budget of about $2 million, funded through USAID's Women in Development office in Washington. It is hoped that the new project will have the opportunity to build upon the lessons drawn from BEST and GEP and, hopefully, the vision to chart a new course. The Peace Accords and their reaffirmation of women's roles as citizens may provide a good opportunity to accelerate, expand, and sustain efforts to improve girls' education.

NOTES

[1]Rigoberta Menchú, "La sobrevivencia de las Culturas Indíigenas," *Revista USAC* no. 2 (1996): 122–126; *Grupo de Ayuda Mutua,* telephone conversation (1997).

[2]SEGEPLAN, *Desarrollo social y construcción de la paz. Plan de acción 1996–2000* (Guatemala, Secretaría Generalde Planificación, November 1996); Mary Hill Rojas, *Assessing the Integration of Gender into the Strategies of USAID/Guatemala and the Central American Program* (Washington, D.C.: WINDTECH, 1997).

[3]SEGEPLAN, *op. cit.,* p. 41.

[4]UNICEF, *Realidad socioeconómica. Con énfasis en la situación del niño y la mujer* (Guatemala: UNICEF, 1994); Gabriela Nuñez, *La iniciativa de la educación de la niña en Guatemala. Una retrospectiva* (Guatemala: SIMAC, Ministerio de Educación, 1997).

[5]Ministerio de Educación, *Anuario estadístico* (Guatemala: MOE, 1992).

[6]Nelly P. Stromquist, Steven J. Klees, and Shirley Miske, *Impact Evaluation: Improving Girls' Education in Guatemala* (Washington, D.C.: Center for Development Information and Evaluation, Agency for International Development, July 1999).

[7]IDEAS, *Guatemalan Girls Scholarship Program* (Guatemala: IDEAS, 1994); Susan Clay, "The Education of Girls in Guatemala: From Oversight to Major Policy Initiative." Paper presented at the Comparative and International Education Society annual conference, San Diego, 21–25 March 1994.

[8]Creative Associates, *Improving Education in Guatemala: A Midterm Evaluation of the BEST Project. Vol. 1. Findings by Evaluation Objectives* (Washington, D.C.: Creative Associates, 1992), p. 11.

[9]Clay, *op. cit.,* p. 10.

[10]USAID, *Guatemala Project Paper. Basic Education Strengthening. Amendment Number 1* (Washington, D.C.: USAID, 1993), p. 24.

[11]USAID, *op. cit.*

[12]Stromquist et al., *op. cit.*

[13]Ray Chesterfield and Fernando Rubio, *Incentives for the Participation of Guatemalan Indigenous Girls in Primary Education. Final Evaluation of the*

Eduque a la Niña Project (Guatemala: Juárez & Associates and Academy for Educational Development, 1996).

[14]Chesterfield and Rubio, *op. cit.*

[15]Julia Richards, *Promoción escolar de niñas rurales Proesa-Xtani* (Guatemala: CARE, 1996).

[16]Ministerio de Educación, *A favor de las niñas. Rincón de recursos para comprender, explicar y facilitar el aprendizaje sobre la situación de la niña* (Guatemala: NOE, 1993).

[17]Ministerio de Educación, *Referencias políticas y estratégicas para la educación, 1993–98* (Guatemala: MOE, c. 1997).

[18]UNICEF, *op. cit.*; SEGEPLAN, *op. cit.*

[19]Ray Chesterfield and Fernando Rubio, *Impact of the BEST Project on Girls' and Mayan Participation in Guatemalan Primary Education* (Washington, D.C.: Juarez and Associates and Academy for Educational Development, 1996), p. 12.

[20]Ray Chesterfield, and Fernando Rubio, *Impact Study of BEST Teacher Effectiveness in Guatemala Primary Education* (Guatemala: Juaréz & Associates and Academy for Educational Development, 1997).

[21]Nuñez, *op. cit.*

[22]Nuñez, *op. cit.*

[23]Clay, *op. cit.*, p. 10.

[24]Creative Associates, 1992, *op. cit.*

[25]Clay, *op. cit.*

[26]Nuñez, *op. cit.*; Ministerio de Educación, *op. cit.*, c. 1997.

[27]USAID, *op. cit.*, p. 53.

[28]Clay, *op. cit.*; Nuñez, *op. cit.*

[29]SEGEPLAN, *op. cit.*, p. 43.

[30]SEGEPLAN, *op. cit.*, p. 45.

[31]Chloe O'Gara, Sharon Benoliel, Margaret Sutton, and Karen Tietjen, *More, But Not Yet Better. USAID's Programs and Policies to Improve Girls' Education in Developing Countries* (Washington, D.C.: Center for Development Information and Evaluation, Agency for International Development, 1998).

[32]IDB, Guatemala, *Proposal for a Loan to Support Education Reform* (Washington, D.C.: Inter-American Development Bank, mimeo, 1997), pp. 15–16.

[33]Diane Elson and Rosemary McGee, "Gender Equality, Bilateral Program Assistance and Structural Adjustment: Policy and Procedures." *World Development* 23, no. 11 (1995): 1987–1994.

REFERENCES

Chesterfield, Ray and Fernando Rubio. *Impact of the BEST Project on Girls' and Mayan Participation in Guatemalan Primary Education.* Washington, D.C.: Juárez & Associates and Academy for Educational Development, December 1996.

Chesterfield, Ray and Fernando Rubio. *Impact Study of BEST Teacher Effectiveness in Guatemala Primary Education.* Guatemala: Juárez & Associates and Academy for Educational Development, 1997.

Chesterfield, Ray and Fernando Rubio. *Incentives for the Participation of Guatemalan Indigenous Girls in Primary Education. Final Evaluation of the Eduque a la Niña Project.* Guatemala: Juárez & Associates and Academy for Educational Development, January 1996.

Clay, Susan. "The Education of Girls in Guatemala: From Oversight to Major Policy Initiative." Paper presented at the Comparative and International Education Society annual conference, San Diego, 21–25 March 1994.

Creative Associates. *Improving Education in Guatemala: A Midterm Evaluation of the BEST Project. Vol. 1. Findings by Evaluation Objectives.* Washington, D.C.: Creative Associates, 1992.

Elson, Diane and Rosemary McGee. Gender Equality, Bilateral Program Assistance and Structural Adjustment: Policy and Procedures. *World Development* vol. 23, no. 11 (1995): 1987–1994.

Grupo de Ayuda Mutua. Telephone conversation, 8 July 1997.

IDB, Guatemala. *Proposal for a Loan to Support Education Reform.* Washington, D.C.: Inter American Development Bank, mimeo, 1997.

IDEAS. *Guatemalan Girls Scholarship Program.* Guatemala: IDEAS, September 1994.

Menchú, Rigoberta. "La sobrevivencia de las culturas indígenas." *Revista USAC* no. 2 (1996):122–126.

Ministerio de Educación. *Anuario estadístico.* Guatemala: MOE, 1992.

Ministerio de Educación. *A favor de las niñas. Rincón de recursos para comprender, explicar y facilitar el aprendizaje sobre la situación de la niña.* Guatemala: MOE, 1993.

Ministerio de Educación. *Un mundo en común. Manual para fomentar la participación equitativa de niñas y niños.* Guatemala: MOE, 1997.

Ministerio de Educación. *Referencias políticas y estratégicas para la educación, 1993–98.* Guatemala: MOE, c. 1997.

Nuñez, Gabriela. *La iniciativa de la educación de la niña en Guatemala. Una retrospectiva.* Guatemala: SIMAC, Ministerio de Educación, May 1997.

O'Gara, Chloe, Sharon Benoliel, Margaret Sutton, and Karen Tietjen. *More, But Not Yet Better. USAID's Programs and Policies to Improve Girls' Education in Developing Countries.* Washington, D.C.: Center for Development Information and Evaluation, Agency for International Development, December 1998.

Richards, Julia. *Promoción escolar de niñas rurales Proesa-Xtani.* Guatemala: CARE, 1996.

Rojas, Mary Hill. *Assessing the Integration of Gender into the Strategies of USAID/Guatemala and the Central American Program.* Washington, D.C.: WINDTECH, April 1997.

SEGEPLAN. *Desarrollo social y construcción de la paz. Plan de acción 1996–2000.* Guatemala: Secretaría General de Planificación, November 1996.

Stromquist, Nelly P., Steven J. Klees, and Shirley Miske. *Impact Evaluation: Improving Girls' Education in Guatemala.* Washington, D.C.: Center for Development Information and Evaluation, Agency for International Development, July 1999.

UNICEF. *Realidad socioeconómica. Con énfasis en la situación del niño y la mujer.* Guatemala: UNICEF, 1994.

USAID. *Guatemala. Project Paper. Basic Education Strengthening. Amendment Number 1.* Washington, D.C.: USAID, August 1993.

Ambiguities in Compensatory Policies
A Case Study from Brazil

FÚLVIA ROSEMBERG

The changes made in the standards for bringing up young children will certainly be remembered as a hallmark of the twentieth century. Care and education of young children has been taking place outside the intimacy of the home environment to an ever-increasing degree, especially since the Second World War. Regardless of their economic backgrounds, young children are increasingly destined to share educational experiences with their contemporaries under adult guidance in collective surroundings such as day-care centers, nursery schools, kindergartens, and preschools. Thus, the bringing up of young children and care for the elderly—two of the remaining traditional family functions—are, at least partially, being moved away from the domestic sphere and from the family's exclusive control.

In this new scenario, the young child's well-being ceases to be the exclusive concern and responsibility of the private sphere, and shifts into the public policy arena. Early childhood care is now public and negotiated between social actors, open to regulation and state control, and subject to scientific inquiry and research. In other words, during this century we have witnessed how the lives of young children have moved into the public sphere or, as Verret affirms, we have witnessed "the collectivization of practices that previously belonged to the private domain."[1] Why should the family let go of its exclusive domain over this function, which was previously considered the only way to guarantee its offspring's physical survival and psychological health? Two correlated factors are frequently mentioned in developed countries: the modification of gender relations and changes in the concept of the young child.

As a matter of fact, a consensus has been reached in recent comparative studies about the evolution of early child care and preschool education policies. These studies consider the evolving decrease in the distance between male and female adult roles and the incentives for greater female participation in the job market to be among the determining factors in the recent expansion of early child care and preschool education provision. Women have always married, worked outside the home, and been mothers, but there have been two changes: First, these activities no longer take place successively but occur either simultaneously or in a new form, which has resulted in a significant number of women with young children working outside the home and living in single-parent families. Second, women from different socioeconomic levels now share this experience, including the middle and upper classes. In multiracial countries, women from different racial groups share the pattern as well.

The feminist movements of the 1960s and 1970s questioned both the ideals of marriage and maternity as being the only destiny for women. Thus, demands for the decriminalization/legalization of abortion, the expression of desire for individual fulfillment outside of the home, and the calling on men to exercise their paternal roles were all-important indicators in the construction of a new role for adult women. A role where, paraphrasing the Brazilian song, *the child does not belong only to the mother and the woman does not belong only to the child.*

As a result, the 1960s and 1970s saw an increase in concrete actions and reflective discussions as well as in the production of knowledge. The increase in the number of facilities—although there were still insufficient facilities for the youngest children—and quality improvements also made them attractive for children of families from the richer sectors of society. Wealthier families began to compete for resources that were previously used by the small middle class and the working class, such as day-care centers and *écoles maternelles* in France, and this led to higher quality and standards. The increase in resources and the improved quality in turn had a potential impact on the number of women who could enter the job market.

These concrete actions were accompanied by and fed into a production of new knowledge, which questioned the psychological paradigms that indisputably associated maternity with humankind's mental health (for example, the earlier research about attachment and Freudianism). This, among other things, led to a reevaluation of the father's role in the care of the small child.

Over the last decades, we have been witnessing a formidable change in the assessment of early child care and preschool education. From being a necessary evil for poor families, early child care and education has become an alternative that changes gender relations. It now allows women to leave the home and also allows the reproductive cycle of the patriarchal family to be broken, thus liberating the mother, the father, and the child from the traps contained in the Oedipal triangle.[2]

However, "women's liberation" does not in and of itself explain the massive shift in attitude. Another important movement of the second half of the twentieth century has been the reevaluation of young children's educational needs and capacities.[3] This movement justifies the search for other institutions in order to enrich the child's socialization even for families in which the mother does not work outside the home. In developed countries, sending a child to preschool does not mean a precocious start on school learning, but allows him or her to have different favorable experiences of psychological development thanks to the provision of an educational environment especially envisioned for this purpose. Thus, a search for part-time or full-time early child care and preschool education that is not restricted to families in which the mother works outside the home can be observed in various countries throughout the world. The young child's newly identified needs are valued to the extent that special institutions are necessary for them to be satisfied.

As one can see, the discourse about early child care and preschool education has also been accompanied by justifications centered on children's needs.[4] When this discourse comes from rich countries, it emphasizes the child's need for social interaction with other children of his or her own age as a result of demographic changes and of the city's new configuration. Young children, with no siblings, locked into apartments in dormitory towns, need the new social spaces offered by day-care centers and kindergartens. This concept of the young child and baby as a social being has penetrated the psychological disciplines over the past few decades and has come to construct a new social image of the infant very distant from the "egocentrism" described by Piaget.

In a mutually reinforcing process, the expansion of quality collective institutions allowed the observation of normal children interacting precociously. The psychological concept of early infancy now sees the baby as an able and social being. This, in turn, reinforced the need for spaces in which the child could develop his or her abilities and sociability. This

process of "coming and going" which . . . characterized the relationship between research and the daycare center contributed to the legitimization

and diffusion of new images of earliest infancy and of its needs . . .
which definitively overthrew the stereotype of the baby as a being who
only needs physiological care . . . ; the precocity of his/her capacity to
produce appropriate actions, to have and sustain significant exchanges
with an adult partner even in the absence of refined communication
instruments has been demonstrated."[5]

To a certain extent, the ability to love and to be capable of responding to parental affection has been attributed to the young child. These are
the main reasons given by modern couples for having children, as has
been affirmed in studies of modern couples in rich societies.[6]

Examining universal standards around early childhood education
shows that there is a tendency for an age group to be given access to educational institutions, but not for all the children of a whole generation to
have access to the same educational experience. When middle-class families gave up part of the responsibility for their young children's upbringing, they did not abrogate their prerogative to impose limits on the extent
of interaction between their children and children from other social sectors. Preschool education systems exhibit sufficient variation to allow
both families and institutions to make a large variety of mutual choices
and rejections, with the exception of a few countries where one objective
of these institutions is to lessen the social distance between its citizens.
In developed countries, children of richer families generally go to better
quality establishments than those of poorer families. As we will see later,
there is also a big difference in the meaning of quality in child care and
preschool education between rich and poor countries.

The ambiguity becomes clear when one focuses on gender relations
and the promise of overcoming inequalities apparent in the mother-child
dyad. When looking inside infant education establishments, one can see
that gender relations have migrated from the private sphere into the public domain. In fact, in most countries, most of the people working in
early child care and preschool education establishments are female educators. Approximately 100 percent of women teachers in preschool education in the developed countries and Latin America were women in
1990, while in Africa and Asia the percentage was only 65 percent and
92 percent, respectively.[7]

If the worldwide movement for collective early child care and
preschool education effectively breaks down the mother-child dyad, it
reinforces the woman-child dyad. This reinforcement not only arises
from the strong presence of women educators in preschool education. It

is also reinforced by the home/family day-care center model found in many countries, in which a woman looks after a group of children in her own home, constituting a form of female labor in the home. These women often have less training than that required for an elementary school teacher, or no training at all, and thus they tend to receive lower wages. "The guardians of under five-year-old children are amongst the workers who receive the lowest wages in the social structure, are less valued, have a lower status . . . [and] more closely resemble missionaries than professionals."[8]

The insufficient educational and professional training given to the educators of small children is especially pronounced in underdeveloped countries and was epitomized by Mina Swaminathan in the expression "the myth of hidden ability."[9] This myth says that all women by nature and due to a biologically given condition have the ability to look after and educate small children in groups without the support of any professional training other than the informal socialization gained in practicing motherhood.

The aspiration to make early childhood and preschool education a universal standard to improve gender equity and childhood well-being faces some dangerous pitfalls. Adult women are confined with small children for long periods of time, and they do not have the exposure to the diversity of sex or ages that are necessary for human social and psychological development. They orient children from a tender age toward educational trajectories that can either be enriching or impoverishing— the poorer the country the greater the risk.

These traps were laid for poor women and children in the underdeveloped regions, especially in Latin America, where access to preschool went from serving 8.5 percent of the children population in 1970 to 51.5 percent in 1995,[10] when governments broadened early child care and preschool education based on the argument of equality of opportunity in elementary education. In the context of the need to universalize elementary education, specialists and politicians attributed two sometimes complementary functions to early child care and preschool education: to prepare the child for elementary school and to make up for deficiencies in the impoverished migrant populations. This latter tendency, which in the 1960s incorporated the theories and ideology of cultural deficit and of compensatory education, was responsible, up to a certain point, for the creation and expansion of special programs directed to poor children in underdeveloped countries. In Brazil, this concept of early childhood education has been considered to be one of the main positions that influenced the expansion of access during the 1980s, designing it according to the adopted universal care profile model proposed by the multinational organizations UNESCO and UNICEF. These issues will be treated in the next section.

THE LOW-COST EARLY CHILDHOOD
AND PRESCHOOL EDUCATION MODEL

Like other underdeveloped countries, Brazil has been bombarded with many consultants, recommendations, and proposals from international and multilateral organizations. Their influence in drawing up and implementing social policies has been considerable. They have been actors in the interplay of tensions, conflicts, and coalitions that have characterized Brazilian social policies aimed at poor sectors of the population. The expansion of low-cost early childhood and preschool education in Brazil in the 1980s resulted from an unfortunate marriage between multilateral organizations and the military governments that were in power in Brazil between 1964 and 1984. This marriage was possible because the engagement took place against the backdrop of the Cold War, and the engagement ring shared by the fiancées was the key concept of "community participation" for implementing programs aimed at poor children.

In her excellent study entitled *Ideology of Community Development in Brazil,* Safira B. Ammann (1982) agrees that the Cold War was the source of the community development theory and of the idea that the poor are the most receptive prey to international communist propaganda. A USAID manual on community education published in Brazil stated it clearly: "In the present ideological struggle, famished peoples are more receptive to international communist propaganda than prosperous nations."[11] Another passage asserted that "the effort to help people achieve a healthier and more economically productive standard of living would eliminate potential sources of communism." This is where the emphasis given to these programs begins, not building from a conceptualization of social policy based on citizens' rights. The similarities between the national security doctrine (the doctrine that oriented political actions of the Brazilian military governments) and the concept of "community development" is not only the result of a bipolar view of the world as a battle between communism and "the free world." It is also based on a notion of society governed by a view of balance and harmony.

In 1956, the United Nations defined "community development" as a "process by which the people's own efforts are united with those of governmental authorities to improve social, cultural and economic conditions in the communities, to integrate these communities into national life, and to give them the capacity to contribute fully to the country's progress."[12] In this view of society, processes of circular causation explain the existence of social inequalities. In other words, the poor are, by deficiency, left out of the process of development. To put an end to this situation, compensatory action is needed (in the areas of health, food, and education), especially addressed to children, to save them from the destiny that poverty has reserved for them.

The concept of "community development" found its way into Brazil through rural missions immediately after the Second World War, and was subjected to regulation by the military government. In 1970, the Center for Coordination of Community Development Programs (CPCD) was set up. It conceived "community development" as an "instrument for popular participation and a system of work aimed at facilitating joint use of resources from the population and the government, and at improving results from both."[13]

The low-cost early childhood education model implemented in Brazil at the end of the 1970s and 1980s was based on a concept of community participation that aimed to diminish government spending in the sector. This model had been incubating inside UNICEF and UNESCO since the end of the 1960s. The longest-lived influence on the new low-cost early child care and preschool education concept came from UNICEF, through the Brazilian National Department for Children (DNCr).[14] It was phased out in 1968.

UNICEF, like any other organization, has been reformulating the principles that guide its proposals and actions. During the 1950s and 1960s, the conceptual bases were laid that gave shape to the low-cost early child care and preschool education model implemented in various countries, including Brazil. Among the various guidelines from the period, I would like to underscore one: emphasis on the community participation strategy to implement social policies aimed at poor children. During the 1950s, UNICEF was still concentrating its efforts on improving health and nutrition for poor children. The organization "was performing true pioneer work for the benefit of African children and mothers. In English-speaking countries, UNICEF contributed to the setting up of advanced care systems that, for the first time, appealed to the participation of the community." Since then, the difficulties encountered in assuring the participation of the inhabitants have already been noted.[15] Even so, the principle of "community participation" was systematically included among guidelines for low-cost early childhood programs. Henry Labouisse, then executive director, referring to the 1965 report of the Executive Office, underscored not only the need for greater attention to preschool activities, but also underscored the format that should characterize the programs. In the same presentation, he emphasized work with disadvantaged populations, using local funds and "non-conventional" methods, attributing a catalyzing role to UNICEF. A 1968 joint UNESCO-UNICEF document on preschool children insists on the need for special attention to young children and recalls the difficulties of implementing formal programs in developing countries. It then suggests "a possible solution that some developing countries are adopting in setting up preschool facilities as annexes to primary schools, using a less elaborate model that is cheaper than [traditional] kindergartens."[16]

An important moment for Latin America was the UNICEF conference held in Santiago, Chile, in 1965. The conference recommended that plans for national development should take into account the overall needs of children and youth, including preschool children. This called for ministries to coordinate their actions and to incorporate the efforts of groups and community movements. These new characteristics formed the bases for the new proposals for low-cost early child care and preschool education in Brazil.

The DNCr represented Brazil at the Santiago Conference, and also attended the UNICEF Executive Committee meeting in 1965. This meeting was convened to discuss the large-scale protection of young (preschool) children.[17] The DNCr prepared a report for this meeting diagnosing the situation of young Brazilian children, and brought back from the meeting the ideas that became the basis of the department's Preschool Children's Assistance Program, presented at the First Inter-American Congress on Preschool Education in Rio de Janeiro in 1968. The document contains the basic guidelines for government proposals for preschool children followed during the 1970s and part of the 1980s.[18]

The 1967 plan is clearly a policy for assistance to young children, and not an educational policy. This distinction was lost, however, when programs were denominated nationwide preschool educational programs. The sober-toned document describes the program as an emergency plan. This tone was lost in subsequent proposals in the 1970s and 1980s. The word *emergency* was replaced by *alternative, non-conventional* (as in Henry Labouisse's 1965 document), or *informal,* as opposed to traditional education. What was initially created because of a lack of funds ended up being treated as a theoretical ideal.

The DNCr proposed setting up recreation centers. Although no such centers were created at the time, they provided the model for future programs. Their objectives were assistance to and development of the whole child. The model broadened the concept of preparation for mandatory schooling, but with a strong preventative connotation. The concept was enlarged to one of mass assistance by extending "low-cost" coverage through the use of simple buildings, unused space or community space, plus the use of voluntary or semi-voluntary work by lay persons, that is, women without professional training.

This same model of expansion of early child care and preschool education had also been gestating within UNESCO since the end of the 1960s. The early child care and preschool education model proclaimed by UNESCO from its founding until the realization of the so-called "Faure Commission"[19] was inspired by the experience of the French *écoles maternelles*. This model, which offers universal quality care, was internationally disseminated through the OMEP (World Organization for Preschool Education). The OMEP, an NGO accredited by UNESCO, received, in turn, continuous assistance from the French Committee of that organization, made up mainly of inspectors from the French *écoles maternelles*. Mme. Herbenière-Lebert, inspector general of the *écoles maternelles*, was OMEP's representative to UNESCO between 1950 and 1968. Herbenière-Lebert's participation was fundamental for the approval of Recommendation 53 on preschool education on the occasion of the Conference of Ministers in 1961 and fundamental to the magisterial statute of 1966. The child care and preschool education model adhered to at such conferences foresaw a multiplicity of functions (prevention, care, socialization, and education), defended quality care adapted to the needs of children and supported in the professional training of the educator. In its recommendations on the magisterial statute at the Conference of Ministers of Education in 1966, the OMEP (through Herbenière-Lebert) included the proposal to bring preschool teachers to the same level as other professors in terms of training, remuneration, and workers' benefits.

A second stage began at the end of the 1960s. It constituted another model, announced for the first time through the Faure Commission in the report published in 1972 and applied more specifically to underdeveloped countries. The model contemplates minimal state investment in the expansion of early child care and preschool education, which should be supported by community participation. The state confines its primary focus and aid to basic education. The theory that informs the model is that of "human capital" along the lines of compensation theories: Early child care and preschool education would make up for the lack of psychosocial and cultural development of the impoverished populations suffering underdevelopment. More economy and planning consultants and specialists were recruited, relegating the assistance of psychologists and pedagogues, which had characterized the former period, to a secondary plane.[20]

In the report of the commission presided over by Edgar Faure, preschool education was identified as the first stage in permanent education. Because it was termed an "essential pre-condition for any educational and cultural policy," its coverage needed to be broadened. The manner suggested to expand spaces was through low-cost, "nonformal" solutions partially assumed by the families. The goal was to "try to organize education for preschool children (beginning at 2 or 3 years old) in a flexible way, seeking to involve the family and the local community in tasks and expenditures. [It] also tried to utilize the modern communications media which can provide great services, mainly for children who live in environments with limited cultural stimulation."[21]

Evaluations of the Ministry of Education's (MEC) project illustrate its resemblance to UNICEF's and UNESCO's proposals. "It is an attempt to implement a true policy for educational compensation that aims to equalize educational opportunities" (Evaluation CFE 2018/74), through the adoption of nonconventional models, seeking to mobilize the entire community (Indication CFE 45/74). As an epigraph to the Preschool Education report, the Faure Commission's recommendations on preschool education also appeared in 1975 and represented a new national perspective developed by the MEC Preschool Education Section (associated with the Basic Education Department). This was the ministry's first national-level program, and it reflected UNICEF's and UNESCO's recommendations in their totality. The program recommends integration of education, nutrition, and health, utilizing available (or idle) physical space in the community. The family and the community should be an integral part of preschool education activities, both to increase understanding of the importance of preschool education and to lower program costs. Mass media should be utilized to reach populations geographically distant from the school.

The new preschool education model was promoted through publications and through seminars with the participation of state secretaries of education. The MEC became a national promoter of the proposals that conformed to recommendations of intergovernmental agencies. Simultaneously with the formulation and dissemination of the new discourse on universal child care and preschool education, a specific preschool education administrative section, complete with new personnel, emerged within the MEC. Despite the persuasiveness of its initial discourse, it has actually had little impact on the educational system. Enrollment increased only slightly, and significant changes in preschool organization that would indicate the implementation of a universal low-cost model were not observed. The educational levels of the teaching staff, the number of children per teacher, and the distribution of enrollments throughout the networks remained the same throughout the period under study (1975 to 1981). Despite the new paradigm, the working standard continued to be elitist.

Despite having developed a national universal preschool education program, MEC did not succeed in implementing it during the 1970s. Instead, the *Legião Brasileira de Assistência* (LBA) (Brazilian Legion for Assistance), a federal foundation linked to the Ministry of Social Welfare, had a direct presence in nearly all the nation's cities. Launched in 1977, *Projeto Casulo* (Project Cocoon) expanded rapidly, surpassing the initial goal of serving seventy thousand children in its first year. Although the facilities were called day-care centers, the model resembled a preschool because it offered predominately half-time openings for children four years and older. Acting indirectly, passing on resources to private institutions and city governments, the LBA managed to implement a national program before the Ministry of Education was able to accomplish the job. The LBA successfully implemented its project because, in addition to having a budget, the project tied its distribution of funds to the institutions and city governments to the fulfillment of operational requirements and it also had technical assistants at the local level who had working experience within the community in social welfare projects. The LBA did not face resistance, while MEC did because it had to work through state education departments that still defended a formal model based on professional qualifications.

To disseminate *Projeto Casulo* during the government of General Geisel (the penultimate military government), the LBA used the discourse of preventing social disorder within "pockets of resentment," that is, among the poor populations mainly in the urban periphery, capable of threatening national security. Like the social policies of that government and in the Cold War context, *Projeto Casulo* incorporated the national security doctrine in its discourse.

The MEC, for its part, managed to implement the universal program only in 1981. It achieved this objective through the changes in another federal foundation, the MOBRAL (*Fundação Movimento Brasileiro de*

Educação de Adultos, Brazilian Movement for Adult Education Foundation), which had also developed nationwide community work experience through micro-level efforts. MOBRAL, which was created in 1970 to carry out adult literacy programs, saw its very existence threatened due to continued high illiteracy rates, as evidenced after the 1980 census. In order to maintain its technical structures, resources, and presence in the municipalities, MOBRAL reorganized and implemented a National Program for Preschool Education, supporting the low-cost community participation model.

Thus, the MEC and the LBA appear to have utilized practically the same young clientele and to have been supported by similar administrative instruments, a network of technicians linked to the federal administration and the distribution of funds through contracts, linked to a centrally defined preschool model.

Later on, both institutions adopted converging models of early child care and preschool education. Aiming to compensate for deficiencies, they subordinated education to social work, defined the same zones and regions as priorities for intervention (the Northeast region and urban peripheries), and based the implemented pedagogical model on the same principal, that is, cost reduction. Both programs were evaluated right after their installation, evaluations that revealed the implications of the low-cost model: inadequate training of personnel, insufficient pedagogical materials, a precariousness of the physical plant, and even problems with the food offered to children.

These evaluations, however, met the same destiny as observations made in Africa in the 1960s. They were not considered at all when the program proposed by UNICEF was implemented. Thus, Brazil, which served approximately 374,000 children up to six years of age in 1970, served 2.5 million children in 1984 (the first school census to include the new preschool programs). When the UNICEF/UNESCO "new model" for low-cost early child care and preschool education reached Brazil, the country did not have a shared solid public experience with early child care and preschool education to counter propose. Early child care and preschool education became a demand of the women's movement only at the end of the 1970s, but received little attention from the academic community when the "new model" was introduced. The "new" low-cost early child care and preschool education model entered into the social ideal, and became, from then on, the dominant model.

Analyzing the federal government's plans during the period, especially in education, Ferrari concluded by expressing perplexity in the face of what he perceived to be an attempt to reconcile various contradictory actions. These actions were centralization of the federal budget, reduction in the percent of the budget for education, extension of obligatory schooling to the seven- to fourteen-year-old age group, expansion of vacancies at the upper levels of schooling, and governmental priority given to preschool education. Expanding low-cost early child care and preschool education through voluntary or underpaid work done by women solved part of the contradiction. As we shall see in the next section, this constituted the cheapest alternative for basic education for certain population groups (the poor and blacks in the Northeast region).

THE EXPANSION: DEMOCRATIZATION OR GROUPING BY DEMOGRAPHICS?

When the growth rates are examined, there is no doubt that the expansion of preschool enrollment in the period could be qualified as spectacular: 991.8 percent in the period 1970–1993, and 206 percent between 1980 and 1993.[22] The growth rates were high across different segments of the population, independent of income level, rural or urban location, racial identity, or sex of the child (Table 1). One could consider this to be democratization of supply. However, the democratization of early child care and preschool education in Brazil cannot be analyzed just from the point of view of its expansion, but must also be looked at from the internal differentiation deriving from this expansion and from the relationship between preschool and basic education.

When we turn our attention to the age composition of the initial enrollments, we see that Brazilian early child care and preschool education has come closer to the model of early schooling through the preschool. The historical series (Table 1) shows that the percent of initial enrollments among children younger than four years of age is small, and care is preferentially part time (four hours daily or less). The adopted model gave little attention to the function of complementary care given to babies (the life stage that requires more care) while mothers work.

Some important conclusions can be drawn from the historical data associated with this increase in the number of initial enrollments from 1983 to 1984. A significant increase occurred in initial enrollments in the rural areas (137.3% between 1983 and 1984); in children older than six years of age (a 198.1% growth rate in initial enrollments between 1983 and 1984); and in residents of the Northeast region (68.8% of new initial enrollments occurred in the Northeast). Of the 397,739 first-time enrollments

Table 1. Characteristics of Expansion of Preschool Education in Brazil, 1969–1993

First Enrollment

Year	Total (thousands)	−4 Years (thousands)	%	6 Years (thousands)	%	+ 6 Years (thousands)	%	Rural (thousands)	%
1969	343	3	1.0	150	43.6	—	—	8	2.5
1970	374	4	1.2	160	42.9	—	—	8	2.2
1971	422	4	1.0	195	46.2	—	—	8	2.0
1972	460	7	1.4	206	44.9	—	—	10	2.3
1973	499	11	2.2	205	41.2	—	—	9	1.9
1974	530	16	3.0	209	39.4	—	—	11	2.0
1975	566	19	3.4	212	37.5	—	—	11	2.0
1976	707	74	10.4	244	34.5	33	4.6	14	2.0
1977	780	83	10.6	269	34.5	33	4.2	18	2.3
1978	945	103	10.9	310	32.8	46	4.9	21	2.3
1979	1,198	128	10.7	403	33.6	69	5.8	27	2.2
1980	1,335	151	11.3	441	33.0	77	5.8	35	2.6
1981	1,544	176	11.4	512	33.2	86	5.6	42	2.7
1982	1,867	189	10.1	638	34.2	95	5.1	83	4.4

Year	Total (thousands)	-4 Years		6 Years		+ 6 Years		Rural	
		%	(thousands)	%	(thousands)	%	(thousands)	%	(thousands)
1983	2,084	10.9	228	32.8	685	5.4	112	5.7	118
1984	2,482	8.1	202	36.3	901	9.4	233	11.3	281
1985	2,524	11.0	272	31.9	804	5.3	131	5.8	143
1986	2,971	10.0	297	4.2	1,017	5.5	165	10.5	312
1987	3,296	9.8	322	3.3	1,098	6.0	197	11.4	375
1988	3,376	9.0	305	30.7	1,036	7.4	251	12.7	431
1989	3,396	9.8	332	33.8	1,148	7.5	253	12.7	431
1990	2,753	9.2	254	35.6	982	6.4	177	10.6	293
1991	3,628	9.4	340	32.7	1,185	8.2	299	14.2	515
1992	3,058	7.8	240	36.0	1,101	7.2	221	13.2	403
1993	4,086	8.7	356	31.4	1,285	11.3	465	17.9	733

Sources: 1969–1975 (Brazil, MEC/SG/SEEC, 1977); 1976–1978 (Brazil, MEC/SG/SI/SEEC, 1981); 1979–1980 (Brazil, MEC/SG/SI/SEEC, 1983); 1981–1983 (Brazil, MEC/SG/SI/SEEC, 1984); 1984 (Brazil, MEC/SG/SEEC, 1986b); 1976–1983 (Brazil, MEC/SG/SAEP, 1985); 1984–1989 (Brazil, MEC/SAG, 1990); 1990–1993 (Brazil, MEC/SAG/CPS/CIP 1992, 1994, 1994a, 1994b, 1994).

examined by the Educational Census of 1984, 81.8 percent were distributed in just seven states: Maranhão (22.7%), Bahia (17.2%), Minas Gerais (12.8%), Ceará (11.0%), Paraná (7.2%), Goiás (5.9%), and Pernambuco (5.0%). Some of these states, especially in the Northeast, extended enrollment mainly to children over six, thanks to the labor of underqualified teachers. These are two aspects worth highlighting: the expansion to include overage children in the preschool system, children who according to the constitution should have been in elementary school, and the expansion based on using underqualified teachers. This process of inclusion and exclusion needs to be described in more detail, paying attention to the complex dynamic of gender subordination and social and racial discrimination that left marks on the profile of Brazilian students attending preschool.

Together with the entry of 397,739 first-time enrollments in 1984, more than 14,528 new teachers with less than secondary education (the level of school training for elementary school teachers) entered the preschool system. Thus, if we accept the 1983 adult/child ratio of 1/23.6, these new teachers, without complete training, were responsible for almost the entire process of expansion. In other words, the 14,528 new teachers without complete training would have absorbed 342,860 new enrollments, or 86.2 percent of the expansion. Not only did underqualified teachers absorb the increased enrollments during this period, as can be observed in the historical data, but the installation of this model is evident in the almost continuous increase in the number of preschool educators who have completed only primary education. In 1993, they made up 20.6 percent of early child care and preschool education teachers (Table 2).

Furthermore, one notes the growth in the percentage of children seven years or older in preschool (Table 3). The failure to make the body of teachers in early child care and preschool education more professional was accompanied by the inverse phenomenon in elementary teaching. While in 1985, 14.4 percent of elementary school teachers had not completed their professional training, in 1987 this number fell to 11.0 percent and reached 10.3 percent by 1993.[23] Thus the devaluation of early childhood education seems to be accompanied by a tendency, even if only a weak one, to more highly value elementary teaching. Early child care and preschool education admits and retains the segments of the population with the highest rates of exclusion from elementary education, poor and black children.

By linking these two observations, I have developed the main thesis

Table 2. Teaching Positions (TP)

Year	Total Teaching Positions	Elementary Only Positions* Number	%	Enrollment/TP Ratio
1969	15,260	1,572	10.3	22.5
1970	16,996	1,872	11.0	22.0
1971	20,720	2,156	10.4	20.4
1972	22,586	2,283	10.1	20.4
1973	24,573	2,809	11.4	20.3
1974	26,355	3,187	12.1	20.1
1975	26,393	2,076	6.3	21.4
1976	33,070	2,059	6.4	21.4
1977	37,600	2,416	6.4	20.7
1978	45,255	2,670	5.9	22.2
1979	51,704	2,916	5.6	23.2
1980	58,788	3,216	5.5	22.7
1981	66,824	3,529	5.3	23.1
1982	81,049	5,012	6.2	23.0
1983	88,149	—	—	23.6
1984	109,514	19,540	17.8	22.7
1985	108,208	—	—	—
1986	123,167	18,872	15.3	24.1
1987	137,702	22,640	16.4	23.9
1988	142,117	22,407	15.8	23.7
1989	147,087	23,756	16.2	23.1
1990	122,427	16,607	13.6	22.5
1991	166,917	31,585	18.9	21.7
1992	136,194	21,448	15.7	22.4
1993	192,340	39,560	20.6	21.2

* Including incomplete secondary school.
Sources: 1969–1975 (Brazil, MEC/SG/SEEC, 1977); 1976–1978 (Brazil, MEC/SG/SI/SEEC, 1981); 1979–1980 (Brazil, MEC/SG/SI/SEEC, 1983); 1981–83 (Brazil, MEC/SG/SI/SEEC, 1984); 1984 (Brazil, MEC/SG/SEEC, 1986b); 1976–1983 (Brazil, MEC/SG/SAEP, 1985); 1984–1989 (Brazil, MEC/SAG, 1990); 1990–1993 (Brazil, MEC/SAG/CPS/CIP 1992, 1994, 1994a, 1994b, 1994).

Table 3. Rates of Schooling for Children Ages 5 to 11, by Age, Sex, and Level of Instruction

Age Groups	Total (thousands)	% Students	% in Preschool	% in Elementary School
All		A=B+C	B	C
5 and 6 Years Old	6,271	64.1	55.6	8.4
7 to 11 Years Old	16,764	92.3	7.3	85.0
7 Years Old	3,279	87.7	20.8	66.9
8 and 9 Years Old	6,739	93.0	6.2	86.8
10 and 11 Years Old	6,745	93.9	1.8	92.1
Males				
5 and 6 Years Old	3,189	63.0	54.6	8.4
7 to 11 Years Old	8,586	89.5	7.6	81.9
7 Years	1,679	86.7	21.3	65.4
8 and 9 Years Old	3,487	87.7	6.4	81.4
10 and 11 Years Old	3,420	92.7	2.1	90.7
Females				
5 and 6 Years Old	3,082	65.2	56.7	8.5
7 to 11 Years Old	8,353	93.2	6.8	86.5
7 Years Old	1,601	88.7	20.2	68.5
8 and 9 Years Old	3,427	93.6	5.7	87.9
10 and 11 Years Old	3,325	95.0	1.4	93.6

Source: Brazil. *Pesquisa Nacional por Amostra de Domicílio, 1995* (Río de Janeiro: FIBGE, 1995).

of this chapter: Early child care and preschool education in Brazil not only does not perform the functions assigned to it in developed countries, it also provides a poor alternative to elementary education, retaining poor and black children who would be candidates for repetition in the early grades of compulsory education. Thus, gender inequality joins race and social class in Brazilian preschool education to exclude some populations from quality education while it includes them in preschool.

Basing itself on the principle of "women's innate ability to be child educators," the low-cost model employed teachers who had no pertinent experience, whether personal or professional, for early child care and preschool education. They knew school from their experiences as children, but many of them had abandoned formal schooling. Brazilian early child care and preschool education came to be, in many cases, an early form of obligatory schooling, and even proposed to teach children literacy. This impoverished model of early child care and preschool education penetrated the poorest regions with the aim of compensating for deficiencies. These poorest regions of Brazil, defined as priorities, are also those areas with a high proportion of blacks. Thus, Brazilian child care and preschool education demonstrates a pattern of exclusion equivalent to that of elementary school. There is a growing population of children being retained in preschool even though they are at the appropriate (and compulsory) age for elementary school: They tend to be boys slightly more than girls (Table 3), and that they tend to be black children from the poorest regions, mostly in Northeastern Brazil (Table 4).

The option to expand early child care and preschool education through a nonformal model, economically dependent on the low salaries of underqualified teachers, primarily in the North and Northeast regions, transformed standards in the supply of early child care and preschool education, not just with regard to regional development, but also in racial terms. Brazil's racial composition varies by region. Nonwhites (the group of persons classified as black and brown), which made up 45.0 percent of the population in 1995, represent 71.3 percent of the residents of the North-Northeast regions and only 15.2 percent of the Southern region.

This diversity in racial composition by region has been explained, in part, by historical factors including the configuration of the system of slave labor at the end of the nineteenth century and immigration policies. According to Hasenbalg, 35 percent of whites lived in the Southeast region in 1872, and 41 percent in 1890,[24] while only 21 percent and 20 percent of blacks and browns resided there on those respective dates. This tendency was accentuated in later years. In 1940, 52 percent, and in 1950, 56 percent of the white population resided in the Southeast. In 1995, according to PNAD data, considering the same division adopted by Hasenbalg (Southeast plus the South), the percentage of whites rose

Table 4. Percentage of 5- to 11-Year-Old Students Attending Preschool by Race, Sex, and Region of Residency.

	Children Attending Preschool	
	5 and 6 Years Old	7 to 11 Years Old
Race (1990)		
Whites	56.3%	36.5%
Black and Mulattos	43.1%	63.5%
Total	2,847,587	1,100,185
Sex (1995)		
Males	49.9%	53.5%
Females	50.1%	46.5%
Total	3,489,222	1,216,454
Region of Residency (1995)		
North*	5.6%	5.3%
Northeast	36.5%	66.2%
Southeast	42.5%	21.8%
South	9.6%	2.5%
Center-West	5.8%	4.1%
Total	3,489,222	1,216,454

* It includes only urban areas in the northern region.
Source: Special tabulations based on Brazil. *Pesquisa Nacional por Amostra de Domicílio, 1990* (Rio de Janeiro: FIBGE, 1990); Brazil. *Pesquisa Nacional por Amostra de Domicílio, 1995* (Rio de Janeiro: FIBGE, 1995).

to 62.0 percent, while only 37.4 percent of nonwhites resided in that region.[25] Thus, it was mainly black children who encountered the non-formal model of early child care and preschool education introduced at the beginning of the 1980s, meaning there was a relationship between the racial profile of the user and the different programs offered.

The option of expanding early child care and preschool education in the North and Northeast regions, through the low-cost model, under the direction of underqualified teachers, conferred a very particular meaning to the coverage indicators. The rates of coverage in early child care and preschool education do not have the same meaning in every state, nor do the rates of coverage for elementary education. In an earlier work, I showed, through an analysis of statistical correlation, that the poorer, less schooled and blacker the federal state is, the higher the percentage of children seven years or older who attend preschool and the higher the percentage of underqualified teachers.[26] As Table 5 shows, these are the states that also present the worst schooling indicators in basic education for children between seven and eleven years old, and the worst results on the Portuguese tests given to children attending first grade at this level. Note that in large areas of these states, early child care and preschool education is quite extensive, ranking among the highest in the country.

In addition, the expansion of early child care and preschool education is not an indicator of either socioeconomic or educational development. Improving socioeconomic or educational development requires improving quality in the expanded preschool education and providing children with qualified teachers. In this sense, early child care and preschool education expansion does not necessarily lead to a process of democratization in education or of equality of opportunity between sexes, races, and different social classes. It could, however, mean a relocation of excluded sectors of society within the educational system. This inclusion, paradoxically, causes exclusion.

CONCLUSIONS

The low quality of early child care and preschool education constitutes a sufficiently generalized phenomenon because of its ties to the social and economic spheres of production. However, in several developed countries, mainly in Europe, a movement in favor of quality has been observed. In the first place, in many countries social dynamics themselves caused the expansion of high-quality supply compatible with the demands of a growing middle-class clientele. Thus, the massive participation of women of different social levels in the labor market, the non-existence (or cost) of domestic employees to provide child care, and the new value attributed to infancy pressured demand for quality standards. In the second place, equal opportunity policies between the sexes in public and private life have also led to improvements in the quality of early child care and preschool education, mainly in the context of the European Union. For example, the European Commission, an executive organ

Table 5. Indices of Socio-Racial Variables and of Schooling by State

State	V1* Average income of head of household 1991	V2** % of blacks in the state (F.U.) 1995	V3*** % of preschool attendance 0 to 4 1995	V4** % of preschool attendance 5 and 6 1995	V5** % of children 7 to 11 in preschool 1995	V6*** Repeaters 1994	V7**** % Teachers with less than secondary schooling in preschool 1993	V8** Rates of elementary school attendance 7 to 11 years 1995	V9***** % of 1st graders passing Portuguese exam 1993
Rondônia	2.6	57.9	9.8	55.1	14.6	0.0	18.5	92.0	55.4
Acre	2.4	71.2	14.5	53.2	5.7	0.3	16.9	89.3	63.4
Amazonas	3.2	71.8	9.7	53.5	19.1		20.2	44.0	63.7
Roraima	3.4	66.5	11.9	68.2	0.0	16.2	27.5	96.3	44.1
Pará	2.5	74.2	13.5	64.1	28.0	0.0	51.0	82.1	60.5
Amapá	3.3	64.7	4.3	55.6	16.7	0.0	11.9	88.2	49.5
Tocantins	2.2	75.4	6.7	40.0	32.6	17.1	50.9	82.6	46.6
Maranhão	1.4	79.2	10.7	58.0	46.2		40.1	67.1	53.3
Piauí	1.5	80.9	16.2	55.9	35.7	14.7	44.3	76.1	48.8
Ceará	1.9	68.6	14.9	59.7	48.0	0.0	41.4	65.2	58.3
RG d Norte	2.0	63.5	18.3	60.2	8.7	2.9	23.3	87.7	58.7
Paraíba	1.7	65.9	11.7	66.4	38.4	34.2	48.3	73.4	68.4
Pernamb.	2.3	62.2	14.7	53.6	25.6	8.1	11.2	79.4	53.7

State	V1* Average income of head of household 1991	V2** % of blacks in the state (F.U.) 1995	V3** % of preschool attendance 0 to 4 1995	V4** % of preschool attendance 5 and 6 1995	V5** % of children 7 to 11 in preschool 1995	V6**** Repeaters 1994	V7*** % Teachers with less than secondary schooling in preschool 1993	V8*** Rates of elementary school attendance 7 to 11 years 1995	V9**** % of 1st graders passing Portuguese exam 1993
Alagoas	1.9	63.8	9.5	46.7	25.7	3.8	43.0	66.0	38.3
Sergipe	2.1	82.5	14.6	63.6	25.7	1.5	33.7	82.9	67.7
Bahia	2.0	78.2	11.3	53.3	46.5		41.5	70.1	60.1
M. Gerais	2.8	45.5	8.6	55.1	20.7	0.0	4.7	89.5	63.7
Esp. Santo	2.9	52.7	11.6	53.2	2.3	0.1	3.2	90.9	54.1
R. Janeiro	4.2	38.7	16.7	66.6	22.7		6.5	87.6	65.9
São Paulo	5.3	23.7	14.6	59.4	7.9		1.8	94.5	71.2
Paraná	3.3	23.7	11.3	43.9	4.0		10.9	93.5	65.1
S. Catarina	3.4	7.3	11.6	55.0	6.2	0.0	19.1	94.4	70.8
RG do Sul	3.5	11.4	10.3	44.0	8.8	0.0	2.6	94.3	69.1
MG do Sul	3.3	37.7	9.6	43.1	6.8	0.0	6.3	90.6	71.5
M. Grosso	3.1	61.0	6.2	41.1	15.8	0.0	12.7	90.9	71.5
Goiás	3.0	56.1	7.0	49.0	32.6		18.6	84.1	55.1
D. Federal	6.8	41.5	18.8	60.9	15.0	0.0	0.9	92.7	73.2

Sources: * Demographic Census in *Anuário Estatístico do Brasil—1994* (FIBGE, 1994); ** PNAD 95; *** MEC/SPE/SEEC, special processings; **** in *Anuário Estatístico do Brasil—1995* (FIBGE, 1996).

of the European Union, has a Consultative Council on Infant Education within its equal opportunity program. In 1992, the Council of Members of the European Community adopted a recommendation on the care of young children that was approved by the twelve member states. This recommendation developed proposals for quality criteria of service provided to young children that even involve incentives for men to act as care providers within child education teams.[27]

The historical process has not evolved in the same way in Brazil. The women's movement's intense participation in the mobilization for child care during the 1970s and 1980s resulted in the child's right to education prior to seven years of age being recognized by the constitution of 1988. Yet, profound social inequalities still maintain, on the one hand, a broad availability of domestic employees (who provide child-care support for middle-class families, possibly minimizing family conflict over child care) and, on the other hand, a profound social segregation in the utilization of social programs. Expansion at low investment rates and the persistence of diversified institutional models generally open up possibilities that simultaneously offer services of extremely uneven quality south of the equator. This inequality in cost and quality penalizes poor and black children in different ways.

It seems urgent to us to eliminate parallel child education tracks in Brazil. It is inadmissible that day-care centers and preschools constitute alternatives to elementary education for poor and black children. The data also suggest the fallacy of thinking that problems faced by elementary education (its low efficiency) arise only at this level of teaching. The socialization of poor and black children into feelings of inferiority begins with day care, where workers with lower educational levels are generally found and children spend their days routinely waiting: waiting to go to the bathroom, for food, or to have their diapers changed.

At this moment, the route that seems most adequate to us to overcome this intricate game of subordination of class, race, gender, and age that has been prejudicial to children through low-quality early child care and education, would be that of training and certification of workers who deal directly with the children. Demanding more education could raise the professional level and dignity of child care and preschool teachers, the majority of whom are women. I will linger a bit on this aspect.

A study of public and popular schools (including day care and preschools), carried out by the Centro de Cultura Luiz Freire (1994) in the metropolitan area of Recife, found that working at these schools, even at low salaries, can mean professional entry for some women. There is some evidence that opening day-care centers does not always respond to the family's need for free time, but instead responds to expanding the labor market for women with low educational levels by allowing them to work in day-care centers and preschools. As Beatty observed in the United States,[28] in Brazil the increase of vacant positions in the national program of the LBA and the MEC opened up other work opportunities for women with low educational levels in the poorest regions of the country.

This broadening of the labor market through nonformal programs also benefits men and women from the middle class, who occupy technical jobs in the administration and supervision of these programs. Since the less qualified person deals directly with children, more support is needed from qualified personnel.

This lack of qualified teachers in early child care and preschool education also touches upon the organization of the public school system, expressed through administrative actions or the reactions of teachers to the school bureaucracy. Among the dynamics of interaction on the part of teachers and directors faced with the challenges of elementary education, we find teachers "on hold" in a waiting period during pregnancy or on the eve of retirement. Walburga Arns Silva referred to preschool, from the teachers' point of view, as a "place of passage." For teachers, working in preschool can mean not having to confront children who are more critical, more active, and more competent. A teacher in day care and preschool, with more pedagogical education, reported that "My goal is to work in elementary teaching, but I'm still not prepared. I need more experience and preparation."[29]

As we have seen, in the period analyzed, the contingent of underqualified teachers simultaneously diminished in elementary teaching while increasing at the preschool level. An improvement in teacher qualifications in elementary teaching is accompanied by a decrease in teacher qualifications in early childhood education. The proportion of overage children also increased at the preschool level, reflecting a retention process of certain groups of students, especially poor blacks and males. Elementary teaching cleanses itself through early child care and education. It retains students who are candidates for "failure" and puts teachers "on hold."

While the low-cost expansion of early childhood education occurred and became institutionalized mainly in the states with majority nonwhite populations, the programs also opened up job opportunities for women with little training from the less privileged layers of society. Some of these women, with children from 0 to 6 years old, are possibly real or potential users of the establishments of early child care and preschool education. Young children could be benefiting indirectly from this broadening of the labor market for their mothers. But what is the cost/benefit relationship? What is the objective of an early child care and preschool education program?

The question emerges when early child care and preschool education, in its process of expansion, also created and reinforced patterns of social and racial exclusion. Even in the public system of early childhood education, poor and black children (slightly more frequently among boys) attend poorer quality schools that provide an inadequate educational program for their age. The poorest quality early childhood educational establishments represent both the worst places for the education and care of children as well as the worst workplaces for adults. They are places where subordination is produced and reproduced. Resisting their destiny as domestic employees, women accommodate themselves under the system's shade by being the underqualified teachers of poor children.

On the macro level, we point out how the standard of racial segregation in the country imprinted a component of racial discrimination on the policy for the implementation of early child care and preschool education expansion. On the micro level, the same standard of spatial segregation allows us to understand the observed socio-racial "ghettoes." This standard is associated with the diverse quality standards in early child care and preschool education programs, in general with education for older children (seven to eleven years old) and with the social and racial prejudices practiced daily in the educational system. I find no possible explanation for the excessive retention of black children in preschool education other than the maintenance of "racial pessimism" that has accompanied us since the nineteenth century ("the apathy, indolence and impudence of the black population"). It is assumed beforehand that this child will have problems in elementary education.

It was thus shown in this study that early child care and preschool education constitutes a social mechanism, among others, that "places the black population at a disadvantage in the competitive process of social mobility."[30] Furthermore, analyses indicate that this process was exacerbated during the implementation of an educational policy for all. This policy was based on the argument of equalizing opportunity for the poor (compensation for deficiency), and for women (early child care and preschool education as an alternative child care that allowed mothers to work). The paradox is that, in all the states that implemented and maintained this low-cost model of early childhood education, the state constitutions stamped antiracist and antisexist pronouncements of equal opportunity into their chapters on education.

Citing Petitat, an author who studied the process of democratization in French secondary education, one cannot reflect on democratization and improved elementary education without analyzing what has been happening in early childhood and secondary education. Neither can one think about changes in educational hierarchies without considering long-term social transformations in society, which heavily influence changes in the educational system. It is by this route that one follows the implications of overcoming these inequalities.

Faced with the distortions announced here in the standards of supply of early child care and preschool education, some suggestions have emerged in Brazil, including that children older than seven be prohibited from attending preschool by norm or legislative act. If this were to occur, it would reemphasize the need to respect the constitution, which determines that elementary education is obligatory for children over seven years old. This measure, however, is not sufficient, since exclusion would dress itself up in another guise. New programs to retain certain sectors of children at inferior educational levels under the responsibility of excluded segments of women, different from preschool or literacy classes, would be easily created. As long as day care is worth less than preschool which is worth less than elementary school, other alternatives for exclusion will be created and re-created. This axiom is especially true if we continue relying on teachers who have not completed their basic education and who, for this reason, receive salaries inferior to those of teachers with diplomas. Hence, the need for the proposed policy that endorses a priority investment in basic and professional training of child educators.

To conclude, I cite William Julius Wilson's proposal for public policies directed at the poor black North American population,[31] a position also defended by Carlos Hasenbalg in Brazil. We need policies, neither racially nor sexually specific, that aim to decrease economic and educational inequalities of early childhood education. A policy to equalize opportunity for white and black children means equalizing the standard of quality (or at least drastically reducing the existing differences) which, as of today, means attending to the professional qualifications of the workers who educate and care for small children in day-care centers and preschools. In the end, these institutions have been defended by the developed countries, arguing that they are potentially liberating of gender hierarchies and that they enrich children's potential and therefore human potential.

The early child care and preschool education model supported by community participation continues to be disseminated by UNESCO. In the publication *L'Education des filles et des femmes: vers un cadre d'action mondial* one can read:

> We are every day more conscious of the need to ensure care and education for small children in order to favor the education of girls and women. This measure not only allows us to guarantee that girls and boys have access to education from an early time, but also liberates girls and adult women, traditionally in charge of the care of small children. But, despite this raising of consciousness, this type of service is almost nonexistent in the majority of countries. During recent years . . . the number of programs directed at small children increased. The communities implanted nonformal structures for the care of small children. . . . A greater number of governments have included early childcare and preschool education in their primary plans . . . NGOs and social welfare organizations have contributed to the installation of early childcare and preschool education with the communities' participation.[32]

NOTES

[1]Michel Verret, *L'Espace Ouvrier* (Paris: Colin, 1979).

[2]Christine Olivier, *Os Filhos de Jocasta* (Porto Alegre: L&PM, 1986).

[3]Recent studies on the origins of the French *école maternelle* point out, in that country, an important change in the social representation of children between four and six years old at the end of the nineteenth century. See J.N. Luc, *L'Invention du Jeune Enfant aux XIX^è Siècle* (Paris: Belin, 1997).

[4]One of the most developed reflections on the impact of demographic changes (mortality and fertility rates) on the forms of raising small children is found in Robert Le Vine, "Fertility and Child Development: An Anthropological Approach," in D. Wagner (ed.), *Child Development and International Development* (San Francisco: Jossey-Bass, 1983), pp. 41–62.

[5]Anna Bondioli and Susanna Mantoviani (eds.), *Manual Critico dell'Asilo Nido* (Milan: Franco Angeli, 1989), pp. 27–28.

[6]G. Neal, H.T. Groat, and J.W. Wicks, "Attitudes about Having Children: A Study of 600 Couples in the Early Years of Marriage," *Journal of Marriage and the Family* 51 (1989): 313–328.

[7]UNESCO, *World Education Report 1993* (Paris: UNESCO, 1993).

[8]Barbara Finkelstein, "The Revolt against Selfishness: Women and the Dilemmas of Professionalism in Early Childhood Education," in Bernard Spodek

et al. (eds.), *Professionalism and the Early Childhood Practitioner* (New York: Teachers College Press, 1988), p. 11.

[9]Mina Swaminathan, "Training Programs for Daycare Workers: A Brief Introduction to the Training Model of Mobile Creches in India," *Preschool Education* 14 (Paris: UNESCO, 1980).

[10]UNESCO, *World Education Report 1991* (Paris: UNESCO, 1991); UNESCO, *World Education Report 1993* (Paris: UNESCO, 1993); UNESCO, *World Education Report 1995* (Paris: UNESCO, 1995); UNESCO, *World Education Report 1998* (Paris: UNESCO, 1998).

[11]David Scanlon, "Raizes historicas do desenvolvimento da educacao comunitaria." In Henri, Nelson (ed). *Educacao comunitaria.* Rio de Janeiro, USAID, 1965, p. 45–58.

[12]In Ammann, *op. cit.,* p. 25.

[13]In Ammann, *op.cit.,* p. 117.

[14]The DNCr was created in 1940 by the Brazilian Ministry of Education and Health to be the supreme coordinating organ of all the activities related to the protection of children, to maternity, and to adolescence.

[15]Charles Egger, "Principales Orientations de la Politique de L'UNICEF: 1947–1979." Paper delivered at Warsaw Colloquio, September 3, 1985, p. 6.

[16]Robert Myers, *A Brief History* (New York: Consultative Group on Early Childhood Care and Development, 1990) (circa).

[17]The Brazilian government's document presented at the meeting of the Executive Board of 1965 was signed by the Brazilian delegate, Dr. Ronaldo Victor de Lamare, then general director of the National Department for Children. It was entitled: "Reaching the Young Child: Children from 2 to 6 Years of Age and Their Present Welfare Situation in Brazil" (UNICEF, E/ICEF/CRP/65-26, June 14, 1965).

[18]The DNCr document emphasizes the influence of UNICEF, pointing out that the proposal had been drawn up "in consonance with UNICEF's interests." The importance of the plan can be seen by the references made to it in the first bibliographies on preschool programs published by the Education Ministry at the beginning of the 1970s. See Brazil, MEC/DEF/SEPRE, *Atendimento ao Pré-escolar.* (Brasília: Ministério da Educação e Cultura, 1977, 2v).

[19]A Faure Commission, officially called the International Commission for the Development of Education, was presided over by Edgard Faure, a former French minister of education appointed in 1969. Its main analyses and recommendations were published in the book *Apprendre à Être* (1972) or, in English, *Learning to Be* (1972).

[20]For this period, we found in the UNESCO documentation traces of the presence of renowned psychologists and pedagogues: Piaget, Wallon, Wall, Zazzo, among others (Rosemberg, 1998).

[21]Edgard Faure, *Apprendre à Être* (Paris: Fayard and UNESCO, 1972), p. 21.

[22]The Brazilian educational data transcribed in the tables come from two sources that adopt a systematic collection of diverse data: IBGE (*Instituto Brasileiro de Geografia e Estatística;* Brazilian Institute of Geography and

Statistics), which, through the *Censos and the Pesquisas Nacionais por Amostra de Domicílios* (Census and National Household Survey), collects information about the user; the SEEC (*Divisão de Estatística de Educação e Cultura do Ministério da Educação,* Division of Statistics on Education and Culture of the Ministry of Education), which, through the *Censos Educacionais* (Educational Censuses) collects data based on a register of teaching establishments. In earlier works (Rosemberg, 1997b), I showed that this latter organism underestimates the frequency of ECCE, given that a significant number of day-care centers and preschools are outside the system, that is, not registered. For this reason, data on teaching tend to show a more advantageous picture, to the extent that "clandestine" schools, those of poorer quality, are generally found off the register.

[23]Fúlvia Rosemberg, *Educação Infantil e Processos de Exclusão.* Research Report (São Paulo; FAPESP, 1997).

[24]It is important to remember that the Southeast region of which Hasenbalg (1979) speaks practically includes the present Southeast and Southern regions, according to the division of the demographic censuses and of the PNAD. It includes the present states of Rio de Janeiro, São Paulo, Paraná, Santa Catarina, and Rio Grande do Sul, and does not include the state of Minas Gerais.

[25]Despite the impact of the men's presence on the valorization of the function being questionable. See Elaine C.L. Saparolli, *Educador Infantil: uma ocupação de gênero feminino.* Master's Thesis (São Paulo: Pontifícia Universidade Católica, 1997).

[26]Rosemberg, *op. cit.*

[27]The report of the evaluation of the Programa Nacional de Educação Pré-escolar in Sergipe states that, in that state, the directors receive a complementary salary proportional to the filling (maximum complement) of vacancies in pre-school classes (Walburga A. da Silva, *Influência da Pré-escola no Processo de Alfabetização: um Estudo de Tendências e Alternativas da Pré-escola Pública de Aracaju,* 1986–1991; Aracaju: UFS, Departamento de Educação, Núcleo de Estudos e Pesquisas em Alfabetização, 1991).

[28]Barbara Beatty, "Child Gardening: The Teaching of Young Children in American Schools," in D. Warren (ed.), *American Teachers: Histories of a Profession at Work* (New York: Macmillan, 1989), pp. 65–97.

[29]Teacher in day care and preschool, with higher education in pedagogy, interviewed by Ana Beatriz Cerizara, 1995. Cerizara, Ana Beatriz. *Formação de Professores em Serviço para a Educação Infantil: Uma Possível Contribuição da Universidade.* Florianopolis: UFSC, 1995, p. 24.

[30]Carlos A. Hasenbalg, "Notas sobre as Relações de Raça no Brasil e na América Latina," in Heloisa Buarque de Hollanda (ed.), *Y nosotras latinoamericanas?Estudos sobre gênero y raça* (São Paulo: F. Memorial da América Latina, 1992), pp. 52–58.

[31]William Julius Wilson, *The Truly Disadvantaged. The Inner City, the Underclass, and Public Policy* (London/Chicago: University of Chicago Press, 1987).

[32]UNESCO, *op. cit.,* 1995, p. 12.

REFERENCES

Ammann, Safira Bezerra. *Ideologia do Desenvolvimento de Comunidade no Brasil.* São Paulo: Cortez Editora, 1982.

Beatty, Barbara. "Child Gardening: The Teaching of Young Children in American Schools." In D. Warren (ed), *American Teachers: Histories of a Profession at Work,* pp. 65–97. New York: Macmillan, 1989.

Bondioli, Anna and Susanna Mantovani (eds.). *Manual Crítico dell'Asilo Nido.* Milan: Franco Angeli, 1989.

Brazil. *Anuário Estatístico do Brasil 1994.* Rio de Janeiro: FIBGE, 1994.

Brazil. *Anuário Estatístico do Brasil 1995.* Rio de Janeiro: FIBGE, 1996.

Brazil. *Diagnóstico Preliminar da Educação Pré-escolar no Brasil.* Brasília: Ministério da Educação e Cultura, 1975a.

Brazil. *Educação Pré-escolar: Uma Nova Perspectiva Nacional.* Brasília: Ministério da Educação e Cultura, 1975b.

Brazil. *Pesquisa Nacional por Amostra de Domicílio, 1990.* Rio de Janeiro: FIBGE, 1990.

Brazil. *Pesquisa Nacional por Amostra de Domicílio, 1995.* Rio de Janeiro: FIBGE, 1995.

Brazil. MEC/DEF/SEPRE. *Atendimento ao Pré-escolar.* Brasília: Ministério da Educação e Cultura, 1977. 2v.

Brazil. MEC/SAG. *A Educação do Brasil na Década de 80.* Brasília: Ministério da Educação e Cultura, 1990.

Brazil. MEC/SAG/CPS/CIP. *Sinopse Estatística de Classes de Alfabetização e Educação Pré-escolar 1990.* Brasília: MEC/SAG/CPS/CIP, 1992.

Brazil. MEC/SAG/CPS/SEEC. *Sinopse Estatística de Classes de Alfabetização e Educação Pré-escolar 1991.* Brasília: MEC/SAG/CPS/SEEC, 1994a.

Brazil. *Sinopse Estatística da Educação Especial 1989.* v. 2 Instituições Especializadas. Brasília: Ministério da Educação e Cultura, 1992.

Brazil. MEC/SAG/CPS/CIP. *Sinopse Estatística de Classes de Alfabetização e Educação Pré-escolar. Censo Educacional 1992.* Brasília: MEC/SAG/CPS/SEEC, 1994b.

Brazil. MEC/SAG/CPS/CIP. *Sinopse Estatística de Classes de Alfabetização e Educação Pré-escolar. Censo Educacional 1993.* Brasília: MEC/SAG/CPS/SEEC, 1994c.

Brazil. MEC/SAG/CPS/CIP. *Sinopse Estatística do Ensino de pré-1º Grau – 69/75.* Brasília: MEC/Departamento de Documentação e Divulgação, 1977.

Campos, Maria Malta, Fúlvia Rosemberg, and Isabel M. Ferreira. *Creches e Pré-escolas no Brasil.* São Paulo: Cortez, 1992.

Centro de Cultura Luiz Freire. Gral. *Uma Estratégia de Sobrevivência na Região Metropolitana do Recife.* Olinda: CCLF, 1994.

Cerizara, Ana Beatriz. *Formação de Professores em Serviço para a Educação Infantil: Uma Possível Contribuição da Universidade.* Florianópolis: UFSC, 1995.

Cochran, Moncrieff, ed. *International Handbook on Child Care Policies and Programs.* Westport and London: Greenwood Press, 1993.

Departamento Nacional da Criança. Divisão de Proteção Social DNCr. *Sugestões para um plano de assistência ao pré-escolar.* Rio de Janeiro: DNCr, 1967.

Egger, Charles. *Principales Orientations de la Politique de l'UNICEF: 1947–1979.* Paper delivered at the Warsaw Colloquio, September 3, 1985.

Faure, Edgard. *Apprendre à Être.* Paris: Fayard and UNESCO (Le Monde Sans Frontières), 1972.

Ferrari, Alceu. "Pré-escola para Salvar a Escola?" *Educação e Sociedade* 12 (1982): 29–37.

Ferrari, Alceu. "Evolução da Educação Pré-escolar no Brasil no Período de 1968 a 1986." *Revista Brasileira de Estudos Pedagógicos* 161 (1988): 55–74.

Finkelstein, Barbara. "The Revolt against Selfishness: Women and the Dilemmas of Professionalism in Early Childhood Education." In Bernard Spodek, Olivia Saracho, and Donald L. Peters (eds.), *Professionalism and the Early Childhood Practitioner,* pp. 10-28. New York: Teachers College Press, 1988.

Hasenbalg, Carlos A. "Notas sobre as Relações de Raça no Brasil e na América Latina." In Heloísa Buarque de Hollanda, *Y nosotras latino-americanas? Estudos sobre gênero e raça,* pp. 52-58. São Paulo: F. Memorial da América Latina, 1992.

Jensen, Jytte. *Men in Child Care Services: A Discussion Paper.* Ravena: European Comunity, 1993 (mimeo).

Le Vine, Robert. "Fertility and Child Development: An Anthropological Approach." In D. Wagner (ed.), *Child Development and International Development.* San Francisco: Jossey-Bass, 1983.

Luc, J.N. *L'Invention du Jeune Enfant aux XIXè Siècle.* Paris: Belin, 1997.

Myers, Robert. *A Brief History.* New York: Consultative Group on Early Childhood Care and Development, n/d (mimeo), circa 1990.

Neal, A.G., H.T. Groat, and J.W. Wicks. "Attitudes about Having Children: A Study of 600 Couples in the Early Years of Marriage." *Journal of Marriage and the Family* 51 (1989): 313–328.

Olivier, Christiane. *Os Filhos de Jocasta.* Porto Alegre: L&PM, 1986.

Petitat, André. *Produção da Escola/produção da Sociedade: Análise Sócio-histórica de alguns Momentos Decisivos da Evolução Escolar no Ocidente.* Porto Alegre: Artes Médicas, 1994.

Rosemberg, Fúlvia. "A LBA, o Projeto Casulo e a Doutrina de Segurança Nacional." In Marcos Cezar Freitas (ed.), *História Social da Infância no Brasil,* pp. 137–158. São Paulo: Cortez/USF, 1997a.

Rosemberg, Fúlvia. *Educação Infantil e Processos de Exclusão.* Research Report. São Paulo: FCC/FAPESP, 1997b.

Rosemberg, Fúlvia. *Educação Infantil na UNESCO.* Preliminary Research Report. São Paulo: FCC/FAPESP, 1998.

Saparolli, Elaine C.L. "Educador Infantil: Uma ocupação de gênero feminino" (Master's thesis). São Paulo: Pontifícia Universidade Católica, 1997.

Serpa, Maria do Carmo Varella. *Atendimento ao Pré-escolar Carente: Utopia ou Realidade? Diagnóstico da Situação em Movimentos Comunitários da Grande Vitória.* Vitória: Master Thesis, Universidade Federal de Espírito Santo, 1992.

Silva, Walburga A. da. *Influência da Pré-escola no Processo de Alfabetização: um Estudo de Tendências e Alternativas da Pré-escola Pública de Aracaju, 1986-1991.* Aracaju: UFS, Departamento de Educação, Núcleo de Estudos e Pesquisas em Alfabetização, 1991.

Swaminathan, Mina. "Training Programs for Daycare Workers: A Brief Introduction to the Training Model of Mobile Creches in India." *Preschool Education* 14. Paris: UNESCO, 1980.

UNESCO. *XXVI Conférence Internationale de l'Instruction Publique.* Paris: UNESCO, 1961.

UNESCO. *L'Education des Filles e des Femmes: Vers un Cadre d'Action Mondial.* Paris: UNESCO, 1995.

UNESCO. *World Education Report 1991.* Paris: UNESCO, 1991.

UNESCO. *World Education Report 1993.* Paris: UNESCO, 1993.

UNESCO. *World Education Report 1995.* Paris: UNESCO, 1995.

UNESCO. *World Education Report 1998.* Paris: UNESCO, 1998.

UNICEF. *Infância e Juventude no Desenvolvimento Nacional na América Latina.* Rio de Janeiro: UNICEF, FUNABEM, 1968.

UNICEF. *Situación de la Infancia en América Latina y el Caribe.* Santiago: Editorial Universitaria, 1979.

UNICEF. *Strategy for Children: A Study of UNICEF Assistance Policies.* New York: UNICEF, 1967.

UNICEF. *UNICEF no Brasil: Ontem, Hoje, Amanhã.* Brasília: UNICEF, 1980.

Verret, Michel. *L'Espace Ouvrier.* Paris: Colin, 1979.

Wilson, William Julius. *The Truly Disadvantaged. The Inner City, the Underclass, and Public Policy.* London/Chicago: University of Chicago Press, 1987.

Conclusions

The chapters presented in the previous pages have explored the unfolding situation within a number of formal educational systems and women-led NGOs in Latin America regarding public policy, actual programs, and research on gender and education in its broadest sense. Several patterns can be discerned from this material and some implications can be drawn for future action and further research.

Public policies concerning gender equity in education are now beginning to emerge in Latin America. Although there is growing interest in the promotion of these policies and improving the education of women and girls, our research could identify only four countries—Argentina, Paraguay, Uruguay, and Bolivia—that have designed specific, comprehensive gender equity policies in education. All countries in the region by now have some form of national office for women and are adopting within their new constitutions a universal proclamation of gender equality. Yet in most cases this initial step has not led to concrete measures to reflect the adopted principles or the agreements reached in international forums during the 1990s.

Gender equity policies have been in effect for only a few years. Argentina, the first country able to include gender equity within its federal education law, encountered serious political opposition at precisely the moment when curriculum changes were about to be implemented nationwide. The Catholic Church raised objections resulting in the resignation of the leader and director of the program. The program lost its autonomy and was incorporated into another unit within the ministry, thus diminishing the importance of the gender equity initiative.[1]

Uruguay, in part because of its long-standing democratic political system and the small size of its population, is the country with the greatest equity of educational opportunity in the region. The gender equity policies there have been successful despite the sociocultural transformation these policies are likely to bring through changes in the curriculum and teacher training.[2] It would seem that societies with strong and established democratic traditions find it easier to extend such rights to women.

In Bolivia, a country with a high percentage of indigenous people, the gender equity initiative includes not only young girls in school but indigenous and rural women, focusing on both formal and nonformal education and calling for the implementation of complementary, supportive programs in both systems. The recommended changes in Bolivia are at present at the level of enacted legislation, leaving open the possibility that gender equity policies might not be implemented if sufficient opposition develops at the national level. Indications of possible dissent have already emerged, as observed by the description of the process in Bolivia. In the case of Paraguay, a country that is initiating its democratic traditions after a long dictatorship, the gender policies have gone beyond the legislation into program implementation.

A key point to consider when following public policies on gender and education is whether they have elements to make official intentions a reality. Often these policies may not be accompanied by sufficient resources or a clear set of proposed actions, thus making them more symbolic gestures than serious plans. As the description of UNESCO efforts in the region shows, there has been limited progress in bringing a gender perspective to the official curriculum of the schools. A careful examination over time of the attainments of educational gender equity policies in the four countries identified in this book should be in the feminist research agenda.

In the countries where gender equity policies have been adopted at the level of legislation, public debate on gender equity in education followed varying strategies and was forged through political alliances suitable to each country's political contexts and circumstances. In the case of Argentina, the ongoing debate on educational reform and decentralization made it possible to include gender equity in the enacted legislation. In the case of Bolivia, public discussion about bilingualism and diversity offered an opportunity to add gender equity to the newly enacted education laws. In Paraguay, gender equity concepts were incorporated in the educational reform as "family education," since it was anticipated that within the public debate about education in that country there would be no wide acceptance of the concept of gender. The variety of strategies pursued to create legitimacy for objectives and goals of gender equity leads us to conclude that there is no established path to produce this type of reform. In each case, the enacted legislation was shaped by the unique context of the particular country, the strength of the feminist movement, and the alliances it established with organizations in civil society as well as with international donors. What does emerge as a pattern is that gender equity policies have utilized other agendas of change (e.g., decentralization, democratization, bilingualism) to insert themselves into the political agenda. Entering the political arena surreptitiously in this manner, gender policies may be passed; on the other hand, their uncertain status as "riders" places them in secondary and vulnerable positions when it comes to implementation.

In years past, most international funding arrived in Latin America after lengthy negotiations with state officials. Today, donor countries are working directly in the region though their own national NGOs, and their bilateral agencies are seeking new kinds of partnerships with actors other than the state. Donor countries are also becoming more powerful in influencing the conceptualization of educational problems and the implementation of educational reform in the region. The growing presence and increasing variety of development agencies gives NGOs, including women-led NGOs, and government officials more choices and more flexibility in finding the right donor to support the programs they are envisioning.

The assessment of educational priorities by donor agencies and their own definition of educational problems continues to focus on basic education, and within basic education, the education of girls has become a priority. The definition of gender issues in education by donor agencies is limited, concentrating on issues of access but not questioning sufficiently the processes within schools by which gender ideologies are experienced and transmitted. With the current challenges brought forth by economic and technological globalization, both donor agencies and national governments are placing much of their attention on issues of quality. At first, this promises an improvement of educational systems, but frequently the consequences for gender issues is that emphasis is placed on concerns for academic performance (primarily in reading and math) as they may affect the productivity of the future labor force, but not on the removal of undesirable messages and experiences along gender and ethnic lines or the fostering of minds critical of their social and cultural environment. It is regrettable that after so many years of agency support for girls' basic education, no educational system in the region has developed a graduated curriculum that introduces gender in increasingly complex ways through the various grades of primary education. An important tension facing educational systems today pits the newly recognized importance of girls' education against the drive for international competitiveness via more technical and less critical curricula and teaching practices.

Since Latin America is dependent on international financing to meet the goals of educating a large segment of its population, the role of research to assess the models being promoted by international agencies and their impact on gender equity is of crucial importance. Throughout the region, schooling is not providing equal opportunities for most groups and there is a stark divide between schooling for the rich and schooling for the poor. The studies presented in this book have identified two types of low-cost interventions that have been promoted in the region. Low-cost models promoting school expansion, such as those pursued through greater access to preschool programs in Brazil, tend to avoid funding in teacher preparation and training. This strategy has the unforeseen consequence of increasing inequality for the poor and those belonging to ethnic minority groups. The other type of low-cost intervention focuses on providing resources directly to groups in need, as in the case of the scholarship programs for indigenous girls and their families in Guatemala, which had a positive effect on the girls' school attendance and likely completion of basic education. The learning achieved in the evaluation of these projects is valuable not only for the donor agencies but also for governments and NGOs seeking international financing. It would seem desirable that when positive results are detected by research, as in the case of scholarships for poor and indigenous girls, such findings become translated into corresponding public policies rather than be left to disappear or decline for lack of sponsors.

It is clear that in the Latin American context, the impact of gender is greatly magnified at its intersection with class and ethnicity. The implication for public policy is that we need action plans that recognize the pervasive impact of gender across the entire population, but also needed are plans that consider specific ways to break barriers caused by the combined impact of ethnicity, social class, and gender. For instance, designing gender equity policies that in addition recognize the existence of groups of girls who are rural and indigenous or girls who are Afro-Brazilian and live in homes identified as extremely poor must become part of future generations of public policies. The question of social exclusion is a serious phenomenon in Latin America. This exclusion runs along clear racial, ethnic, and social class lines. But it would be a serious mistake to ignore the deep nature of gender exclusion both within and independent of affiliation to the traditionally disadvantaged groups in the region.

The quality of the analysis that can be made is highly dependent on the educational statistics available to the research community. Official statistics about student enrollment and completion in the region are still imprecise and often underplay the educational failure of many students. UNICEF, working in collaboration with governments in Latin America, has made an important first step by agreeing on universal indicators of educational access, completion, and repetition. Such common and more accurate statistics describing the educational achievements of the population are at this time available for only selected countries in Latin America. Cooperating with other international organizations, UNESCO can become an ally in the establishment of gender equity policies in education by carefully measuring the low completion rates of the poor in basic education in Latin America and by widely publicizing these rates. Moreover, a new effort needs to be started to provide an accurate portrait of middle-school completion rates for young men and women in the various countries of the region. We do have increased knowledge, however, of the importance of having at least middle-school education for improving social mobility and access to well-being.

In the past decade, there has been a dramatic organizational growth of NGOs, linked to preparation for and participation in international conferences on gender issues and to advances in computer-mediated communications. For example, a major portion of the work of REPEM is done through electronic newsletters and virtual workshops. As organizations of civil society and community institutions, women-led NGOs are demonstrating growing political maturity. Their capacity for mobilization to monitor the implementation of public policies is evidence of organizational strength and growth in the understanding of what it takes to bridge the space between political rhetoric and action. Their lobbying of both government officials and representatives of development agencies reflects a more effective political participation. The active mobilization of NGOs and the growing presence of these organizations in forums where important decisions are made concerning women and education have the potential to influence policy makers at national levels.

Political alliances within the international women's movement have strengthened women-led NGOs. Our research shows that women-led NGOs tend to network with similarly minded NGOs within their countries, regionally, and across the world. These networks have been solidified and expanded through participation in the various regional and international conferences of the women's movement. Participation in these regional and international forums has been made possible by lateral development agencies, international agencies affiliated to the UN, and private foundations—particularly the Ford Foundation, which has financed the participation of NGO leaders in regional and world conferences sponsored by UN agencies.

NGOs are emerging as central players in the process of changing the social relations of gender. Their work goes beyond the actual workshops, training, and community services they might provide. In this book we attempted to highlight the types of knowledge that are transmitted and acquired through women-led NGOs; we also emphasized the important nature of informal learning. Further research is needed to determine the transformation of education as a result of the knowledge-producing effects of women's participation in educational programs within NGOs. Often, women who have participated in workshops dealing with subjects such as micro-enterprises or domestic violence work in single-sex environments and, as women, they can talk with other women, thus expanding exponentially the work done by NGOs. While conducting this important but little studied form of activism, the leaders of NGOs find themselves in a constant tension between problems, solutions, and conceptual advancement that helps to refine their understanding of gender-related problems. Through the analysis of women-led NGOs we were able to observe the intersection between community-level leadership, the state, and international development agencies. As NGOs negotiate for funding, there is always the possibility that they can be co-opted by the particular interests of the state or international funding agency. The tension is already a subject of discussion within feminist NGOs in the region, within whose ranks there is a vocal minority that favors autonomous action, even it if means not having resources for larger programs.

Another area of promise and needed research concerns the growing interaction between NGOs and universities. The new and emerging alliance between women in NGOs and women in the academy can be helpful in theory development and for strengthening as well as reflecting upon experiential training, ways in which gender is embedded in the organization of society, the settings in which gender-based structures of social authority are enacted and contested, and the linkages between gender transformation and state action. Academic women and others interested in gender issues stand to gain much knowledge from understanding better the particular problems of NGOs and their constant tension between addressing practical and strategic needs. The practice of NGOs, complex as it is, brings clear challenges to theories that tend to be cast on ideal models or situations. Collaboration with NGOs can help to strengthen academic contributions to theory in those areas.

In most countries across Latin America, research on gender-related topics takes place almost exclusively in the gender studies centers of major universities supported by international cooperation; rarely does this research permeate the rest of the university. Gender as a category of social analysis is achieving greater legitimacy under the auspices of international cooperation, but theory building— to fit the socioeconomic and cultural realities of the region—is only in its beginning stages, as is our understanding of its impact, which will be found in research that remains to be done. Particularly in developing countries, such as those in Latin America, there is an imperative to work on women's survival and practical needs. These actions merit close scrutiny to assess the extent to which solving these problems can contribute to embarking on more strategic action. The growing cooperation between activist NGOs and reflective academicians is a welcome development with much promise.

The process of implementing gender equity policies will be accelerated further by increasing cooperation between NGO leaders and academics. In addition, a more proactive stance is required from the various governments in the region. In general, their response to international agreements signed in the 1990s has been modest. As we have seen, very few countries have formulated and implemented gender equity policies. When international development agencies produce in-country agreements with developing countries, they do not use their leverage to ask that countries comply with such agreements. Were they to do so, educational policies in all countries would reflect a wider array of measures to address issues of gender equity in education. Implementation within each country is largely the result of political organizations in civil society and their capacity for lobbying for the changes they seek. In this regard, knowledge fostered by women-led NGOs to produce leadership skills among women (such as the training attempted in Chile) is essential to produce leaders capable of engaging in persistent and resilient action.

Another area of needed research concerns what types of partnerships best assure national and local support for the long-term implementation of programs, and specifically how to evaluate whether the project of a funding agency has a credible national partner likely to ensure the success of the effort. It is presumptuous for an international donor agency to come into the local arena with preconceived notions of who will provide political support at the community, regional, or national level. It is equally presumptuous to expect success because controversial issues tend to be avoided in the project design. One particularly large and well-funded project did not achieve success for exactly these reasons: In the case of the USAID project in Guatemala, the necessary support from parents and civil society that might have assured the continuation of the program and its long-term acceptance was not sought. Just as assumptions were made about community support, they were made also about the support from the private sector—assumptions that in the end were not realized. In looking for partners that could influence policy at the national level and provide access to decision makers, the USAID project in Guatemala relied on private-sector and business leaders. The assumption was that if the private sector understood the focus of the policy, it would provide the necessary long-term support and would mobilize others to influence government policy. The Guatemala case study shows that the private sector often intervenes not to promote national social goals but to advance their own business priorities. In contrast to U.S. policies of international cooperation, the assistance provided by the Netherlands is designed to strengthen groups within civil society and to provide technical training for these groups so that they can lobby for the reforms they envision.

Partnerships can work in two ways. If international agencies deal directly with the government, they are giving more decision-making power to the government. But if the government is not genuinely interested, it can block or weaken implementation of gender policies or ensure that they do not survive past the termination of project funding. The other type of partnership, one that has been the most important ally of women in providing resources and ideas, is the alliance between international agencies and local or national NGOs. Among the international donors, our research in the specific case of the schooling of girls and the nonformal education of adult women found that the Spanish Agency for International Cooperation and two major Dutch NGOs co-financed by their respective government have been the most important allies in the establishment and implementation of gender policies in education.

Several strategies most influence the rate and scope of change in gender in education. One is intensive and sustained staff training within the development agencies and donor governments, including top managers and leaders. This is certainly happening, but its voluntary character prevents training from permeating the entire personnel structure of these agencies. Another strategy is to strengthen the links between the universities and women-led NGOs. A third is to link systematic and sustained training for teachers to the implementation of local programs for gender equity and educational improvement; an essential component in this effort must be the production of new nonsexist and antisexist educational materials. A fourth is to build gender as an analytical construct in theories of social change. Our theories of national development stand to grow and mature as they become more sensitive to the role, functions, and potential of half of the population. Such theories of national development will benefit also from recognizing and incorporating analytically the role of NGOs and international funding agencies.

A sustained commitment to all these strategies is needed if we are to make progress in achieving gender equity and transformation in education. The chapters in this book have highlighted the pertinence of these strategies. They have emphasized the crucial importance of acting holistically when centering on gender and education. Incorporating the educational needs of adult women into public policy is as important as a focus on girls' education. The involvement of civil society through the engagement in women-led NGOs is a helpful complement to state action. The mutual support of local action and global agencies can create further energies for the success of public policies.

NOTES

[1]Gloria Bonder, "El programa nacional de igualdad de oportunidades en la educación de Argentina: Lecciones aprendidas en el plano teórico y estratégico." Paper presented at the Pre-LASA 98 Conference, "Gender and Education in Latin America," University of Illinois, Chicago, 22–23 September 1998.

[2]Carmen Tornaría, "Políticas de género en la reforma educativa uruguaya." Paper presented at the Pre-LASA 98 Conference, "Gender and Education in Latin America," University of Illinois, Chicago, 22–23 September 1998.

REFERENCES

Bonder, Gloria. "El programa nacional de igualdad de oportunidades en la educación de Argentina: Lecciones aprendidas en el plano teórico y estratégico." Paper presented at the Pre-LASA 98 Conference, "Gender and Education in Latin America," University of Illinois, Chicago, 22–23 September 1998.

Tornaría, Carmen. "Políticas de género en la reforma educativa uruguaya." Paper presented at the Pre-LASA 98 Conference, "Gender and Education in Latin America," University of Illinois, Chicago, 22–23 September 1998.

Contributors

Jeanine Anderson was born in the United States. She holds a Ph.D. in anthropology from Cornell University. She has lived in Peru since 1970, having first arrived to carry out fieldwork for a doctoral dissertation. She has been a researcher for the Peruvian Ministry of Education and program advisor for the Ford Foundation regional office for the Andes and the Southern Cone countries. She participated in founding NGOs for the promotion of women and gender equity in Peru, and has been an active participant over several years in regional South American networks and events concerned with women and local governments, women and social policy, and gender and education. Currently, she is an associate professor of anthropology at the Catholic University of Peru, where she is also affiliated with the gender studies program.

María Bonino is from Uruguay. She is a sociologist and consultant in project evaluation for different agencies. She is the coordinator of the Monitoring Committee for the Beijing Accords for Uruguay. She is also in charge of the CONFINTEA Follow-up Initiative on Gender and Education for Latin America, Asia and Africa for REPEM-GEO. Some of her recent publications include *Género y pobreza en Uruguay* (CIEDUR, 1999); *Una propuesta de desarrollo local en Bajo Valencia* (Montevideo, IPRU, 1998); and *Una propuesta de indicadores para evaluar proyectos de género* (IAF-SADES, 1998).

Carmen Colazo is Paraguayan, a lawyer, and a graduate of Information Science at the Universidad Nacional de Córdoba in Argentina. She has been a university professor in Argentina and Paraguay and a researcher in law and communication focusing on gender for several NGOs. She has consulted for the women's caucus of the constitutional convention of Paraguay in 1992, and she directed the office of social development for the Ministry of Health and Welfare between 1991 and 1993. She organized the Women: Health and Development Program. She was a founding member of the Ministry of Women and the first director of education of such ministry since 1993. Some of her publications are *Los partidos políticos en el Paraguay,* and *Desarrollo de los temas educación, comunicación y mecanismos de participación* as part of Paraguay's Ministry of Women official documents presented in the IV International Conference on Women in Beijing.

Regina Cortina is a faculty member and researcher in the School of Education at New York University. She received her Ph.D. in education from Stanford University. Her research has focused on the training and employment of teachers and on issues of equity and politics in education policy. Cortina continues to work on Mexican education and is working on a book, *The New Politics of Mexican Education,* which focuses on the recently enacted law to decentralize public education in Mexico and its effects on local control, equity, and democratization. Her recent publications include "Presencia de la mujer en la educación: Perspectivas de género en la política educativa," in Stromquist (ed.), *Gender Dimensions in Education in Latin America* (1996), "The Impact of International Organizations on Educational Policy in Latin America," in Randall and Anderson (eds.), *Schooling for Success: Preventing Repetition and Dropouts in Latin American Primary Schools* (1999).

María Clara di Pierro is from Brazil. She holds a degree in geography from the University of São Paulo and a master's in education degree from the Pontificia Universidade Católica de São Paulo. She is presently working on her Ph.D. at the same institution. Her research area is on Brazil's adult public policies. She has written extensively on the subject in articles and book chapters. She has also worked with *Ação Educativa,* an NGO that focuses on education and informs, researches, consults, prepares materials, and trains educators. She is also a member of the coordinating task force to support literacy programs in Brazil. She coordinates the Brazil regional office of the Adult Education Council for Latin America and the Caribbean (CEAAL).

Celia Eccher is a social worker from Uruguay. She is a graduate of the Universidad de la República del Uruguay. She is a feminist educator who has participated in many panels and workshops, and has taught different courses. She considers that her best learning experience comes from her interaction with Uruguayan women in small communal productive organizations in the countryside. She is currently the coordinator of the Red de Educación Popular entre Mujeres de América Latina y el Caribe and the regional coordinator of DAWN (Development Alternatives with Women for New Era) for Latin America.

María Luisa Jáuregui has worked for UNESCO since 1973. A sociologist by training, María Luisa has a vast international experience. She worked in the Paris UNESCO headquarters until 1991 when she asked to be transferred to the regional office in Chile, where she could directly focus on educational programs in Latin America and the Caribbean. Her main focus areas have been literacy programs and adult and youth professional and technical education. In all these areas, María Jauregui has spent a great deal of effort to achieve equal opportunity in access to education for girls and boys as well as for young and adult females and males.

Steven J. Klees completed his Ph.D. at Stanford University in 1975 with an emphasis in the economics of education. He has taught in the United States at Cornell University, Stanford University, Florida State University, and is currently a faculty member at the University of Maryland. He has also taught at Palermo University in Argentina, UNAM in Mexico, the Federal University of Rio Grande do Norte in Brazil, as well as on two occasions receiving a Fulbright Scholar Award to teach at the Federal University of Bahia in Brazil. His research is in the area of education and economic policy and concerned with issues of inequality and social progress.

Martha Lanza is from Bolivia. She was an expert on gender and education issues for the Embassy of the Netherlands in Bolivia. Between 1994 and 1997, she was in charge of the Gender and Education Office of the Undersecretariat for Gender of the Human Development Ministry in Bolivia. During her term, the issue of gender equity was incorporated into the educational reform process in Bolivia. She also participated in the Program to Prevent Violence in schools. She was one of the organizers of the International Seminar on Gender and Education in Bolivia, where important progress was made to develop and implement school retention programs for girls in rural areas.

Laura Cecilia Lazarte is a social scientist from Bolivia. She holds an undergraduate degree from the Universidad Católica Boliviana and a postgraduate degree from the Facultad Latinoamericana de Ciencias Sociales. Currently, she is responsible for the Gender and Education section of the Undersecretary for Gender and Family of the Ministry of Planning and Sustainable Development of Bolivia. She has been the coordinator of the National Initiative to Prevent Violence in Schools in Bolivia. She has presented at numerous conferences, including the International Seminar on Gender and Education held in La Paz in 1996. She has several publications on equal opportunity in education and violence and gender discrimination in and out of the classroom. In 1997, she published a *Guía para Prevenir la Violencia en la Escuela.*

Rosa Mendoza is from Peru. She recently received a master in international and intercultural management from the School for International Training (Vermont, USA). Previously, she graduated in Education and received a Diploma in Gender Studies from the Catholic University in Peru. She is currently in charge of the Training Department of *Escuela para el Desarrollo,* a Peruvian NGO specialized in organizational development and training of NGO professionals in topics related to development and NGO management. She has recently finished a research in gender and organizational cultures in Peruvian NGOs. Her topics of interest include gender, ethnicity, international development, and education.

Shirley J. Miske holds a Ph.D in education and was a teacher and school administrator in Guatemala and China. Currently she is a consultant for UNICEF, USAID, and various NGOs on program design, research, training, and evaluation in basic education, especially for girls and women. Miske has worked in Latin America, Asia, and Africa, and has taught graduate education courses at the University of Minnesota and Michigan State University. Other research interests include qualitative research methods and methodology, organizational theory, and women's studies and gender issues in higher education. Miske has contributed to *Education and Development: Tradition and Innovation* and is on the editorial board of the *Asian Journal for Women's Studies.*

Helen Porter is a Ph.D. student in the School of Education at New York University. She received an M.S.Ed. in reading and elementary education from Hunter College. She also holds teaching certification in reading, elementary education, and social studies from New York State. Currently, she teaches first grade in the inner city of New York, where she has worked for the past eight years as a classroom teacher, reading teacher, and staff developer. She is interested in developing effective literacy education programs worldwide.

Fúlvia Rosemberg is Brazilian. She holds a docorate in psychology from the University of Paris. Currently, she is a researcher at the Carlos Chagas Foundation and a graduate professor in the Universidad Católica de São Paulo. Her research focuses on gender hierarchies, race, and gender in education. Some of her recent publications include "Gender Subordination and Literacy in Brazil," "Education, Democratization and Inequality in Brazil," "Education, Inequality and Race in Brazil," and *Contemporary Trends and Ambiguities in the Upbringing of Small Children.*

Nelly P. Stromquist is professor of education and an affiliated scholar in the Center for Feminist Research at the University of Southern California, Los Angeles. She received her M.A. in political science from the Monterey Institute of Foreign Studies and her Ph.D. in education from Stanford University. Stromquist specializes in international development education, which she observes from a sociological perspective using critical and feminist theories to inform her analysis. Her research addresses questions of gender, social equity policy, adult education, and innovations in developing countries, particularly Latin America and West Africa. She is the author of numerous articles and several books. Her most recent work includes authoring the book *Literacy for Citizenship: Gender and Grassroots Dynamics in Brazil* (1997) and editing *Women in the Third World: An Encyclopedia of Contemporary Issues* (Garland, 1998) and *Gender Dimensions in Education in Latin America* (1996). She is past president of the Comparative and International Education Society.

Alejandra Valdés is a social planner and an educator from Chile. She has also studied public policy at the University of Chile. From 1991 to 1998, she was a member of the Women Leadership School at the Instituto

Nacional de la Mujer in Chile. She coordinated the school, taught classes, and did research. She has also worked as consultant on gender and leadership projects for government agencies and NGOs. She is a faculty member at the Universidad Bolivariana, where she is also involved in leadership training. In the 1980s, she coordinated REPEM in Chile and actively worked on networks for educators among NGOs and women's organizations. She also elaborated a leadership program for the Seasonal Workers Program and Women's Rights Program of the Chilean Ministry of Women (SERNAM). Among her publications, we find *Un indecente deseo: Escuela de formación de líderes mujeres* (1995), *A contramano: Estudio evaluativo del impacto de la escuela de líderes* (1997), and *El feminismo en la esfera transnacional o la globalización del feminismo* (1998).

Malú Valenzuela y Gómez Gallardo is Mexican. She obtained a bachelor's degree in psychology and later specialized in teacher's training and educational research at the Universidad Nacional Autónoma de México. She will soon obtain her master's degree in Adult Education in the Universidad Pedagógica Nacional in Mexico. She is also a faculty member in that institution. In 1986, she was a founding member of GEM and currently sits on its board of directors. She coordinated the "Another Form for Being Mothers and Fathers" project. Among her recent publications, we have "Frente a la modernización—el olvido: La situación de la educación de las personas adultas en México" and "Nuevos rostros y esperanzas para viejos desafíos en la educación de adultos en México," both published by the Universidad Pedagógica Nacional. She also had an active role in the writing of the *Woman as an Educator* document presented at the International Conference of the Nine Most Populated Countries in the World, organized by UNESCO.

Index

REFERENCE BOOKS IN INTERNATIONAL EDUCATION

EDWARD R. BEAUCHAMP, *Series Editor*

EDUCATION IN THE PEOPLE'S
REPUBLIC OF CHINA,
PAST AND PRESENT
An Annotated Bibliography
by Franklin Parker
and Betty June Parker

EDUCATION IN SOUTH ASIA
A Select Annotated Bibliography
by Philip G. Altbach, Denzil
Saldanha, and Jeanne Weiler

TEXTBOOKS IN THE THIRD WORLD
Policy, Content, and Context
by Philip G. Altbach
and Gail P. Kelly

TEACHERS AND TEACHING
IN THE DEVELOPING WORLD
by Val D. Rust and Per Dalin

RUSSIAN AND SOVIET EDUCATION,
1731–1989
*A Multilingual Annotated
Bibliography*
by William W. Brickman
and John T. Zepper

EDUCATION IN THE ARAB GULF
STATES AND THE ARAB WORLD
An Annotated Bibliographic Guide
by Nagat El-Sanabary

EDUCATION IN ENGLAND
AND WALES
An Annotated Bibliography
by Franklin Parker
and Betty June Parker

UNDERSTANDING EDUCATIONAL
REFORM IN GLOBAL CONTEXT
Economy, Ideology, and the State
edited by Mark B. Ginsburg

EDUCATION AND SOCIAL CHANGE
IN KOREA
by Don Adams
and Esther E. Gottlieb

THREE DECADES OF PEACE
EDUCATION AROUND THE WORLD
An Anthology
edited by Robin J. Burns
and Robert Aspeslagh

EDUCATION AND DISABILITY
IN CROSS-CULTURAL PERSPECTIVE
edited by Susan J. Peters

RUSSIAN EDUCATION
Tradition and Transition
by Brian Holmes, Gerald H. Read,
and Natalya Voskresenskaya

LEARNING TO TEACH
IN TWO CULTURES
Japan and the United States
by Nobuo K. Shimahara
and Akira Sakai

EDUCATING IMMIGRANT CHILDREN
*Schools and Language Minorities
in Twelve Nations*
by Charles L. Glenn
with Ester J. de Jong

TEACHER EDUCATION IN
INDUSTRIALIZED NATIONS
Issues in Changing Social Contexts
edited by Nobuo K. Shimahara
and Ivan Z. Holowinsky

EDUCATION AND DEVELOPMENT
IN EAST ASIA
edited by Paul Morris
and Anthony Sweeting

THE UNIFICATION OF
GERMAN EDUCATION
by Val D. Rust and Diane Rust

WOMEN, EDUCATION, AND
DEVELOPMENT IN ASIA
Cross-National Perspectives
edited by Grace C.L. Mak